Embodied Practices

Embodied Practices

FEMINIST PERSPECTIVES ON THE BODY

edited by
KATHY DAVIS

SAGE Publications
London · Thousand Oaks · New Delhi

This edition first published 1997

Chapters 2, 4, 6, 8, 9, 10 and 12 were originally published in
The European Journal of Women's Studies, 1996, 3(3).
Chapter 3 was originally published in *The European Journal of
Women's Studies*, 1997, 4(2).
Chapter 5 was originally published in *The European Journal of
Women's Studies*, 1996, 3(4).
Chapter 11 was originally published in *The European Journal
of Women's Studies*, 1997, 4(1).

SAGE Publications Ltd
6 Bonhill Street
London EC2A 4PU

SAGE Publications Inc
2455 Teller Road
Thousand Oaks, California 91320

SAGE Publications India Pvt Ltd
32, M-Block Market
Greater Kailash – I
New Delhi 110 048

British Library Cataloguing in Publication data

A catalogue record for this book is available
from the British Library

ISBN 0 7619 5362 0
ISBN 0 7619 5363 9 (pbk)

Library of Congress catalog card number 97-067935

Typeset by Type Study, Scarborough
Printed in Great Britain by The Cromwell Press Ltd,
Broughton Gifford, Melksham, Wiltshire

CONTENTS

Notes on Contributors

ANNA AALTEN teaches feminist anthropology at the Department of Anthropology of the University of Amsterdam. She has written numerous articles on women's labour, feminist methodology and the development of feminist anthropology. In 1991 she published the book, *Zakenvrouwen. Over de grenzen van vrouwelijkheid in Nederland sinds 1945* ('Business-women. Crossing the Boundaries of Feminity in the Netherlands since 1945'). Her current interest is in the relationship between gender, culture and constructions of the body.

RACHEL A. BLOUL lectures in sociology at the Australian National University, Canberra, specializing in gender, ethnicity and social theory. Her PhD analysed the disruptions in gender and power relations brought about by post-colonial immigration among North African migrants in France, with a particular focus on the construction of masculinity. She has published several articles on gender and ethnicity. Her forthcoming publications include papers in B. Metcalf (ed.), *Making Muslim Space in North Africa and Europe* (University of California Press) and in J. Kahn (ed.) *Beyond Nationalism and Ethnicity* (University of Hawaii Press). Her present research looks at the role of gender in the globalization and ethnicization of Muslim discourses. She is also preparing a book on the feminist socio-logical imagination(s).

GON BUURMAN has been a photographer for over 15 years. She has received many commissions from ministries and foundations for her work. Her first book, *Poseuses* (1987), which contained a series of portraits of women, was highly acclaimed in the Netherlands and abroad. In *About Love* ('Over liefde') (Ploegsma / De Brink, 1995), she focused on the themes of love, desire and loneliness in relationships between people 'of every colour, sex or sexuality'. Her most recent book, *With Desire* ('Uit Verlan-gen') (Schorer / van Gennep, 1996) was commissioned by the Dutch Gay and Lesbian Movement in honour of their fiftieth anniversary.

KATHY DAVIS was born in the US and has taught (medical) sociology, psychology and women's studies at various European universities. She is currently a senior lecturer in the Women's Studies Department at Utrecht University. She is the author of *Power under the Microscope* (Forum, 1988) and *Reshaping the Female Body* (Routledge, 1995), and co-editor of several books on gender, power and discourse. She is currently working on masculinity, plastic surgery and men's bodies.

JULIA EDWARDS is a lecturer in politics at the University of Glamorgan. She is the author of *Local Government Women's Committees* (Avebury Press, 1995) and a number of publications on equal opportunities and local government. She is currently researching women's participation in local government and access to public services.

JOANNE FINKELSTEIN teaches cultural studies and sociology at Monash University, Australia. She is the author of *Dining Out: A Sociology of Modern Manners* (Polity Press, 1989); *The Fashioned Self* (Polity Press, 1991), *Slaves of Chic: An A–Z of Consumer Pleasures* (Minerva, 1994), and *After a Fashion* (Melbourne University Press, 1996).

INEKE KLINGE was trained as a biologist and specialized in immunology. She has been working as a Research Fellow at the Dutch National Cancer Institute and since the mid-1980s she has developed Women's Studies in Science in Utrecht. Her current research entitled 'Bones and Gender' addresses the representation of the female body in biomedical practices concerning osteoporosis. She has co-ordinated an international EU-funded research project on women's views on the Human Genome Project. She is co-ordinator of the Dutch Research Network of Women's Studies in Science and Medicine and Chair of the WISE division: Women, Science and Technology. She has published on feminist science studies, the position of women in science and technology, medicalization of the female body, and women and gene technologies.

GESA LINDEMANN teaches sociology at the Johann Wolfgang Goethe-Universität Frankfurt/Main. Her research interests include the body, the sociology of the emotions, gender difference, and the difference between human/non-human as a constituting principle of modern society. As well as many articles on the construction of body and gender, her recent publications include *Das paradoxe Geschlecht. Transsexualität im Spannungsfeld von Körper, Leib und Gefühl* ('The Paradoxical Gender') (1993) and, co-edited with Theresa Wobbe, *Denkachsen. Zur theoretischen und institu-ionellen Rede vom Geschlecht* (Axes of Thinking) (1994).

LINDA MCKIE is a senior lecturer in health education at the University of Aberdeen. Her research interests include the body in public and health policies and the social construction of the body in health promotion. She is the author of a number of articles on equal opportunities and health promotion. With Sophie Bowlby and Sue Gregory she edited *Concepts of Home*, a special issue of *Women's Studies International Forum* and *Gender, Power and the Household* (forthcoming, MacMillan).

HARRIETTE MARSHALL is a principal lecturer in the Psychology Division at Staffordshire University. She is a member of the editorial group for the journal *Feminism & Psychology*. Her main research interests include identity, issues around gender, ethnicity and the role of psychology in relation to inequalities.

MONICA RUDBERG is professor at the Institute for Educational Research, University of Oslo. Her main interests are in the intersection between gender studies and youth studies. She is currently involved in a three-generation study of young women and men. Her latest book, in collaboration with Harriet Bjerrum Nielsen, is *Psychological Gender and Modernity* (Scandinavian University Press, 1994).

ANNE WOOLLETT is Reader in Psychology at the University of East London. Her research interests are in the role of families in children's development, and in women's experiences of childbirth, parenting and parenting problems. With Ann Phoenix and Eva Lloyd she edited *Motherhood: Meanings, Practices and Ideologies* (Sage) and with David White she wrote *Families: A Context for Development* (Falmer).

DUBRAVKA ZARKOV studied sociology, anthropology and women's studies in Beograd (Serbia) and the Netherlands. She is currently doing her PhD on the female body and nationalist processes in the former Yugoslavia, at the Centre for Women's Studies, Nijmegen, the Netherlands.

Preface

The photograph on the cover of this book was taken by Gon Buurman. It shows a young woman and an older woman dancing in a garden. They are mother and daughter. The young woman is also a professional dancer. But it is the mother who knows how to do the tango. So, with an expression of concentration and determination (do I still know how to do this?), she begins to instruct her daughter. Together, they engage in some mundane gender-bending in the most traditional and heterosexist of all dances. The image brings together many of the themes of this book: differences between women, cultural discourses about the body, power and domination, subversive body practices and more. It manages to be playful and serious, both at the same time.

The publication of *Embodied Practices* represents the growing interest in the body of contemporary feminist scholarship. The book is aimed at a broad audience of scholars interested in the body and, more generally, in issues concerning femininity and masculinity in various fields, from women's studies, cultural studies, sociology and psychology, to philosophy and the humanities.

Most of the chapters in this book originally appeared in the Special Issue on the Body in *The European Journal of Women's Studies* (Volume 3, Issue 3, August 1996). Three chapters were published in subsequent issues of the journal – those by Gesa Lindemann, 'The Body of Gender Difference' (Volume 3, Issue 4, November 1996), Kathy Davis, 'My Body is My Art: Cosmetic Surgery as Feminist Utopia?' (Volume 4, Issue 1, February 1997), and Anna Aalten 'Performing the Body, Creating Culture' (Volume 4, Issue 2, May 1997). The introductory chapter 'Embody-ing Theory: Beyond Modernist and Postmodernist Readings of the Body' and the chapter by Dubravka Zarkov, 'Sex as Usual: Body Politics and the Media War in Serbia' appear for the first time in this book.

I would like to thank the members of the editorial board of *The European Journal of Women's Studies* and Karen Phillips of Sage for supporting this project. A final word of thanks goes to Margit van der Steen who came up with the idea to begin with and has been a constant source of encouragement and practical help.

Kathy Davis

1 Embody-ing Theory

Beyond Modernist and Postmodernist Readings of the Body

Kathy Davis

Several years ago a well-known sociologist, Arthur Frank, remarked that bodies were 'in' (1990: 131). The past decade has marked an enormous upsurge of interdisciplinary interest in the body, both in academia and in popular culture. Conferences on the body abound and no annual meeting in the social sciences, cultural studies or humanities would be complete without at least one session devoted to the body. A whole series of 'body' books has emerged with titles like *A Political Anatomy of the Body* (Armstrong, 1983), *Five Bodies* (O'Neill, 1985), *The Body and Social Theory* (Shilling, 1993), *The Body & Society* (Turner, 1984), *Body Matters* (Scott and Morgan, 1993), *The Body Social* (Synnott, 1993), or just *The Body* (Featherstone, Hepworth and Turner, 1991). Add to this, three lengthy volumes by Michel Feher et al. (1989) on the history of the body from antiquity to the present and a special interdisciplinary journal, *Body & Society*, and it becomes clear that the body has clearly captured the imagination of contemporary scholars.

Different explanations have been put forth for this recent 'body craze'. For some, the concern is regarded as a reflection of the culture at large. Others view the current interest in the body primarily as a theoretical development. And, for still others, feminism is held responsible for putting the body on the intellectual map.

BODY CULTURE

Scholars like Bryan Turner, Mike Featherstone and John O'Neill take the line that the current popularity of the body is due to changes in the cultural landscape of late modernity. While the body has always been a matter of social concern (take, for example, nineteenth-century fears in Europe and the US that the societal 'stock' was degenerating through malnutrition and a high birth rate among immigrants and African-Americans), the meanings surrounding the body have changed. With the demise of industrial capitalism and the rise of consumer culture in the second half of the twentieth century, the Protestant work ethic with its emphasis on hard work, thrift and sobriety gave way to a celebration of leisure, hedonism and unbridled consumption (Turner, 1984; Featherstone, 1983).

> The imagery of consumer culture presents a world of ease and comfort, once the privilege of an elite, now apparently within the reach of all. An ideology of personal consumption presents individuals as free to do their own thing, to construct their own little world in the private sphere. (Featherstone, 1983: 21)

The body is the vehicle *par excellence* for the modern individual to achieve a glamorous life-style. Bodies no longer represent how we fit into the social order, but are the means for self-expression, for becoming who we would most like to be. In an era where the individual has become responsible for his or her own fate, the body is just one more feature in a person's 'identity project' (Giddens, 1991).

Interest in the body also goes hand in hand with recent medical advances and improved sanitation. Life expectancy is greater than in previous centuries and the result in most Western societies is a rapidly greying population. Health care issues have become increasingly relevant, particularly for the elderly. Paradoxically, as we become more able to turn back the clock, a wide-spread cultural anxiety about bodily decay and death have emerged. Individuals are prepared to go to great lengths to achieve a body which looks young, thin, sexual and successful, while ageing, ill, or disabled bodies are hidden from view (Shilling, 1993). Previously-held notions of the human life course proceeding according to socially constructed stages (childhood, middle age, old age) have been replaced by the notion that age is nothing but a mask concealing the 'real' person underneath (Featherstone and Hepworth, 1991).

The denial of mortality is exacerbated by recent developments in technology. Transplant surgery, pacemakers, in vitro fertilization and plastic surgery have joined the more routine techniques of dieting and exercise, offering the individual increasingly dramatic possibilities for taking his or her body in hand. Our bodies have become the ultimate cultural metaphor for controlling what is within our grasp (Crawford, 1984: 80; Bordo, 1993). The notion that the body is a machine – to be repaired, maintained or enhanced (Finkelstein, 1991) – is reflected in computer technologies which blur the boundaries between body and machine, between physical and virtual realities (Shilling, 1993).

BODY THEORY

While the desire to map cultural trends may account for much of the recent enthusiasm about the body, many scholars regard the interest in the body, first and foremost, as a *theoretical* intervention. Traditionally, science has been reluctant to deal with the material body, displaying what Scott and Morgan (1993) refer to as an 'anti-body bias'. Philosophers have tended to disparage bodies in favour of the mind, while theologians have decried the body as the enemy of the soul (Synnott, 1993). Social scientists have tended to focus on social structures, institutions and collectivities, relegating the actual body to the domain of biology (Turner, 1984). Human beings are portrayed as disembodied actors rather than living, breathing, flesh-and-blood organisms (Freund, 1988). As O'Neill (1985: 48) puts it, sociologists seem to prefer to imagine that if society rules us, it does so through our minds, while we rule our bodies rather than being ruled by them.

Shilling (1993) suggests that the body has not been entirely absent, but rather an 'absent presence' in the social sciences. For example, psychologists study body images and self concept. Anthropologists deal with cultural meanings which are attributed to the body (Douglas, 1966, 1973). Sociologists have discussed the body as a carrier for the 'self' (Goffman, 1959; Giddens, 1991). The body is treated obliquely, as a symbol for something else: 'nature', desire or biology. In this context, the recent interest in the body can be viewed as a long overdue attempt to redress an imbalance. By 'bringing the body back in', social scientists are retrieving a neglected topic and making it the focus rather than the implicit backdrop of their analyses.

Michel Foucault has probably done more than any other contemporary social theorist to direct attention to the body. In his highly influential attack on humanism, he replaces the notion of the self-conscious subject as a mainstay of history with the concern for how bodies are arbitrarily and often violently constructed in order to legitimate different regimes of domination (1978, 1979, 1980, 1988). The body became the primary site for the operation of modern forms of power – power which was not top-down and repressive, but rather, subtle, elusive and productive. Power, once the province of the state, now came to be regarded as part and parcel of the micro-practices of everyday life. Foucault's studies on the regimes of the prison, the asylum and the clinic, as well as the history of sexuality, were seminal in understanding the body as object of processes of discipline and normalization. Through his work, the body came to be seen more generally as a metaphor for critical discussions which link power to knowledge, sexuality and subjectivity.

Arthur Frank (1990, 1991) has provided the most convincing explanation for the body 'revival' in social theory, however. He attributes interest in the body as theoretical object to contradictions in academic discourse which have emerged in the wake of postmodernity. The contradictory impulses of modernist certainty and postmodernist uncertainty, which are central to contemporary social theory, have been carried out in perspectives on the body as well.

In modernist discourse, the body represents the hard 'facts' of empirical reality, the ultimate justification for positivism and the Enlightenment quest for transcendental reason. The body is the 'only constant in a rapidly changing world, the source of fundamental truths about who we are and how society is organized, the final arbiter of what is just and unjust, human and inhumane, progressive and retrogressive' (Frank, 1990: 133). However, the enormous diversity in the appearance and comportment of the body in different cultures is also used by social scientists as an argument for social constructionism. Cultural variation in embodiment and bodily practices show just how untenable the notion of a 'natural body' is, making the body an ideal starting point for a critique of universality, objectivity or moral absolutism.

This same contradiction can be found in postmodern discourse on the body. Although the material body is replaced by the body as metaphor, the conflict between the body as bedrock or the body as construct remains. On the one hand, the body is treated as the ideal location from which to criticize Enlightenment philosophy and its tendency to privilege the experience of the disembodied, masculine, Western elite. By 'embody-ing' knowledge, critics deconstruct the faulty universalist pretensions of such 'grand narratives' as merely one version among many. On the other hand, postmodern scholars, inspired by Foucault, take the body as the site *par excellence* for exploring the construction of different subjectivities or the myriad workings of disciplinary power.

Thus, both modernist and postmodernist scholars alternately propose the body as secure ground for claims of morality, knowledge or truth *and* as undeniable proof for the validity of radical constructionism.

For Frank, it is precisely this use of the body for contradictory theoretical agendas which accounts for its current place of honour in contemporary social theory. In his view, the tension between the body as 'reference point in a world of flux and the epitome of that same flux' (Frank, 1991: 40) is inherent in *any* perspective on the body. As such, it serves to fan the flames of controversy, thereby ensuring that the body remains a subject of ongoing theoretical concern for both modernist and postmodernist scholars alike.

FEMINISM AND THE BODY

A final explanation for the body revival is *feminism* – a scientific imperative which emerged in the wake of women bringing themselves back in (Frank, 1991: 41). While many of the 'new', male body theorists seem somewhat reluctant to draw upon feminist scholarship on the body, they generally acknowledge the influence of feminism as a political movement on the emergence of the body as a topic. The body became a political issue as feminists struggled to gain control over their fertility and their right to abortion (Gordon, 1976; Dreifus, 1978). Feminists brought the body to the forefront in their analyses of power relations under patriarchy (Firestone, 1970; Mitchell, 1971; MacKinnon, 1982). And, as feminists entered the academy, they brought their analysis of gender and power to bear on how women's (and men's) bodies were conceptualized in scientific discourse.

For feminist scholars, scientific indifference towards the body was much more than an oversight, bias or 'absent presence', however. Theorists like Susan Bordo (1987), Evelyn Fox Keller (1985), and Moira Gatens (1996) have analysed scientific neglect of the body as a product of the dualisms of Cartesian thought and the centrality of rationality in modernist science. From Plato to Bacon, the mind–body dualism has permeated Western thought, dividing human experience into a bodily and a spiritual realm (Bordo, 1993). The female body becomes a metaphor for the corporeal pole of this dualism, representing nature, emotionality, irrationality and sensuality. Images of the dangerous, appetitive female body, ruled precariously by her emotions, stand in contrast to the masterful, masculine will, the locus of social power, rationality and self-control. The female body is always the 'other': mysterious, unruly, threatening to erupt and challenge the patriarchal order through 'distraction from knowledge, seduction away from God, capitulation to sexual desire, violence or aggression, failure of will, even death' (Bordo, 1993: 5). In short, the female body represented all that needed to be tamed and controlled by the (dis)embodied, objective, male scientist (Keller, 1985).

By exploring the relationship between gender and the mind/body dichotomy in Western science, feminist scholars have shown that the 'antibody bias' masked a distinctively masculine fear of femininity and a desire to keep the female body and all the unruliness which it represented at bay. Thus, feminist scholarship provided a critique of modernist science with a distinctively political thrust. When feminists called for a social theory of the body, they meant a theory which took gender and power into account. For them, 'bringing the body back in' meant both addressing *and* redressing the 'fear of femininity' which had made science such a disembodied affair in the first place.

In the past three decades an enormous amount of feminist research on the female body has been generated from a diversity of disciplines, theoretical perspectives and methodologies.[1] The female body has been the subject of numerous empirical studies in a wide variety of specific contexts. These studies focus on how women experience their bodies, on how women's bodies are implicated in various social and cultural practices and on symbolic representations of the female body. The history of women's bodies has been mapped in various areas of social life and attention has been devoted to how institutions and cultural discourses shape women's embodied experiences.

The specific character of women's embodied experiences of menstruation, pregnancy and menopause have been explored (O'Brien, 1981; Martin, 1987). Reproductive control has been a favourite topic among feminist scholars – from contraception, abortion and sterilization (Gordon 1976; Petchesky, 1986) to the new reproductive technologies like IVF (Stanworth 1987; McNeil et al., 1990; van Dyck 1995). Beginning with the ground-breaking *Our Bodies, Our Selves* (The Boston Women's Health Book Collective 1971), women's health has occupied a central place on the feminist research agenda (Ehrenreich and English, 1979; Roberts, 1981; Lewin and Olesen, 1985) with attention given to, on the one hand, indifference on the part of the medical profession to women's bodily complaints, and, on the other hand, to the negative consequences of medicalization and the often dangerous medical interventions in women's bodies. Medical discourse has played an important role in constructing the female body as, by nature, unstable, deficient, diseased or unruly (Bleier, 1984; Keller, 1985; Showalter, 1987; Jordanova, 1989; Scheibinger, 1989; Jacobus et al., 1990). From hysteria and nymphomania in the nineteenth century to the twentieth-century variants of postnatal depression, pre-menstrual syndrome, anorexia nervosa and menopause, women's bodies have been regarded as more susceptible to pathologies than their male counterparts. Constructions of the female body as more tied to nature than the male body have been instrumental in justifying women's being barred from higher education (Ehrenreich and English, 1979; Morantz-Sanchez, 1985) to, more recently, being exonerated from murder due to their raging hormones (Bransen, 1986).

Sexuality has been a primary focus of feminist scholarship on the body (Vance 1984; Rich, 1980; Haug, 1987). Feminist scholars have explored women's sexual desire and experiences, paying special attention to the normative constraints of heterosexuality. In the past two decades pathbreaking work has been done on sexual violence: from child abuse, rape, wife-battering, or the exploitation of sex workers (Herman, 1981; Stanko, 1985; Mort, 1987; Marcus, 1992; Edwards, 1993) to the mass rape of women during wartime or the international slave trade in women (Brownmiller, 1975; Barry, 1981). State policies and legislation concerning body issues like abortion, pornography, prostitution or social welfare have been critically scrutinized in their capacity to undermine women's right to bodily self-determination (Petchesky, 1986). Legal discourse has drawn upon the female body in ways which curtail women's autonomy or detract from their credibility (Eisenstein, 1988; Smart, 1995).

Women's experiences with the appearance of their bodies have been explored – from the more routine beauty practices (Chapkis, 1986; Bartky, 1990), fitness regimes (Radner, 1995) and fashion (Wilson, 1985) to dieting, the recent epidemic of female eating disorders (Chernin, 1981; Orbach, 1986; Brumberg, 1988; Bordo, 1993) and the cosmetic surgery 'rage' (Wolf, 1991; Davis, 1995). Feminist research in cultural studies has provided a wealth of studies on representations of the female body in film and television, showing how cultural images in the media normalize women by presenting images of the female body as glamorously affluent, impossibly thin and invariably white (Bordo, 1993).

Contemporary feminist theories have historically drawn upon the body in order to understand gender and sexual difference (Nicholson, 1994). Scholars have shown how the female body is implicated in the construction of femininity (Brownmiller, 1985; Smith, 1990; Bartky, 1990) as well as how differences are constituted along the lines of social class, 'race', eth-nicity, nationality, sexuality, able-bodiedness and more (Young, 1990a). The female body is the object of processes of domination and control as well as the site of women's subversive practices and struggles for self-determination and empowerment (Bordo, 1993; Davis, 1995).

Feminist scholarship has begun to trace the interconnection between racism and the body, showing how the body has been central to the con-struction of 'race' (hooks, 1990, 1994; Collins, 1990; Gilman, 1985). In the early nineteenth century scientists justified colonial expansion with bio-logical arguments about the superiority of European 'racial' types. The bodies of African women played a significant role in the imaginations of male European scientists who represented them as wild and unruly con-tinents to be explored and tamed (Gilman, 1985; Fausto-Sterling, 1995). The non-white woman was thought to be endowed with an uncontrolled, animalistic sexuality – a myth which justified the use of black women for slave breeding and exempted them from the possibility of being raped (Davis, 1981; Carby 1987; Smith, 1990). 'Racial' differences are drawn to produce dichotomies of 'Otherness' and power hierarchies among women. For example, the light-skinned, Western ideal of feminine beauty is predicated on African woman with dark skin, broad noses and kinky hair (Collins, 1990). In order to represent Woman, white Western women require an inferior 'Other' – the woman of colour or women from non-Western countries (Spivak, 1988).

In addition to being used in the construction of 'racial' differences, the female body has always been the target of nationalist discourses of com-munity. Women's bodies have historically been used as a metaphor for nation – as, for example, Delacroix's famous rendition of Marianne as a bare-breasted, flag-bearing heroine, leading the French nation into battle. The female body not only represents freedom and liberty, but is the sym-bolic marker of the boundary between 'us' and 'them'. It is mobilized to fan the flames of ethnic conflict and militarism (Wobbe, 1995; Cooke and Woollacott, 1993).

Even this cursory look at contemporary feminist research on the body indicates that the body is hardly new, let alone in the process of making a comeback.[2] For feminist scholars, the body has always been – and continues to be – of central importance for understanding women's embodied experiences and practices and cultural and historical construc-tions of the female body in the various contexts of social life.

In the rest of this chapter, an attempt will be made to set out the dis-tinctive features of a feminist perspective on the body. Despite differences in topic, theoretical orientation and methodological approach, feminist approaches to the body invariably attend to three problematics: *difference*, *domination*, and *subversion*. These themes are implicated in the analysis of women's bodily experiences and embodied practices as well as in studies of how the female body is constructed in different cultures, social contexts and historical epochs. I shall now take a closer look at these issues and, in particular, the kinds of debates which have been generated within feminist scholarship on the body. Conclusions will be drawn for directions which feminist scholarship might profitably take – directions which I hope the reader will find in the remaining chapters of this book.

SEXUAL DIFFERENCE AND 'OTHER BODIES'

The problem of difference has played a central role in feminist scholarship on the body. On the one hand, feminist scholars have been wary of any attempt to use the body as an explanation for socially-constructed differences between the sexes. On the other hand, they have been critical of approaches which treat the body as generic, thereby ignoring the specific features of women's embodiment. This has led to two separate – and opposing – strands within feminist theory on the body.[3]

In the first strand, the body is rejected altogether as a basis for explaining difference. It is argued that notions of bodily difference are all too easily drawn upon to naturalize differences based on gender, 'race' or sexuality. As explanation, bodily difference legitimates social inequality as unavoidable, 'normal' or immutable. Differences among individuals are obscured, while one difference is exaggerated as the only one which counts. A focus on bodily-based difference goes hand in hand with essentialism and homogenization.

Initially, the sex/gender distinction seemed to resolve the problem of the body. Simone de Beauvoir's (1952) famous statement that 'women are made and not born' launched a whole generation of feminist scholars, intent on dispelling the doctrine of 'natural' difference and showing that differences between the sexes were socially rather than biologically constructed. This paved the way to a wealth of studies devoted to deconstructing biological notions of sexual or 'racial' difference and exploring how representations of natural bodies, more generally, are deployed to legitimate social relations of domination and subordination.

While the sex/gender distinction was essential to feminist scholarship, it had some disadvantages as well. One disadvantage was that the body remained an under-theorized backdrop. Feminist theory concentrated on the cultural meanings attached to the body or the social consequences of gender rather than on how individuals interacted with and through their bodies.

In recent years, scholars have begun to question the sex/gender distinction. While the distinction has allowed feminists to formulate commonalities in women's experiences without reverting to a biological determinism, it does not do justice to the historically variable shapes which the body takes. Gender appears to be socially constructed, while the sexed body is not. This leaves the material body as a substrate upon which gender is expressed – a kind of 'coat rack' (Nicholson, 1994): 'Here the body is viewed as a type of rack upon which differing cultural artifacts, specifically those of personality and behavior, are thrown or superimposed' (1994: 81).

Judith Butler (1989, 1993) has been highly influential in breaking down the distinction between biological bodies and socially constructed gender difference. She provides the most radical refusal of gender difference, arguing that the distinction between male or female bodies is itself entirely arbitrary – an artifact of a social order organized by normative heterosexuality. Just as there are myriad forms of 'gender', there are different 'sexes'. For Butler, women are neither born, nor made; they appropriate the cultural prescriptions on sex. The body is the domain where individuals enact sex – often in compliance with heterosexual norms, but sometimes in ways which disrupt these norms, thereby causing 'gender trouble'.

In the second strand, difference is treated as essential for understanding embodiment – that is, individuals' interactions with their bodies and through their bodies with the world around them. Approaches which ignore differences in embodiment are rejected as falsely universalist and unable to do justice to the particularities of individuals' bodily experience. Conditions of embodiment are organized by gender, 'race', sexuality and more, resulting in different possibilities and constraints on individuals' body practices.

French feminism has been most influential in taking sexual difference as a starting point for exploring the specific features of feminine embodiment. Beginning with Hélène Cixous's appeal for woman to 'write her body' in order to escape the constraints of phallocratic language, difference feminists like Luce Irigaray and Julia Kristeva have looked for ways to give expression to women's bodies as the site of pleasure and arousal, sensuality or maternal *jouissance* (for example, Cixous, 1976; Irigaray, 1985; Kristeva, 1980). These appeals to differences in women's bodily and sexual experience or to unique modes of feminine desire not only provide insight into the materiality of feminine embodiment, but demonstrate that feminine embodiment is not simply oppressive, but can be heretical and even empowering as well (Allen and Young, 1989).

For other scholars, phenomenology has provided a useful theoretical starting point for making sense of the lived experience of having a female body. In her ground-breaking essay, 'Throwing Like a Girl', Iris Marion Young (1990b) explores the phenomenology of feminine body comportment, motility and spatiality. She shows how the constraints of femininity in contemporary Western societies make it impossible for women to use their full bodily capacities in a free and open engagement with the world.

Both French poststructuralist and phenomenological approaches to embodiment have been charged with essentialism and for giving priority to experience, particularly of the maternal or heterosexual variety. They do not do justice to structured or systematic differences in women's experiences of embodiment.

Iris Young (1990a) has attempted to weave insights of poststructuralist feminism with a theory which takes differences between women based on class, racial or ethnic background, geographical location, sexuality, or able-bodiedness into account. In my view she has provided the most promising theoretical perspective on embodied difference to date. It is a perspective which tackles the necessity of acknowledging differences in embodiment, while avoiding the pitfalls of difference feminism. For Young, the body is central to how dominant cultures designate certain groups (elderly, homosexual, fat, female, people of colour and so on) as Other. Subordinate groups are defined by their bodies and according to norms which diminish and degrade them as 'drab, ugly, loathsome, impure, sick or deviant' (Young, 1990a: 123). By imprisoning the Other in her/his body, privileged groups – notably, white, Western, bourgeois, professional men – are able to take on a god's eye view as disembodied subjects. They become the ones who set the standards and judge rather than the ones who are judged against standards they can never hope to meet. This 'aesthetic scaling of bodies', as she calls it, is not only central to the construction of difference, it is the mainstay of processes of domination as well.

DOMINATION AND THE FEMALE BODY

Feminist scholarship on the body invariably links women's embodied experience with practices of power. From the sexualization of the female body in advertising to the mass rape of women in wartime, women's bodies have been subjected to processes of exploitation, inferiorization, exclusion, control and violence. The female body is symbolically deployed in discourses of power – discourses which justify social inequality and power hierarchies based on gender and other forms of bodily difference.

Although power is standard fare for any feminist perspective on the body, these perspectives vary, depending on how the body is conceptualized (as material entity, as text or as negotiated practice) or the kind of theoretical framework which is used to account for the social, cultural and symbolic conditions of feminine embodiment (Davis, 1995).

Initially, feminist scholars regarded power as a fairly straightforward matter of male domination and female subordination in a patriarchal social order (Davis et al., 1991). Feminist scholarship focused on how women's bodies have been regulated, colonized, mutilated or violated. Women were viewed as the victims of oppression and all women were oppressed in and through their bodies. The female body in all its materiality was regarded as the primary object through which masculinist power operated. A feminist body/politics was advocated which attacked all oppressive body practices and ideologies. The aim was, ultimately, to provide directions for collective forms of resistance. A set of specifically feminist aesthetics or empowering alternatives to the patriarchal body regimes was proposed to help individual women to develop more 'authentic' and empowering relationships to their bodies.

In the wake of the 'linguistic turn', the focus in feminist theory on the body shifted from women's experience of oppression to how images of the female body were implicated in power relations. Drawing upon Foucauldian notions on power, the female body became a text which could be read as a cultural statement about gender/power relations. The concern for commonality in women's bodily practices was replaced by a preoccupation with the multiplicity of cultural meanings which could be attributed to the female body – notably through scientific texts, the popular media or everyday common sense. Emphasis shifted from power as exploitation, coercion or manipulation to the subtle, pervasive and ambiguous processes of discipline and normalization through cultural representations. Given our 'embeddedness' in cultural discourses which define the female body as inferior and in need of constant surveillance, it was not surprising that the focus became collusion and compliance rather than collective forms of (feminist) protest.

Susan Bordo (1993) provides one of the most thorough and powerful cultural readings of how domination is enacted upon and through female bodies. She explores how cultural constructions of femininity intersect with the Cartesian legacy of mind-over-matter and contemporary body discourses of control and mastery to produce a normalizing politics of the body. Caught between the tensions of consumer culture, the cultural ambivalence toward female appetites and the backlash against women's power, women in Western culture believe that by controlling or containing their bodies and their appetites, they can escape the pernicious cycle of insufficiency, of never being good enough. They can take on 'male' power – power-as-self-mastery – and, paradoxically, feel empowered or liberated by the very bodily norms and practices which constrain or enslave them. While Bordo acknowledges women's possibilities for resistance, she is deeply sceptical about using notions like choice, freedom or agency to describe women's interactions with their bodies. Ostensibly liberatory practices are constantly in danger of being 'reabsorbed' in the dominant cultural discourse of liberal individualism. While Bordo admits that the 'old' oppressor/oppressed model of power needs to be replaced with a more sophisticated understanding of power, she warns feminists to keep their sights firmly fixed on the systematic, pervasive and repressive nature of modern body cultures. In our present 'culture of mystification' – a culture which constantly entices us with false promises of power and pleasure – we need to be concerned with domination rather than freedom and with constraint rather than choice.

FEMALE AGENTS AND SUBVERSIVE BODIES

While domination has been the primary theoretical focus of feminist perspectives on the body, it is not without its drawbacks. Some feminists have argued that a one-sided attention to the constraints of the body culture obscures women's active and – at least to some extent – knowledgeable engagement with their bodies. Others have claimed that the symbolic possibilities for a transgressive body politics have been given short shrift within feminist body theory. Taken together, these critiques have introduced the notions of agency and subversion into feminist scholarship on the body.

The first strand of scholarship has attempted to redress the imbalance in feminist theory on the body by producing a wealth of empirical studies which explore the active role individuals play in contemporary body regimes. By focusing on how individuals throughout history and in all walks of life have ongoingly negotiated the possibilities and limitations of their embodied experience, the body emerges as a site for mundane acts of resistance and rebellion as well as compliance (Fisher and Davis, 1993; Scott and Morgan, 1993; Sault, 1994; Terry and Urla, 1995). For example, practices like religious dress restrictions or veiling, which at first glance appear repressive and confining, prove upon closer inspection to be the site of women's attempts to actively give shape to their lives (MacLeod, 1991; Arthur, 1993; Lomawaima, 1995).

At a theoretical level, attempts have been made to conceptualize agency and the female body. Dorothy Smith (1990) has, for example, posited the notion of women as 'secret agent' behind the gendered discourses of femininity. When women confront cultural discourses which instruct them that their bodies are inferior, a gap is created between the body as deficient and the body as an object to be remedied. Dissatisfaction becomes an active process, whereby women engage with their bodies as an object of work, for 'doing femininity'. The notion of biographical agency has been elaborated in Davis (1995). By exploring women's struggles with cultural discourses of feminine beauty and their ambivalences in deciding to have their bodies altered surgically, a framework is developed for understanding bodily practices like cosmetic surgery as both an expression of the objectification of the female body and an opportunity to become an embodied subject.

In the second strand of thought, attention has shifted from agency and the mundane embodied practices of individuals to symbolic possibilities of subverting cultural gender norms through the body. It is argued that practices like cross-dressing, 'gender bending' or transsexuality disrupt or subvert the homogenizing cultural norms of gender. The example of Madonna, the female body builder or the male transvestite are potential sources of 'gender trouble' (Butler, 1989), precisely because they upset our normative conceptions of the appropriate female or male body and provide inspiration for a transgressive body politics (Epstein and Straub, 1991; Garber, 1992; Halberstam and Livingstone, 1995). While these practices may themselves shore up stereotypical notions of femininity (the drag queen being a case in point) and are not necessarily empowering for the individuals who engage in them, they do create symbolic space. It is the possibility for experimenting with alternative identities which has fired the imagination of many feminist scholars, providing the theoretical impetus for a (post)feminist perspective on the body.

The recent emergence of 'Queer Theory' attests to this new trend. Initially developed in response to the pathologization of same-sex desire, queer theory provided a voice for gay activists and queer culture. Strongly influenced by Foucault and constructionist theory, literary criticism and cultural studies, queen theory has moved on to become one of the most potent critiques of modernist thought (including some strands of feminism). It attacks all forms of binary thinking, including dualistic conceptions of sex and gender. The assumption that there are two genders which are invariantly bound by the genitals is banished in favour of a view which treats every body as a statement, text or performance of gender. Queer theory attacks the 'hegemonic centrism of heterosexism' and brings homosexual iconography to the forefront of postmodern cultural critique (Whittle, 1996). More generally, it is a synonym for any method which messes up ('queers') the normal, including normal business in the academy (Warner, 1993).

(Post)feminist theorists of the body like Elspeth Probyn (1992), Judith Butler (1993) and Elizabeth Grosz (1994, 1996) have embraced queer theory as a radical perspective for rethinking feminist body theory and developing an alternative politics of the body. It offers a way of celebrating a politics of creative subversion without retreating to identity politics or the tactics of collective rebellion which belonged to body / politics in the 1970s. Politics becomes aestheticized and, unsurprisingly, the body takes on a central role in the transgressive aesthetic of performance and display. Feminist body politics entails experimentation, boundary crossing and an ongoing determination to shock and unsettle.

Some feminist scholars have been more sceptical, arguing that this new form of transgression is merely rebellion without content, a self-conscious posturing which lacks moral sense. As Elizabeth Wilson puts it, it is 'not transgression that should be our watchword, but transformation' (1993: 116). While such critique provides a welcome word of warning, queer theory remains, nevertheless, a powerful invitation to take subversion through the body seriously and explore the possibilities for an alternative body politics.

EMBODIED THEORY

I began this chapter by considering the recent 'body revival' in (male-) stream social sciences and humanities. At first glance, this interest would seem to be an indication that three decades of feminist scholarship on the body have finally paid off. The (male) homeless mind has apparently found his body and joined the land of the living. Feminists can now, together with critical male academics, create a truly embodied science – a science which takes account of the body in everyday life as well as in social theory.

Unfortunately, a second look shows that such relief on the part of feminists would be premature. The body may be back, but the new body theory is just as masculinist and disembodied as it ever was. While it acknowledges the importance of feminism in helping to make the body a topic, actual feminist scholarship on the body is notably absent from much of the literature within the 'new body theory'. If reference is made to feminist theory at all, it tends to be limited to the classics (Shulamith Firestone or Kate Millet), while the more recent theoretical interventions by Iris Marion Young, Susan Bordo or Elizabeth Grosz are ignored. This is not merely a sin of omission, but affects the content of the theories which are produced to explain the importance of the body in contemporary social life. Critiques of Western consumer culture and body technologies are incorrectly assumed to impinge upon modern selves in search of their identity projects without any consideration being given to gender, ethnicity or other socially-constructed differences. Critics of the anti-body bias in science chalk the problem up to 'our' Cartesian legacy with its mind/body dualism and abhorrence for irrationality, emotions and the particulars of everyday life, thereby assuming that a little postmodern theory will suffice to bring the body back. Postmodernism, with its critical demolition of dichotomies like mind/body, nature/culture and emotionality/rationality has certainly helped to make the body a popular topic. However, postmodern perspectives on the body have not been unproblematic. Postmodern theorizing about the body has all too often been a cerebral, esoteric and, ultimately, disembodied activity. The danger is that theories on the body distance us from individuals' everyday embodied experiences and, ultimately, from the dangers and pleasures of the body itself (Morgan and Scott, 1993: 18–19).

Feminist theory on the body provides an essential corrective to the masculinist character of much of the 'new' body theory precisely because it takes difference, domination and subversion as starting points for understanding the conditions and experiences of embodiment in contemporary culture. Bodies are not generic but bear the markers of culturally-constructed difference. Understanding what embodiment means to individuals depends upon being able to sort out how sexual, 'racial' and other differences intersect and give meaning to their interactions with their bodies and through their bodies with the world around them. Conditions of embodiment are organized by systemic patterns of domination and subordination, making it impossible to grasp individual body practices, body regimes and discourses about the body without taking power into account. By assuming that the theorist is also embodied, feminist theory opens up possibilities for exploring new ways of doing theory – ways which use embodiment as a theoretical resource for an explicitly corporeal epistemology or ethics (Braidotti, 1994; Grosz, 1994; Gatens, 1996).

This raises the question whether feminist scholarship which – in contrast to (male-)stream body theory – introduced gender/power relations to the analysis of the body, has also created theoretical frameworks which are embodied. Having reached the end of my foray into recent feminist scholarship on the body, I must admit that I am left with some reservations. In conclusion, I will, therefore, touch briefly on two problems which in my view stand in the way of developing embodied theories on the body.

The first problem concerns the grounding of theories on the body in the concrete embodied experiences and practices of individuals in the social world. While there has been a wealth of feminist scholarship devoted to exploring the particularities of embodiment, recent feminist theory on the body has displayed a marked ambivalence towards the material body and a tendency to privilege the body as metaphor. Priority is given to the deconstructive project – that is, to dismantling the mind/body split in Western philosophy or debunking gendered symbols and dichotomies rather than to attending to individuals' actual material bodies or their everyday interactions with their bodies and through their bodies with the world around them.

Bodies are not simply abstractions, however, but are embedded in the immediacies of everyday, lived experience. Embodied theory requires interaction between theories about the body and analyses of the particularities of embodied experiences and practices. It needs to explicitly tackle the relationship between the symbolic and the material, between representations of the body and embodiment as experience or social practice in concrete social, cultural and historical contexts.

The second problem concerns the reflexivity of theorizing the body. As topic, the body evokes a range of emotions among feminist scholars, ranging from unease and ambivalence to passion and fascination. Like any theory on the body, feminist theory is entangled in a set of irresolvable tensions which emerge in the wake of contradictions between modernist and postmodernist projects (Frank, 1990). It is essential, for example, to deconstruct the body as bedrock of sexual difference, but also to validate difference in order to do justice to individuals' embodied experiences. It is necessary to focus on the systematic features of domination as enacted through the female body (Bordo, 1993), but also to uncover the myriad ways that women engage in subversion, in and through their bodies. And, it is mandatory that feminist scholarship takes an explicitly political stance, but also avoids being moralistic or overly-political, thereby ignoring the aesthetic features of contemporary body practices.

It seems to me – and here I agree with Frank – that feminist theory needs to be less concerned with achieving theoretical closure and more interested in exploring the tensions which the body evokes. This would entail using the tensions evoked by the contradictions mentioned above as a resource for further theoretical reflection. It would mean embracing rather than avoiding those aspects of embodiment which disturb and/or fascinate us as part and parcel of our theories on the body. In the process of becoming more self-conscious and reflexive, feminist theory on the body will also become more embodied.

ABOUT THE BOOK

The book has been divided into two parts. The first part is called 'The
Female Body: Difference and Power'. Each contribution shows how sexual
and other differences are constructed through the female body and how
these differences are implicated in asymmetrical relations of power. While
some of the authors focus particularly on domination through the female
body, others are concerned with how the body provides avenues for resistance or subversion.

The book opens with a chapter by Anne Woollett and Harriette Marshall
which explores how young women from different ethnic backgrounds
living in the East End of London talk about their bodies in relation to sexuality, contraception and AIDS. In contrast to mainstream psychological
theory which treats adolescents as generic individuals on the universal
road to sexual maturity, Woollett and Marshall argue for a contextualized
theory which takes the specific meanings of autonomy and responsibility,
as played out through the body, into account. Their analysis of group discussions shows how gender, social class and ethnicity shape the meanings
young women attribute to their bodies as well as the significance of autonomy and responsibility in their lives. These meanings provide the context
for their struggles to attain independence and maturity in the context of
their everyday lives.

In the next chapter, Anna Aalten traces shifting conceptions of femininity and the female body in classical ballet. The Cartesian split between
body and mind is a staple in most forms of dance, where performers are
trained to control their muscles, restrain their appetites and overcome
exhaustion or pain. Aalten draws upon Butler's notion of performativity
to explore the ongoing stylization of the female body to fit the norm of
weightlessness and aetheriality. At the same time, she takes issue with the
notion that ballet is strictly repressive, arguing that it offers possibilities
for empowerment and pleasure, for performers and audiences alike.

Ineke Klinge draws upon medical discourses on osteoporosis (brittle
bones) to explore how different representations of the female body are produced. Drawing upon the feminist social studies of science and the long-
standing critique of the 'natural body', she shows how competing
traditions of bio-medical research emerge within a specific, historical
context. The tradition which focuses on menopause as the culprit for
osteoporosis creates a 'hormonal body', while the 'mineral body' is the
result of a tradition which takes the 'ageing process' as its starting point.
She discusses the disciplinary power of each representation, while
showing how each (dis)allows possibilities for agency and contestation.

Gesa Lindemann explores the limits of the social constructionist view
on the body which is so popular in contemporary feminist theory, arguing
that male and female bodies have their own logic. Taking Lacqueur's distinction between a 'one-sex' and a 'two-sex model', she shows that sex
does make a difference. She uses the phenomenon of transsexuality as a

case in point, thereby showing that embodiment is different depending on whether the body one starts with is a female or male one.

Taking recent debates in France on genital excision and veiling as a starting point, Rachel Bloul shows how sexual and ethnic politics intertwine in representations of Black African and Arab/Muslim women. She shows how contradictions are built into French discourses of cultural difference used to explain each problem. While veiled Arab/Muslim women are positioned as victims in need of protection by French men, black African mothers and female practitioners of excision are cast as seductive Others who are the ignorant, but complicit perpetrators of barbaric crimes. Her analysis is seminal in understanding how colonial discourses of 'cultural difference' and the female/ethnic 'Other' produces power relations between the sexes as well as among women.

Dubravka Zarkov provides a chilling analysis of how the female body can become a metaphor in the context of war and national or 'ethnic' conflict. In former Yugoslavia the civil war is intertwined with a highly nationalistic media war. Zarkov shows how the tabloid press in Serbia deploys images of feminine purity and defilement to fan the flames of 'ethnic' conflict in former Yugoslavia. The normalization of the war and the discourse of the Serbs as the ultimate victims of the war are produced through constructions of the female body – in this case, the body of the prostitute.

Gon Buurman's photographic essay is located strategically between the two sections of the book. She provides an unusual and refreshing view of disabled bodies. In Western culture, physical impairment or disability is treated as a burden, evoking shame and pity. Her images, on the contrary, present disability in a context of pleasure, sexuality and seductiveness. This is a powerful example of feminist critique and feminist intervention, all in one.

The second part of the book is 'Feminist Interventions in Body/Politics'. It explores different kinds of feminist strategies for transformation – from collective action to (self-) critical theory.

Julia Edwards and Linda McKie take an all-too-familiar body problem: the absence of women's toilets – and turn it into an issue for feminist body politics. Despite the fact that women need twice as many toilets as men, the provision is inadequate. The authors show how a web of gendered power relations exists which inhibits open debate about toilets, trivializing it with embarrassed laughter or silencing it with innuendo. A case is provided of a campaign for more and better provision of women's toilets. Despite myriad obstacles, this campaign can serve as an instructive model for how women might collectively mobilize around body issues.

Fashion – the mainstay of femininity – is the subject of Joanne Finkelstein's article. Drawing upon recent scholarship in the field of cultural studies and French feminist theory, she explores the liberating as well as conservative aspects of fashion. Fashion has often been criticized for being shocking, frivolous or 'politically incorrect'. For most feminists fashion is regarded as ideologically suspect. Historically, it has ill-served women for whom identity and status are defined through their appearance. Finkel-stein is critical of this stance, however, for it rests on a misconception of what fashion is all about. Inherently ambivalent, fashion has the capacity to be both a manifesto of rebellion and a mirror to convention. It is this capacity to be more than a particular representation that calls for an aes-thetic rather than a materialist stance, for an appreciation of the contra-dictions rather than a moralistic condemnation.

Kathy Davis takes up radical body art as a site for exploring the possi-bilities of technology for envisioning alternative feminist body/politics. Her case in point is Orlan, a French performance artist who has had her face surgically constructed in a series of video-taped operation/perform-ances. Davis shows how such projects may be situated in a postmodern feminist body/politics and considers their usefulness as a critical response to the cultural dictates of feminine beauty and women's involvement in cosmetic surgery. While such experiments may well contribute to the post-modern project of deconstructing natural bodies and fixed identities, the price is women's embodied experience – a price which is too steep for an alternative feminist body/politics.

Monica Rudberg provides a delightful look at Mary Shelley's *Franken-stein* as an account of masculinist epistemology. She draws upon some of the French feminist criticisms of the masculine epistemophilic project with its denial of sexual difference. She takes issue with theorists like Simone de Beauvoir who treat the female body as a 'smelly swamp' while the male body is the 'fine, uncomplicated, neat' finger, arguing that women are not obliged to transcend their bodies or go through the male body to under-stand their own. The female body itself may provide some possibilities for a less fearful and, indeed, more passionate science. By mapping the relationship between gender, the material body and the research project, she suggests that there may be hitherto unexplored possibilities for femin-ist epistemological projects.

This collection provides a glimpse of some of the possibilities which embodied scholarship on the body can offer. It sets the agenda for a femin-ist scholarship on the body which integrates women's lived bodily ex-perience with a concern for how the female body is implicated in gender/power relations. New forms of bodily discipline and subversion are explored and possibilities for engaging in self-critique and reflection are offered. Taken together, the contributions attest to the scope and diver-sity of feminist interventions in the realm of body/politics, both in theory and in practice.

NOTES

I would like to thank Willem de Haan for his constructive comments on an earlier version of this chapter and Anna Aalten for many inspiring discussions on the body and indispensable help in untangling theoretical knots.

1. Ironically, men's bodies tend to be absent from much of contemporary feminist scholarship on the body. The attempt to develop explicitly feminist analyses of the body have – somewhat paradoxically – shored up the dualism which links bodies and bodily matters to women and femininity. Although there are now plenty of studies on men and masculinity, the male body receives short shrift. Notable exceptions are Morgan (1993) and Connell (1995).
2. It goes well beyond the scope of this introduction to do justice to this scholarship. I have sufficed with a brief – and admittedly incomplete – inventory of some of the main topics of interest as well as the widely cited sources.
3. Many scholars have questioned this opposition, of course, arguing that equality and difference presuppose one another or that the notion that we need to choose should be deconstructed. See, e.g., Scott (1988).

REFERENCES

Allen, Jeffner and Iris Marion Young (eds) (1989) *The Thinking Muse. Feminism and Modern French Philosophy*. Bloomington: Indiana University Press.

Armstrong, David (1983) *The Political Anatomy of the Body: Medical Knowledge in Britain in the Twentieth Century*. Cambridge: Cambridge University Press.

Arthur, Linda Boynton (1993) 'Clothing, Control, and Women's Agency: The Mitigation of Patriarchal Power', pp. 66–84 in Sue Fisher and Kathy Davis (eds) *Negotiating at the Margins. The Gendered Discourses of Power and Resistance*. New Brunswick: Rutgers University Press.

Barry, Kathleen (1981) *Female Sexual Slavery*. New York: Avon.

Bartky, Sandra (1990) *Femininity and Domination. Studies in the Phenomenology of Oppression*. New York: Routledge.

Bleier, Ruth (1984) *Science and Gender: A Critique of Biology and Its Theories on Women*. Oxford: Pergamon Press.

Bordo, Susan (1987) *The Flight to Objectivity: Essays on Cartesianism and Culture*. Albany: SUNY Press.

Bordo, Susan (1993) *Unbearable Weight. Feminism, Western Culture, and the Body*. Berkeley: University of California Press.

Boston Women's Health Book Collective, The (1971) *Our Bodies Our Selves*. New York: Simon and Schuster.

Braidotti, Rosi (1994) *Nomadic Subjects: Embodiment and Sexual Difference in Contemporary Feminist Theory*. New York: Columbia University Press.

Bransen, Els (with Ingrid Baart) (1986) 'Het premenstruele syndroom', pp. 18–34 in Ingrid Baart and Marlene Baerveldt (eds) *Dokteren aan vrouwen. Medikalisering van vrouwenlevens*. Amsterdam: SUA.

Brownmiller, Susan (1975) *Against Our Will: Men, Women and Rape*. New York: Simon and Schuster.

Brownmiller, Susan (1985) *Femininity*. New York: Fawcett Columbine.

Brumberg, Joan Jacobs (1988) *Fasting Girls. The History of Anorexia Nervosa*. Cambridge, MA: Harvard University Press.

Butler, Judith (1989) *Gender Trouble: Feminism and the Subversion of Identity*. New York: Routledge.

Butler, Judith (1993) *Bodies That Matter: On the Discursive Limits of 'Sex'*. New York: Routledge.

Carby, Hazel (1987) *Reconstructing Womanhood. The Emergence of the Afro-American Woman Novelist*. New York: Oxford University Press.

Chapkis, Wendy (1986) *Beauty Secrets*. London: The Women's Press.

Chernin, Kim (1981) *The Obsession: Reflections on the Tyranny of Slenderness*. New York: Harper & Row.

Cixous, Hélène (1976) 'The Laugh of Medusa', *Signs* 1(4): 875–93.
Collins, Patricia Hill (1990) *Black Feminist Thought. Knowledge, Consciousness and the Politics of Empowerment*. New York and London: Routledge.
Connell, R.W. (1995) *Masculinities*. Berkeley: University of California Press.
Cooke, Miriam and Angela Woollacott (eds) (1993) *Gendering War Talk*. Princeton: Princeton University Press.
Crawford, Robert (1984) 'A Cultural Account of "Health": Control, Release and the Social Body', pp. 60–103 in J. McKinlay (ed.) *Issues in the Political Economy of Health Care*. New York: Tavistock.
Davis, Angela (1981) *Women, Race and Class*. New York: Random House.
Davis, Kathy (1995) *Reshaping the Female Body. The Dilemma of Cosmetic Surgery*. New York: Routledge.
Davis, Kathy, Monique Leijenaar and Jantine Oldersma (eds) (1991) *The Gender of Power*. London: Sage.
de Beauvoir, Simone (1952) *The Second Sex*. New York: Alfred A. Knopf, Inc.
Douglas, Mary (1966) *Purity and Danger: An Analysis of Concepts of Pollution and Taboo*. London: Routledge & Kegan Paul.
Douglas, Mary (1973) *Natural Symbols*. New York: Vintage Books.
Dreifus, Claudia (ed.) (1978) *Seizing Our Bodies. The Politics of Women's Health*. New York: Vintage Books.
Edwards, Susan S.M. (1993) 'Selling the Body, Keeping the Soul: Sexuality, Power, and Theories and Realities of Prostitution', pp. 89–104 in Sue Scott and David Morgan (eds) *Body Matters*. London: The Falmer Press.
Ehrenreich, Barbara and English, Deirdre (1979) *For Her Own Good*. London: Pluto Press.
Eisenstein, Zillah (1988) *The Female Body and the Law*. Berkeley: University of California Press.
Epstein, Julia and Kristina Straub (eds) (1991) *Body Guards. The Cultural Politics of Gender Ambiguity*. New York: Routledge.
Fausto-Sterling, Anne (1995) 'Gender, Race, and Nation. The Comparative Anatomy of "Hottentot" Women in Europe, 1815–1817', pp. 19–48 in Jennifer Terry and Jacqueline Urla (eds) *Deviant Bodies. Critical Perspectives on Difference in Science and Popular Culture*. Bloomington and Indianapolis: Indiana University Press.
Featherstone, Mike (1983) 'The Body in Consumer Culture', *Theory, Culture & Society* 1(2): 18–33.
Featherstone, Mike and Mike Hepworth (1991) 'The Mask of Ageing and the Postmodern Life Course', pp. 371–89 in Mike Featherstone, Mike Hepworth and Bryan S. Turner (eds) *The Body. Social Process and Cultural Theory*. London: Sage.
Featherstone, Mike, Mike Hepworth and Bryan S. Turner (eds) (1991) *The Body. Social Process and Cultural Theory*. London: Sage.
Feher, Michel, Ramona Naddaff and Nadia Tazi (1989) *Fragments for a History of the Human Body*, Parts I–III. New York: Zone.
Finkelstein, Joanne (1991) *The Fashioned Self*. Cambridge: Polity.
Firestone, Shulamith (1970) *The Dialectic of Sex*. New York: Bantam Books.
Fisher, Sue and Kathy Davis (eds) (1993) *Negotiating at the Margins. The Gendered Discourses of Power and Resistance*. New Brunswick: Rutgers University Press.
Foucault, Michel (1978) *The History of Sexuality, Volume 1*. New York: Pantheon.
Foucault, Michel (1979) *Discipline and Punish*. New York: Vintage Books.
Foucault, Michel (1980) *Power/Knowledge: Selected Interviews and Other Writings, 1972–1977*. New York: Pantheon.
Foucault, Michel (1988) *Politics, Philosophy, Culture: Interviews and Other Writings, 1977–1984*. New York: Routledge, Chapman, Hall.
Frank, Arthur W. (1990) 'Bringing Bodies Back In: A Decade Review', *Theory, Culture & Society* 7: 131–62.

Frank, Arthur W. (1991) 'For a Sociology of the Body: An Analytical Review', pp. 36–102 in Mike Featherstone, Mike Hepworth and Bryan S. Turner (eds) *The Body. Social Process and Cultural Theory*. London: Sage.

Freund, Peter E.S. (1988) 'Bringing Society into the Body', *Theory and Society*, 17: 839–64.

Garber, Marjorie (1992) *Vested Interests: Cross-Dressing and Cultural Anxiety*. New York: Routledge, Chapman and Hall.

Gatens, Moira (1996) *Imaginary Bodies: Essays on Corporeality, Power and Ethics*. New York and London: Routledge.

Giddens, Anthony (1991) *Modernity and Self-Identity. Self and Society in the Late Modern Age*. Cambridge: Polity Press.

Gilman, Sander L. (1985) 'Black Bodies, White Bodies: Toward an Iconography of Female Sexuality in Late 19th Century Art, Medicine and Literature', *Critical Inquiry* 12: 204–42.

Goffman, Erving (1959) *The Presentation of Self in Everyday Life*. New York: Doubleday Anchor.

Gordon, Linda (1976) *Woman's Bodies, Woman's Right. A Social History of Birth Control in America*. Middlesex: Penguin Books.

Grosz, Elizabeth (1994) *Volatile Bodies: Toward a Corporeal Feminism*. Bloomington: Indiana University Press.

Grosz, Elizabeth (1996) *Space, Time and Perversion. Essays on the Politics of the Body*. New York: Routledge.

Halberstam, Judith and Ira Livingstone (eds) (1995) *Posthuman Bodies*. Bloomington: Indiana University Press.

Haug, Frigga (1987) *Female Sexualization*. London: Verso.

Herman, Judith (1981) *Father-Daughter Incest*. Cambridge, MA: Harvard University Press.

hooks, bell (1990) *Yearning*. Boston: Southend Press.

hooks, bell (1994) *Outlaw Culture. Resisting Representations*. New York: Routledge.

Irigaray, Luce (1985) *Speculum of the Other Woman*. Ithaca: Cornell University Press.

Jacobus, Mary, Evelyn Fox Keller and Sally Shuttleworth (eds) (1990) *Body/Politics*. New York and London: Routledge.

Jordanova, Ludmilla (1989) *Sexual Vision: Images of Gender in Science and Medicine Between the Eighteenth and Twentieth Centuries*. New York: Harvester Wheatsheaf.

Keller, Evelyn Fox (1985) *Reflections on Gender and Science*. New Haven: Yale University Press.

Kristeva, Julia (1980) *Desire in Language*. New York: Columbia University Press.

Lewin, Ellen and Virginia Olesen (eds) (1985) *Women, Health and Healing*. London: Tavistock Publications.

Lomawaima, K. Tsianina (1995) 'Domesticity in the Federal Indian Schools: The Power of Authority over Mind and Body', pp. 197–218 in Jennifer Terry and Jacqueline Urla (eds) *Deviant Bodies. Critical Perspectives on Difference in Science and Popular Culture*. Bloomington and Indianapolis: Indiana University Press.

MacKinnon, Catherine (1982) 'Feminism, Marxism, Method, and the State: An Agenda for Theory', *Signs* 7(3): 515–44.

MacLeod, Arlene Elowe (1991) *Accommodating Protest. Working Women, the New Veiling and Change in Cairo*. New York: Columbia University Press.

McNeil, Maureen, Ian Varcoe and Steven Yearly (eds) (1990) *The New Reproductive Technologies*. London: Macmillan.

Marcus, Sharon (1992) 'Fighting Bodies, Fighting Words: A Theory and Politics of Rape Prevention', pp. 385–403 in Judith Butler and Joan W. Scott (eds) *Feminists Theorize the Political*. New York: Routledge.

Martin, Emily (1987) *The Woman in the Body. A Cultural Analysis of Reproduction*. Boston: Beacon Press.

Mitchell, Juliet (1971) *Women's Estate*. Middlesex: Penguin.

Morantz-Sanchez, Regina Markell (1985) *Sympathy and Science*. Oxford: Oxford University Press.

Morgan, David (1993) 'You Too Can Have a Body Like Mine: Reflections on the Male Body and Masculinities', pp. 69–88 in Sue Scott and David Morgan (eds) *Body Matters*. London: The Falmer Press.

Morgan, David and Sue Scott (1993) 'Bodies in a Social Landscape', pp. 1–21 in Sue Scott and David Morgan (eds) *Body Matters*. London: The Falmer Press.

Mort, F. (1987) *Dangerous Sexualities*. London: Routledge.

Nicholson, Linda (1994) 'Interpreting *Gender*', *Signs* 20(1): 79–105.

O'Brien, Mary (1981) *The Politics of Reproduction*. Boston: Routledge & Kegan Paul.

O'Neill, John (1985) *Five Bodies*. Ithaca: Cornell University Press.

Orbach, Susie (1986) *Hunger Strike. The Anorectic's Struggle as a Metaphor for our Age*. London and Boston: Faber and Faber.

Petchesky, Rosalind Pollack (1986) *Abortion and Woman's Choice*. London: Verso.

Probyn, Elspeth (1992) *Sexing the Self. Gendered Positions in Cultural Studies*. New York and London: Routledge.

Radner, Hilary (1995) *Shopping Around. Feminine Culture and the Pursuit of Pleasure*. New York: Routledge.

Rich, Adrienne (1980) 'Compulsory Heterosexuality and Lesbian Existence', *Signs* 5(4): 631–60.

Roberts, Helen (ed.) (1981) *Women, Health, and Reproduction*. London: Routledge and Kegan Paul.

Sault, Nicole (ed.) (1994) *Many Mirrors. Body Image and Social Relations*. New Brunswick: Rutgers University Press.

Scheibinger, Londa (1989) *The Mind Has No Sex: Women in the Origins of Modern Science*. Cambridge, MA: Harvard University Press.

Scott, Joan W. (1988) 'Deconstructing Equality-versus-Difference: Or, The Uses of Poststructuralist Theory for Feminism', *Feminist Studies* 14(1): 33–50.

Scott, Sue and David Morgan (eds) (1993) *Body Matters. Essays on the Sociology of the Body*. London: The Falmer Press.

Shilling, Chris (1993) *The Body and Social Theory*. London: Sage.

Showalter, Elaine (1987) *The Female Malady*. London: Virago.

Smart, Carol (1995) *Law, Crime and Sexuality*. London: Sage.

Smith, Dorothy (1990) *Texts, Facts and Femininity. Exploring the Relations of Ruling*. London and New York: Routledge.

Smith, Valerie (1990) 'Split Affinities: The Case of Interracial Rape', pp. 271–87 in Marianne Hirsch and Evelyn Fox Keller (eds) *Conflicts in Feminism*. New York: Routledge.

Spivak, Gayatri Chakravorty (1988) *In Other Worlds. Essays in Cultural Politics*. New York and London: Routledge.

Stanko, Elizabeth (1985) *Intimate Intrusions: Women's Experience of Male Violence*. London: Routledge & Kegan Paul.

Stanworth, Michelle (1987) *Reproductive Technologies. Gender, Motherhood and Medicine*. Minneapolis: University of Minnesota Press.

Synnott, Anthony (1993) *The Body Social. Symbolism, Self and Society*. London: Routledge.

Terry, Jennifer and Jacqueline Urla (eds) (1995) *Deviant Bodies. Critical Perspectives on Difference in Science and Popular Culture*. Bloomington and Indianapolis: Indiana University Press.

Turner, Bryan S. (1984) *The Body & Society*. Oxford: Basil Blackwell.

Vance, Carol (1984) *Pleasure and Danger: Exploring Female Sexuality*. London: Pandora.

Van Dyck, José (1995) *Manufacturing Babies and Public Consent. Debating the New Reproductive Technologies*. Basingstoke: Macmillan.

Warner, Michael (1993) 'Introduction', pp. vii–xxxi in Michael Warner (ed.) *Fear of a Queer Planet. Queer Politics and Social Theory*. Minneapolis and London: University of Minnesota Press.

Whittle, Stephen (1996) 'Gender Fucking or Fucking Gender? Current Cultural Contribution to Theories of Gender Blending', pp. 196–214 in Richard Ekins and Dave King (eds) *Blending Genders. Social Aspects of Cross-Dressing and Sex-Changing*. London and New York: Routledge.

Wilson, Elizabeth (1985) *Adorned in Dreams*. London: Virago.

Wilson, Elizabeth (1993) 'Is Transgression Transgressive?', pp. 107–17 in Joseph Bristow and Angelia R. Wilson (eds) *Activating Theory: Lesbian, Gay, Bisexual Politics*. London: Lawrence & Wishart.

Wobbe, Theresa (1995) 'The Boundaries of Community: Gender Relations and Racial Violence', pp. 88–104 in Helma Lutz, Ann Phoenix and Nira Yuval-Davis (eds) *Crossfires. Nationalism, Racism and Gender in Europe*. London: Pluto Press.

Wolf, Naomi (1991) *The Beauty Myth. How Images of Beauty Are Used Against Women*. New York: William Morrow.

Young, Iris (1990a) *Justice and the Politics of Difference*. Princeton: Princeton University Press.

Young, Iris Marion (1990b) *Throwing Like a Girl and Other Essays in Feminist Philosophy and Social Theory*. Bloomington and Indianapolis: Indiana University Press.

The Female Body

DIFFERENCE AND POWER

2 Reading the Body

Young Women's Accounts of their Bodies in Relation to Autonomy and Independence

Anne Woollett and Harriette Marshall

This article examines the ways in which young women living in East London position the body in terms of their lives and relations with others and the implications of their representations for mainstream psychological approaches to adolescent development. Mainstream psychological approaches, as articulated in stage and 'Sturm und Drang' theories, characterize adolescence as a time when young people move from a state of dependence on parents to individuation and independence from others (Erikson, 1968; Noller and Callan, 1991; Coleman and Hendry, 1990; Apter, 1991). Concomitant with this emphasis on independence is the notion that young people gradually take on responsibility for themselves and their actions and make their own decisions (Griffin, 1993; Smetana and Asquith, 1994; Hendry et al., 1993).

An important area in which this mainstream psychological blueprint is played out is in relation to the body. Adolescence is marked by physical and bodily changes as young people reach sexual maturity and heterosexual relations are construed as central to young people's lives, and as replacing those with parents and with same-sex friends (Coleman and Hendry, 1990; Moore and Rosenthal, 1993). The body is also seen as central to conceptualizations of adolescence because of perceived threats to social order and moral panics about issues such as single mothers and the spread of AIDS or as related to 'problems' such as anorexia (Griffin, 1993; Phoenix, 1991).

Although representations of the body play a central part in mainstream psychological theorizing about adolescence, the meaning and social constructions of biological/physical changes have been neglected. However, as many feminist writers make clear, the notion of representation does not refer to a system of signs directly mapping on to reality nor is there an underlying essence to the meaning of the body and bodily actions. Instead, it can be argued that the body and bodily actions and interactions carry different meanings and can be 'read' in various ways (Cowie, 1990; Haraway, 1984).

Attributions of maturity, responsibility and independence figure largely in psychological approaches to what young people do with their bodies as well as in accounts produced by young people themselves. This is evident in their discussions of where they go and how they spend their time, how they interact with others and their concern with sexual activity (Moore, 1987; Allen, 1987; Griffiths, 1987; Sharpe, 1994).

However, closer examination of the accounts of young people indicates variations in readings of the body: the signification of the body is gendered and is deciphered in diverse ways by young people from different socio-economic and ethnic groups (Griffin, 1993; Sharpe, 1994; Lees, 1993; Moore and Rosenthal, 1993). For this reason this article concentrates on the representations of the body of young working-class women from a variety of ethnic backgrounds.

Participants were 44 working-class young women. They were aged 14–16 years and attended three schools in East London. They came from a variety of ethnic and 'racial' backgrounds, but largely they defined themselves as white, Afro-Caribbean/black and Asian (families originating from the Indian subcontinent). All spoke fluent English and had received much or all of their education in the UK.

The young women participated in discussion groups: these were same sex as young women preferred to discuss potentially sensitive issues in a same-sex context. Groups typically comprised four or five young women who had volunteered to take part. The discussions were semi-structured and informal, and the topics for discussion included education and career choices, relations with parents and other young people, ideas about healthy living, including contraception, and sex education. The same areas of questioning were used in each case, although not necessarily in the same order. Two white women in their 30s acted as discussion leaders. All young women gave their consent to be tape recorded, and the confidentiality of the discussions was assured by the researchers. The tapes were later fully transcribed.

ANALYSIS

In order to allow themes relating to the body to emerge from the discussion, a form of thematic analysis was adopted. Instances where the discussion turned to aspects of the body, its meaning and significance, were extracted from the transcripts. Close and repeated readings of the extracts, their content and use of words suggest that the themes on which young women drew varied considerably and they expressed a variety of complex and sometimes contradictory ideas and assumptions. These often centred around dualisms such as the private/the public; the individual/the individual in relation to another/others; and rationality/emotionality.

The themes which thus emerged from the young women's accounts most consistently and are examined here are:

1. the body as one's own;
2. taking responsibility for one's body;
3. the body as sociosexually active/preserved as inactive.

In the analysis that follows these three key themes are presented with the use of illustrative extracts. AG indicates Asian, BG black, and WG white young women. Numbers are used to identify different members of each discussion group. Questions and comments from the discussion leaders are indicated by Int.; . . . denotes that the full text has been edited down.

The Body as One's Own

The theme articulated most frequently and most emphatically by young women was that 'one's body is one's own'. Young women assumed an individualistic approach in which it was argued that a young woman has the right to make her own decisions about her body (Allen, 1987; Smetana and Asquith, 1994). Young women resisted ideas of collective moralities and ideologies such as those which recognize the viewpoints of others and the rights of others to influence how they use or make decisions about their bodies.

Young women's individualistic approach can be seen in the first extract in their discussion of abortion. They take up the argument that their bodies are their own, yet also elaborate on the ways in which their ideas might be modified by contexts and situations.

> *Int*: Whose decision is it [to have an abortion]?
> BG1: The woman's.
> BG2: It depends as we were saying like. If you got raped.
> BG3: I think it's the woman's decision.
> BG5: No man's got the right to tell you.
> BG2: No no, you ain't listening to me are you, right. That's what I say, no one can't tell you to have your baby aborted or not to have it aborted.
> BG5: The choice is yours.
> BG2: Yeh it means then that the choice is yours but then at the same time, if you are having a steady relationship with a boy and you get pregnant. You can't just take it upon yourself to go and get his baby aborted.
> BG3: Yeh cause the boy might even want the baby.
> BG2: Yeh cause after all the boy might say 'Yeh have my baby and I'll look after it and bring it up.' But that's what I'm saying it will be a different case. Now if it's rape you ain't gonna go and look for the man who raped you and ask him. At that time you'd just wanna get it out of the system, get rid of the baby and whatever else and try and start fresh.
>
> (Extract 1)

The notion of the body as one's own is consonant with more general ideas about becoming independent and making one's own decisions. While the young women said they often talked to their parents and asked advice, this depended on the topic: they did not often talk to parents or seek advice about issues related to the body, such as sex and marriage. The young women tended to view the body as 'a private matter' (using terms such as 'it's none of their business [who I spend time with]', 'I wouldn't involve them [parents]') and described their decision-making in terms such as 'I'll handle things myself', 'I'll find out for myself'. In the following extract (2), an Asian young woman expresses her difficulty in talking to her mother about sex even though she feels close to and respects her mother (Moore, 1987; Noller and Callan, 1991).

> *Int*: Do the rest of you feel you can talk to your mum or dad about anything?
> *AG2*: I can't talk to my mum about everything, not everything, I've got my limits.
> *Int*: So what can't you talk about?
> *AG2*: My relationship with other friends and things like that. I don't tell her everything . . . I tell my friends more, like my friend here she knows everything about me, more than my mum like. Not that she doesn't understand, it's just that I feel weird going to my mum and saying some of the stuff I tell my friend, you know. I don't think she'd understand or anything. It's just probably out of respect, probably, don't you think? So because I think as you get to our age, older, you don't talk to parents as much.
> *Int*: What did you mean by respect?
> *AG2*: I dunno I think, I probably think twice about what I say to my parents because I don't want to say something wrong. Because that will spoil our relationship and it might come up into an argument and you don't want an argument. I don't want anything to go wrong. . . .
> *Int*: Do you ever talk to a parent or parents about sex?
> *AG5*: I was gonna the other day actually, but I just sort of sat there thinking 'No, I can't do it'. I'd rather talk to a mate because say you come with a question or something. Whereas your parents have been through it you might think it's easier, but I'd rather talk to a friend about it and like, you know.
>   (Extract 2)

The accounts of relations between young women and their parents centred on young women's ability to take independent action. Going out was a major source of tension for young women from all ethnic groups, and is illustrated in the following extract (3). Being able to stay out is seen as an indication of independence, the body as one's own, and of parents accepting their maturity.

> *AG3*: They don't accept you growing up or something like that. You know they don't think 'She's grown up and she wants to do this or she wants to do that.'
> *Int*: In what way does it show itself?
> *AG5*: Overprotection in't? I think.
> *Int*: Do you have any examples?
> *AG2*: I see all my mates, they go out at night if there's a party or something, it's always night. Now I ask my mum 'Look', I say 'the party starts at 8.' You know they're always thinking 'No that's too late, you can't go out. That's too young.' But then if you think about it you are 16 years old and you know you should be able to really.

AG5: They've got to have limits and that.
AG2: I don't think they realize that you are growing up really.

(Extract 3)

Being able physically to take one's body where one wishes and when one wishes is taken as signifying maturity. If a young woman's parents accept her right to do so, then this is taken as a sign that they accept her as an independent and adult being. Yet at this point, once again the gendered reading of the body is seen. In the following extracts (4 and 5) young women suggest that parents view a girl's body as more vulnerable and more at risk than a boy's. The possibility of rape is seen as shaping the differential reading of the vulnerability of young women's bodies. This contrasts with the readings of young men's bodies: they are seen as able 'to get away with anything'.

Int: So what are the big problems [with your parents]?
BG3: Going out. I think because when sometimes when they let me go out and I take liberties, I don't come back on time.
BG2: My mum might not want me going there cause of the particular person or the area or the time of night that I'm going.
Int: So do you think your parents are concerned about your safety then?
All: Yeh.
BG2: Overprotective and she admitted that.
Int: Do you think it's the same as it is for boys?
BG2: No, boys get away with anything.
BG4: It's worse for girls.
BG1: Because of rape and all that what goes on and bad people on the streets at night time.
Int: So why do you go off and do your own thing?
BG2: Everybody goes through that stage where they're around that age and they are thinking in their mind 'I want to do what I wanna do.'

(Extract 4)

The gendered reading of parents' concerns for young people's safety may be resisted, as in the following extract (5), in which young women argue that boys are at risk as much as girls.

Int: Are there things your parents don't want you to do?
WG3: Like getting in on time. If you want to stay up late at night you've got to be in at a certain time.
Int: So why do they want you home at a certain time?
WG2: They're worried about you, especially girls as well. It's better for boys. They think that boys can look after themselves without getting into trouble.
WG1: They say that boys can look after themselves but I don't think so.
WG2: Yeh it's just the same for boys and girls. Boys and girls can get into as much danger.
WG1: You've got to be able to walk down the street on your own haven't you?
WG4: Going out. I want to go out to nightclubs and mum's worried about me getting home safely.
WG5: Yeh having to be in early especially when all me mates can go out late.
WG4: 'Yeh' you say 'but mum', and she says 'I don't care about anyone else.'

(Extract 5)

The resistance of the white young women in this extract (5) to a gendered reading of safety was also found in discussion groups with Asian young men which indicated that they are aware of physical threats to the body, although in somewhat different forms, through muggings, racialized attacks, and being out on the streets at night (as Brannen et al., 1994 report). Contextual issues such as these shape young people's discussion of the extent to which they wish to stake their claim to independence by going out when and where they want to.

However, despite the resistance by some young women to gendered readings of the body as illustrated earlier, it is young women whose lives and independence are constrained by their own and their parents' fears (Sharpe, 1994; Brannen et al., 1994). Young women take up the theme of the body as one's own stating that how they use their bodies is their 'own decision'. But in recognizing gendered readings of the body and the physical risks of being out late at night, young women acknowledge the limitations on the extent to which they can realize independence. Such accounts indicate the need for mainstream psychological theorizing about adolescence to engage more fully with such gendered meanings and constraints on the extent to which independence is played out through the body.

Taking Responsibility for One's Body

Closely related to the theme of one's body being one's own was the theme of taking responsibility for one's body. Taking responsibility was seen as part of growing up and being a mature person and was drawn on in accounts in a variety of settings. While young women recognized the benefits of a healthy lifestyle, they argued that such decisions about the body were a matter for the individual.

Taking responsibility for one's body was a theme much in evidence in discussions about engaging in sexual activity with others and specifically in discussion of the benefits of contraception in preventing pregnancy and avoiding the risk of AIDS. Young women were strongly committed to contraception as an aspect of taking responsibility for one's own body. However, their readings of their own and young men's responsibility for the reproductive body indicate some of the difficulties they experience. They argued that young men were resistant to finding out about and taking responsibility for contraception. This raised issues about power in sexual relations as well as putting women's health at risk.

> AG5: Later on in life I reckon they'll realize 'Oh god I wish I'd sat down and actually like you know listened to them, paid attention.' Because like it'll be them using the stuff not us. I mean if people find a packet of condoms in a girl's purse, 'Oh yeh, she's easy, you know.'
> Int: Would you choose to supply the contraception or would you rely on the other person?
> AG2: No I'd take it myself.

AG5: I'd take it myself yeh.

AG1: Yeh just in case.

AG3: They'd probably try and put it off, you know.

AG5: You know it's their pride in't.

AG3: Yeh their pride, you know. And it's okay, look you're not going to get anything from me, you know.

AG5: Yeh, 'Don't worry whatever, I'll tell you when I'm coming.'

AG1: It's your health at risk as well. Like your life, let's say if that boy did have AIDS or whatever.

AG5: You ain't gonna know about that are you?

AG1: No.

AG2: And you're gonna be the one at risk. I mean if he has got AIDS okay, and you become pregnant, well if you . . .

AG3: And you become HIV positive. And you get yourself HIV positive because they didn't tell you. You trusted them and, you know, they broke that trust.

AG5: That's the boys for you in it though?

Int: Do you think boys don't know how to take responsibility for . . .

AG5: Some of them do.

AG2: You can't really, you can't say all boys because . . .

AG3: Well girls are different as well. It depends on every individual.

(Extract 6)

The body is discussed in relation to another's body through sexual inter-action. Yet within the notion of the body-in-relation, is the repeated use of the theme of taking responsibility for one's own body: so, for example, young women state that it is up to them to think about contraception and to be prepared with condoms. However, in doing so they risk the negative attribution of being 'easy' and unrestrained with respect to the body. This contradiction and the positioning of young women in a 'no win' situation has been noted many times (e.g. Lees, 1993; Griffin, 1993; Moore and Rosenthal, 1993).

The limits of individual responsibility and control are also discussed in the following extract (7) in which young women discuss negotiating 'safe sex' with young men, requiring as it does a trust and confidence in young men's knowledge and concern for a woman's body.

BG5: I don't think boys know much about sex anyway. That's getting it in and taking it out.

Int: So why do you think they have such a limited knowledge?

BG1: Well they don't really gotta know, have they, cause it's not nothing for them though is it?

BG3: They don't have to worry about getting pregnant.

BG2: Sometimes they get funny about wearing a condom in't. Like 'If you're gonna do it, let's do it properly.' That kind of talk.

Int: Do they know about AIDS?

BG2: If they really care for you then they should.

BG5: They should both because girls can't pass AIDS to another girl can they? It's boys that passes AIDS mainly to the girls and the girls to the boys.

BG1: If the boy really cares for you then he'll wanna like protect you but if he don't care and he knows he's gonna leave you then he'll just say that's cool.

(Extract 7)

Tensions between taking responsibility for one's body and acceptance of the body-in-relation can also be seen in other contexts, such as young women's acceptance of some constraints placed upon their ability to take one's body physically where one wishes, as illustrated in extracts 3–5.

So, although young women view taking responsibility for the body as an aspect of increasing maturity and independence, they also point to a number of sources of tension because responsibility for the body-in-relation cannot be achieved independently but requires negotiation with others, including parents and sexual partners. Some of the ways in which the young women tried to resolve such tensions are discussed in the following section.

The Body as Sociosexually Active/Preserved as Inactive

A third theme is that of the body as a commodity, as sociosexually active, to be given over to others. The body as sociosexually active is viewed by most young women as a 'natural' part of growing up and becoming adult. This is in spite of the tensions in negotiating 'safe sex' with young men and concerns about trust, which were discussed above in extracts 6 and 7. Heterosexual activity is seen as 'given' and as an important part of young women's lives, although there was little discussion about sexual pleasure or of the significance of sexual activity for young women. This seemed to be because the benefits of engaging in sexual relations and of hetero-sexuality were 'taken for granted' and hence did not need to be discussed, as well as reflecting difficulties in finding ways to talk about 'taken for granted' ideas (Griffin, 1993; Segal, 1994; Macpherson and Fine, 1995).

Giving over one's body to others in sexual activity takes the form of becoming aware of and interested in boys, dressing up, going out, finding a boyfriend, or getting to know someone who is 'fancied'. In extract 8 maturity is read in terms of increasing awareness of and interest in boys and recognition that they might be interesting classmates.

> *AG3*: In the first year it used to be really different. Boys and girls, we used to sit on different sides of the room.
> *AG4*: And when we had to go to assembly they'd stick their bags between the girls.
> *AG3*: If you had to sit next to the boys and they'd go –
> *AG4*: It was so childish.
> *AG2*: If a boy touched me I'd go 'Ugh, he touched me' and things like that.
> *AG3*: It was like boys are there and girls are here, really childish. Thinking about it now it's really childish but now, yeh, we've matured as well.
> *AG2*: Now boys are more mature than –
> *AG3*: Not all of them but yeh.
> *AG2*: But most of them, especially nowadays.
> *AG3*: Yeh now it's different. Some of our really good friends are boys like, not all girls. Like we have really good friends that are boys.
> *Int*: Do you spend most of your time with other girls or mixed groups?
> *All*: Mixed.
> *Int*: Is that a good thing?
> *All*: Yeh.
> *AG2*: Yeh but if you'd have told us that about two years ago we'd have

thought 'No we'll stick to our girlfriends.' But like now we don't care. It's part of growing up really isn't it.

(Extract 8)

The discussion in this extract (8) indicates the power of the heterosexual imperative in defining 'normal' development (Griffin, 1993; Griffiths, 1987). However, elsewhere young women discuss some difficulties they experience in engaging in heterosexual relations. These include establishment of trust (as in extracts 6 and 7) and the ways in which engagement in heterosexual activity could conflict with young women's commitment to maintaining their independence (Allen, 1987; Bhavnani, 1991; Sharpe, 1994; Mirza, 1992). In extract 9 young women do not question the value of sexual activity. They do, however, question and resist young men's approaches to sex and personal relationships.

BG1: Yeh they [boys] should be made to know [about contraception]. But like when they are our age all they wanna do is go out and get experience.
BG2: They are not sitting down like us. If some of us go out and have sex we're gonna sit down and think 'I wonder if I'm gonna get pregnant.' They're just gonna sit there and think 'Oh well how many girls can I get?' or you know they run bets with each other.
BG5: The boys of our age are really immature. It's when they get to 17 and 18 that they take it more serious.
BG2: It's like it's just experience. It's like sex has just come into their heads and so they're going out to see which one's the best compared to this one.
BG2: They're saying 'I've done this, I've done that and everything else, sex, sex, sex.' It's said to make themselves sound big.
Int: So do girls do that?
BG3: No.
BG2: Well you can't really can you, you get a bad name.
BG5: Boys don't get called names that are bad, do they?
BG4: They feel good.
BG2: You can only tell like the close friends. Like the ones you think can keep their mouth closed to a certain extent.
BG4: But they don't go around boasting to you.
BG2: Can you imagine girls going around 'Oh I had sex with him last night and blah, blah, blah.' Because then a girl, as soon as it gets round the story always gets tangled up and she gets a label on her as a slag or a tart or slut or something like that. Whereas with a boy he just gets a bit more macho.

(Extract 9)

Young women do offer resistance to the heterosexual imperative by continuing to value close relationships with young women with whom they can discuss intimate topics (as in extract 2), by recognizing the gendered readings of sexual activity and distancing themselves from young men. One way in which distance is maintained is through stereotyping young men as universally untrustworthy and unconcerned about young women's bodies (as in extracts 6 and 7). Alternatively, as in the following extract (10), specific young men are singled out as trustworthy and with whom a young woman can relate. This then enables young women to engage with the notion of the body as sociosexually active as pleasurable and unproblematic.

Int: Do you think that young people talk about sex with boys?
WG4: Sometimes you can trust them, you can can't you?

WG3: But you never know what they're gonna say, like 'Oh guess what Kim said.'
WG1: Girls seem to mature more quickly than boys do, but you get some boys that are mature and some that are really immature.
WG5: Yeh they're all right when they are on their own, they talk to you.
WG2: It's when they get with their friends then they get all loud. There's something about being with their friends, but when they're on their own they seem like all nice.

(Extract 10)

Young women argue for taking responsibility for one's body because the risks of sexual activity are greater for them: pregnancy interferes with their independence and their opportunity to have careers and enjoy themselves (Griffin, 1985; Allen, 1987). However, there are tensions between taking responsibility for one's body and another theme on which young women draw, that of shared/joint decision-making. In the next extract (11) young women argue that decisions about contraception should be 'joint', the result of discussion and negotiation, but when this is not possible, the ultimate decision is 'up to the female'.

Int: Do you think girls take it [contraception] more seriously or not?
WG1: Yes.
Int: Why do you think they do?
WG2: Because if anything happens they're the one that's gonna get pregnant, they're the ones that are gonna have to live with it. But the boys are not, they're just gonna be able to walk away.
Int: Who do you think in a relationship should make the decision about contraception?
WG4: Should be a joint decision but then again if the male partner doesn't wanna use it and the female does, then it's really up to the female then cause she's the one that could end up getting pregnant.
Int: What if your partner doesn't want to use a condom? How would you react if your partner says 'I'm not wearing one of those'?
WG2: You'd say 'Well you creep, you don't care about me that much to make sure that I don't get pregnant.'

(Extract 11)

A different construction of the body is drawn on by some Asian young women indicating the diversity of representations of the body among young women and the ways in which gendered and racialized representations intersect. This construction relates to virginity which Asian young women (but no black or white young women) discussed in terms of the body preserved as inactive being something to be proud of. In extract 12, they distinguish between 'having sex' and 'making love', that is sexual relations as signifying commitment as well as/rather than as sexual pleasure. They talk about the body as sociosexually active prior to marriage or some firm commitment as a personal loss of dignity and as being 'used'. This is especially the case if the relationship breaks down and knowledge of women's sexual activity comes into the public domain.

AG5: My mum's sort of no sex before you get married. I mean say you are going out with a person before you actually get married and then say you have sex with him or what have you, and say you split up, you're lost. I mean I reckon virginity is pretty important in a girl's life and once you've lost it, you know, especially if you don't get married to that person it really hurts I reckon. So I mean like that's my point of view, whether other people think different I don't know.

AG1: Yeh, you feel used in't.

AG3: Virginity is something to be proud of and I don't know why girls say, 'Oh I'm still a virgin.' You know they think it's something to be ashamed about.

AG2: You know, you're sweet 16 and you're still a virgin, 'Oh my god, that's tragic.'

AG3: They sit there talking about, 'Oh I had sex with my boyfriend last night, oh you know.'

AG2: We hear this in our class everyday don't we?

AG3: It makes you sick. Having sex and making love is different. Because making love with someone you love and you know. It's different from them having sex just for the sake of it you know.

(Extract 12)

In their discussion of the body as sociosexually active/preserved as inactive young women's readings are shaped by ethnicity as well as gender. This can also be seen in the ways in which Asian young women link dress and hence how the body is presented with their ethnic identities (Woollett et al., 1994). In the context of arranged marriages and constraints on sexual relations between young people, young Asian women question assumptions about the normality of the body as sociosexually active. However, in spite of these examples of different readings of the body, in many respects Asian young women drew on themes of independence, responsibility and maturity in similar ways to other participants in the study.

DISCUSSION

A number of themes about the body are drawn on by young women: those which seemed predominant are outlined in the analysis above. The body as one's own was frequently used as indicative of more general notions of independence. However, when used in conjunction with taking responsibility for one's body certain tensions arose. These occurred in part because gendered readings of the body constrain young women's ability to make decisions about their bodies. The notion of the body as vulnerable (physically or morally), or the body-in-relation, require that young women do not always make their own decisions, but negotiate with parents about going out and with young men about issues such as contraception and decision-making in heterosexual relations. The impact of gendered readings of the body was also evident in the third theme, the body as sociosexually active/preserved as inactive, in which the benefits of heterosexual activity were set against young women's concerns about their reputations and about becoming pregnant and AIDS. As we have suggested, these three themes are interlinked. We consider the use and interrelations of the themes for young women and psychological theorizing.

At the core of young women's use of the three themes is the implicit acceptance of individualism, 'individual freedom' and the 'need' to make one's 'own' decisions. These individualistic assumptions serve to express an ideology and morality which contrasts with more collective moralities based on concerns for others or consideration of the broader implications of individual actions, for example for the young woman's sexual partner, her child or the wider family. While individualism is sometimes taken as contradictory to discourses of morality, the young women in this study use it in the sense of a morality or guiding principle, which 'should' underlie their decision-making (Moore and Rosenthal, 1993).

However, as indicated in the analysis, there are contradictions in the use of these predominant themes for young women when viewed within contextual considerations. Young women's readings are centred around a number of dualisms, of which we have paid particular attention to the public/private. Becoming independent, making one's own decisions, taking responsibility for one's body and engaging in sexual activity tend to be construed as within the private domain and as, for example, 'none of their [parents'] business'. But they also have 'public' implications insofar as public knowledge that a young woman is engaging in sexual activity (too much, of the 'wrong' kind or with the wrong person), has implications for her reputation and whether her behaviour is viewed as 'deviant' (Griffin, 1993). The dualism employed in the themes makes for an obvious contradiction when considered in the context of the moral panic over 'single/young mothers'. This indicates public concern and intervention concerning young women's engagement in sexual activity in spite of a political climate in the UK which is still fiercely individualistic.

A further contradiction is evident in the widespread societal assumptions that relations between the sexes in Western democracies are now more equal and decision-making about issues such as contraception is shared. These assumptions contrast with the unequal and traditional double standards for judging women's sexual activity.

We have emphasized the gendered readings of the body throughout this article. In this sense we are in agreement with feminist writers working in disciplines including women's studies, cultural studies and sociology, who have questioned decontextualized and universal theorizing (Butler, 1993; Collins, 1990; Farganis, 1994; Ramazanoglu, 1993). These contrast with 'stage' theories and 'universal' constructions of 'normal' adolescence common in mainstream psychology. These universal constructions are achieved in part by a reliance on limited samples (generally white, middle-class and US subjects) from which mainstream psychology argues that the central task of adolescence for *all* young people is that of achieving independence and it is this which marks maturity. As a result, gendered subjectivities and readings of the body, and power relations between young people as they achieve maturity and define themselves as independent, are neglected or denied (Bhavnani, 1991; Macpherson and Fine, 1995).

Our analysis suggests that, in their reading of the body, young women do draw extensively on the achievement of maturity, independence, separation from parents and engagement in heterosexual relations. In this respect young women's ideas reflect mainstream psychological constructions of 'normal' adolescent development. However, at the same time, we also highlight the inadequacies of psychological theorizing which does not acknowledge the gendered nature of ideas about independence and maturity and which fails to recognize social constructions of women's bodies and sexuality, and constraints on their ability to make independent decisions. Mainstream psychological theories also fail to address social class. The young women who participated in this study could all be categorized as working class and all lived in the inner city. As a result, the representations of young working-class women who are often omitted from mainstream psychology are included, although it was not possible to examine the impacts of social class on their readings of the body and their representations of independence and maturity.

This analysis of gendered readings also argues for the importance of *not* assuming that all young women share the same readings of the body and conceptualizations of independence, responsibility and maturity. In their accounts young Asian women suggest that the presentation of the body and the implications of taking independent action (in terms of their own reputation and those of their families) are related to and need to take account of *both* their gender *and* their ethnicity. In addition, for Asian young women living in families where arranged marriages are an accepted practice, engagement in sexual relations is often less women's 'own' decision but relates to family considerations and to the value placed on collective as distinct from individualistic ideas. Psychological accounts of development in adolescence need to take account of gender, of ethnicity and the ways in which they intersect and interplay.

Therefore, we stress the importance of engaging with varied meanings and constraints on the realization of independence as played out through the body. This is of particular relevance to young women in general, and to young Asian and black women (and men) for whom immediate contextual concerns cannot be ignored or avoided. We would argue that it remains of central importance to continue to challenge universalistic and decontextualized theorizing in mainstream psychological approaches to adolescence on the basis of their exclusivity and reproduction of gender and ethnic inequalities.

NOTE

The research for this chapter was conducted with an award from the Economic and Social Research Council (R 000 23 2456) 'Parenthood and Parenting Practice in a Multi-Ethnic Setting' to Anne Woollett, Harriette Marshall and Paula Nicolson from the University of Sheffield. We would like to thank Bianca Raabe for assistance with interviewing.

REFERENCES

Allen, I. (1987) *Education in Sex and Personal Relationships*. London: Policy Studies
    Institute.
Apter, T. (1991) *Altered Loves: Mothers and Daughters during Adolescence*. Hemel
    Hempstead: Harvester.
Bhavnani, K.K. (1991) *Talking Politics: A Psychological Framing for Views from Youth
    in Britain*. Cambridge: Cambridge University Press.
Brannen, J., K. Dodd, A. Oakley and P. Storey (1994) *Young People, Health and Family
    Life*. Milton Keynes: Open University Press.
Butler, J. (1993) *Bodies that Matter: On the Discursive Limits of 'Sex'*. London: Rout-
    ledge.
Coleman, J. and L. Hendry (1990) *The Nature of Adolescence*. London: Routledge.
Collins, P. H. (1990) *Black Feminist Thought: Knowledge, Consciousness, and the Poli-
    tics of Empowerment*. London: Unwin Hyman.
Cowie, E. (1990) 'Woman as Sign', in P. Adams and E. Cowie (eds) *The Woman in
    Question*. London and New York: Verso.
Erikson, E. H. (1968) *Identity: Youth and Crisis*. London: Faber.
Farganis, S. (1994) *Situating Feminism: From Thought to Action*. London: Sage.
Griffin, C. (1985) *Typical Girls: Young Women from School to the Job Market*. London:
    Routledge.
Griffin, C. (1993) *Representations of Youth: The Study of Youth and Adolescence in
    Britain and America*. Cambridge: Polity Press.
Griffiths, V. (1987) 'Adolescent Girls: Transition From Girlfriends to Boyfriends?',
    in P. Allat, T. Keil, A. Bryman and B. Bytheway (eds) *Women and the Life Cycle:
    Transitions and Turning Points*. London: Macmillan.
Haraway, D. (1984) 'Primatology is Politics by Other Means', in R. Bleir (ed.) *Femin-
    ist Approaches to Science*. London: Pergamon.
Hendry, L. B., J. Shucksmith, J. G. Love and A. Glendinning (1993) *Young People's
    Leisure and Lifestyles*. London: Routledge.
Lees, S. (1993) *Sugar and Spice: Sexuality and Adolescent Girls*. Harmondsworth:
    Penguin.
Macpherson, P. and M. Fine (1995) 'Hungry for Us: Adolescent Girls and Adult
    Women Negotiating Territories of Race, Gender, Class and Difference',
    Feminism & Psychology 5: 181–200.
Mirza, H. S. (1992) *Young, Female and Black*. London: Routledge.
Moore, D. (1987) 'Parent–Adolescent Separation: The Construction of Adulthood
    by Later Adolescents', *Developmental Psychology* 23: 298–307.
Moore, S. and D. Rosenthal (1993) *Sexuality in Adolescence*. London: Routledge.
Noller, P. and V. Callan (1991) *The Adolescent in the Family*. London: Routledge.
Phoenix, A. (1991) *Young Mothers*. Cambridge: Polity Press.
Ramazanoglu, C. (1993) *Up Against Foucault: Explorations of some Tensions between
    Foucault and Feminism*. London: Routledge.
Segal, L. (1994) *Straight Sex: The Politics of Pleasure*. London: Virago.
Sharpe, S. (1994) *Just Like a Girl: How Women Learn to be Women. From the Seventies
    to the Nineties*. Harmondsworth: Penguin.
Smetana, J. G. and P. Asquith (1994) 'Adolescents' and Parents' Conceptions of
    Parental Authority and Personal Autonomy', *Child Development* 65: 1147–62.
Woollett, A., H. Marshall, P. Nicolson and N. Dosanjh (1994) 'Asian Women's
    Ethnic Identity: The Impact of Gender and Context in the Accounts of
    Women Bringing up Children in East London', *Feminism & Psychology*
    4: 101–14.

3 Performing the Body, Creating Culture

Anna Aalten

About a year ago I went to the Music Theatre in Amsterdam to watch the Dutch National Ballet. They were doing the famous *Giselle*, a ballet first performed at the Parisian Opéra in 1841. In those days the leading role was danced by Carlotta Grisi and the ballet was an instant success. It has been on the repertoire of every major ballet company in Europe and the United States ever since, always popular and never ceasing to fill the house.

Giselle is the story of a farmer's daughter, Giselle, who falls in love with the aristocratic Albrecht. Albrecht seduces her without revealing his identity. Later, when she finds out who he is, she kills herself by piercing his sword through her heart. After her death Giselle joins a group of *willis*, the revengeful ghosts of betrayed virgins. Guided by their ruthless queen Myrtha, the *willis* set out to kill Albrecht, but Giselle's love reaches across the grave and she saves him.

Although I am a great lover of dance in whatever form, attending this performance was still something I had to think about first. My hesitation had to do with the research I am conducting on representations of femininity and the body in classical ballet. Descriptions of scenes at professional schools of dance and dance troupes (Mazo, 1974; Gordon, 1983) and autobiographies of female dancers (Flett, 1981; Brady, 1982; Bentley, 1982; Kirkland and Lawrence, 1986) do not give a particularly favourable impression of how women are presented on stage or how the bodies of female dancers are dealt with. In order to be able to dance a convincing Giselle, female dancers submit to gruelling training and need perfect control of their bodies. Bearing this in mind, how could I appreciate a performance of this ballet?

However, during the performance, I enjoyed the aesthetics of dance and I felt admiration for the dancers' technical skills. I was also touched at the moments when Giselle depicted in dance her love for Albrecht and her yearning to save him. There is a strange paradox in the fact that as a viewer I experience an immense pleasure watching this ballet performance – a pleasure that does not seem to be in accordance with my awareness of the degrading images of femininity on stage and the unhealthy practices behind it. This paradox will be the starting point for my reflection on the relationship between bodies and cultures as they become manifest in ballet.

FEMINIST STUDIES AND DANCE

In 1992 two books on the history of dance were published, both written
from an explicitly feminist perspective. The British journalist Christy
Adair was the author of *Women and Dance: Sylphs and Sirens* and the
German sociologist Gabriele Klein of *Frauen Körper Tanz. Eine Zivilisationsgeschichte des Tanzes*. Looking back now, I think these books were a turning
point in the feminist disdain of the world of dance and its performers up
to that point. At last dance and dancers were considered an interesting
field for feminist research. Of course in the late 1980s we had read Judith
Lynne Hanna's book on *Dance, Sex and Gender* (1988) and Ann Daly's
inspiring article on classical ballet as a discourse on difference (1987/88).
And in the early 1990s we enjoyed Jane Cowan's case study of *Dance and
the Body Politic in Northern Greece* (1990) and Cynthia Novack's feminist
analysis, *Sharing the Dance*, on contact improvisation as an innovative force
in American dance (1990). However, in contrast to these authors, Adair
and Klein provided feminist frameworks that would make it possible to
rewrite dance history. In this sense, both studies can be called 'ground
breaking'.

Adair's book called attention to the elitist, sexist and racist tendencies
in the world of Western theatrical dance. In her introduction Adair presented herself as a feminist with a lifelong passion for dance. Her aim was
to expose the confining and hierarchical practices in dance and to focus
attention on women's achievements. For the most part, her book is a historical overview emphasizing the contribution women have made to the
history of theatrical dance in Europe and the United States. In the first few
chapters she put the developments in dance into a larger social historical
framework.

According to Adair, ballet as an art form has been in close alliance with
the ruling classes ever since its first manifestations at the French courts of
King Louis XIV. Class and gender are both important social variables that
order the power relations within the world of dance. Adair addressed the
social arrangements that have colonized dancers' bodies, permitting
women to be performers while excluding them from the more powerful
positions of choreographer or director (Adair, 1992: 40–119). She also
pointed out that black dancers have virtually no opportunities to join the
established, all-white dance companies, thus being marginalized to the
circles of 'ethnic' dance (Adair 1992: 160–182).

Klein's focus was a different one. She made an effort 'to understand and
explain the history of dance in relation to the history of the human body'
(1992: 12). These objectives sound rather grand, but the scope of the book
is limited to the developments in German theatrical dance. Following in
the footsteps of Norbert Elias, the German sociologist who saw history as
an ongoing process of increasing civilization, Klein examined how dance
has been influenced and shaped by social forces. The treatment of the
human body in particular historical periods was her main focus.

Klein stated that in the course of European history, periods of *'Körper-entfesselung'*, the liberation of the human body, alternate with periods of *'Körperdisziplin'*, the restriction of the human body. Placing the development of dance in a social context, she showed how nineteenth-century views of the body as something to be controlled are reflected in the ideals of Romantic ballet. On the basis of developments in dance in Germany, Klein wrote a history of the continuous growth of bodily discipline, accompanied by the confirmation of patriarchal power relations. The *'Freikörperkultur'*, an inspiration for German modern dancers in the first half of the twentieth century, freed the body of the constraints of corsettes, pointe shoes and a dance technique that could ruin a dancer's health. But in its place came an even stronger form of restraint, that of self-discipline and self-control.

Adair and Klein both took the subordination of women as their starting point. Women were conceptualized as victims of patriarchal relationships in the world of dance and their representation on stage was regarded usually as oppressive. At the same time both authors tried to show that women have played a very important part in the development of dance and that their role should be described and acknowledged. At the end of her book Adair turned to the new generation of dancers who, often inspired by feminism, question the ideal of the dancer's body and the dancer's look in their choreographies. In her last chapter she stated hopefully: 'Deconstruction of the representations of women in dance enables rejection of restrictive, offensive images of women, because it involves analysis of images in terms of differences and multiplicities of representations' (Adair, 1992: 199). Research on the images and representations of femininity in dance and on the training methods and attitudes towards the body can stimulate different, less oppressive forms of dancing. Klein also looked at dancers' search for a new aesthetic, exploring the borders of their own corporeality: dancers who cross the social and cultural boundaries between femininity and masculinity. Their quest will lead to a fundamental critique of the seemingly so self-evident connection between women and the body in Western culture.

DANCE, GENDER AND THE BODY

Some time ago I started a research project on 'Femininity and the Body of the Ballerina in Western Theatrical Dance'. As an anthropologist with a strong commitment to feminist studies and a lifelong fascination for dance and dance practices, I have watched numerous performances and I have experience of dance styles ranging from classical ballet to Argentinian tango and African dance. I see dance as having potential to reflect culture, along the same lines as anthropologist Ted Polhemus who once called dance 'a liqueur which is distilled of the stuff of culture' (1993: 9). He states that:

Dance is a stylised, highly redundant schema of a people's overall physical culture which is itself the embodiment of that particular people's unique way of life – their culture in the broadest sense of the term. Dance is the meta-physics of culture. (Polhemus, 1993: 8)

In my research, therefore, I want to consider classical ballet as a form of ethnic dance (Kealiinohomoku, 1983: 544–5). This means that ballet is a reflection and representation of specific cultural notions, which it (re)creates at the same time. In doing so, I am aware that I go against all the conventions in theatre studies, but if challenged I think I can make a case for my choice.

I take as my point of departure the body and femininity, joining Klein and Adair in their exploration of these research themes. It was Gabriele Klein's detailed account of the increasing control of the human body in Western society that first called my attention to this aspect of dance. To Christy Adair's work I owe my interest in the relations between social inequalities and the world of dance that is also part and parcel of my anthropological background. Although I read *Women and Dance* and *Frauen Körper Tanz* with pleasure and respect the authors' endeavours tremendously, I find the women-as-victims model a serious stumbling block when trying to understand the complexity of gender relations in dance. Therefore, unlike both of them I have chosen an actor-oriented approach. It is my conviction that when theories portray human beings narrowly as the vehicles through which discourses gain expression, they neglect their potential to confront, negotiate and manoeuvre in their worlds.

Looking for the theoretical tools to study dance, gender and the body from an actor-oriented approach, I came upon the work of the American philosopher Judith Butler. Her notion of gender as a performative act, 'instituted through the stylization of the body' (Butler, 1990b: 270), facili-tates an analysis of the relations between gender and the body. Moreover, Butler ascribes a dimension of agency in her conceptualization of the body as a 'materializing of possibilities' (Butler, 1990b: 272).

My research project makes use of several different methods. The first is the use of biographies and autobiographies of dancers. Secondly, I analyse performances of Dutch dance companies and finally I gather life stories of Dutch professional (ex-)dancers, specifically concerning the training methods at Dutch ballet academies and their own dancing practices. In doing so, I combine the anthropological tradition of focusing on the human subject as the creator of his or her world with the feminist and dance studies' attention for the representation of femininity. My aim is to study the construction of the body of the female dancer in relation to rep-resentations of femininity. Since the research has not been completed and none of my methods have resulted in any clear-cut answers yet, this article should be regarded as an elaboration of the main research questions, and not as its answer.

SEX, GENDER AND THE BODY

In feminist studies, bodies and cultures have long been separated on a con-
ceptual level by the distinction between sex and gender. 'Sex' is everything
concerned with the bodily differences between women and men, while
'gender' is about the cultural elaboration of these differences. In the past,
the distinction between sex and gender has been extremely useful in the
battle against biological determinism evident in so many of the analyses
of female–male relationships. However, recently the distinction has been
seriously questioned. Feminist social scientists became aware of the con-
textuality of the body and the necessity to study it in its own cultural
frameworks (Haug et al., 1987; Martin, 1987; Jacobus et al., 1990; Bordo,
1993). The work of feminist biologists has revealed that sex and sexual
differences are far less obvious or natural than we had been assuming all
along (van den Wijngaard, 1991; Birke, 1986). The distinction between sex
and gender was also questioned on a philosophical level by Judith Butler
(1987, 1990a, 1993), among others.

In an effort to develop a theory of gender inspired by Simone de
Beauvoir's famous formulation 'one is not born, but rather becomes a
woman' (de Beauvoir, 1972), Judith Butler proposed seeing gender as 'the
corporeal locus of cultural meanings both received and innovated' (1987:
128). But if we define the body as a locus of meanings, which aspects of
this body are hence natural or free of cultural imprint? Or, to quote Butler:

> Indeed, how are we to find the body that preexists its cultural interpretation?
> If gender is the corporealization of choice, and the acculturation of the cor-
> poreal, then what is left of nature, and what has become of sex? If gender is
> determined in the dialectic between culture and choice, then what role does
> 'sex' serve, and ought we to conclude that the very distinction between sex
> and gender is anachronistic? (1987: 129)

To answer these questions, Butler returned to de Beauvoir's work in
combination with the ideas of Wittig, Foucault and phenomenologists
such as Merleau-Ponty (Butler, 1987).

At first glance, de Beauvoir's famous statement seems to adopt a Cartesian mind/body dualism, presenting the view of a disembodied agent
taking on a gender. However, upon examining it more closely it becomes
clear that in saying that one becomes a woman, de Beauvoir

> does not imply that this 'becoming' traverses a path from disembodied
> freedom to cultural embodiment. Indeed, one is one's body from the start, and
> only thereafter becomes one's gender. The movement from sex to gender is
> internal to embodied life, a sculpting of the original body into a cultural form.
> (Butler, 1987: 131)

Instead of reproducing the Cartesian view of a body that must be transcended, de Beauvoir introduces the notion of the body as a situation.
There are at least two ways of interpreting this notion. The first is to see

the body as a material reality: as something that is there and can be held. Yet even as a material reality a body is never just there; it always has a meaning, because it has already been defined in a social and cultural context. The second way of interpreting the notion of the body as a situation is to regard having a specific body as an obligation to take up these social and cultural definitions and come to terms with them.

Butler rightly states that the acceptance of the notion of the body as a situation poses a serious problem regarding the distinction between sex and gender, because,

> If we accept the body as a cultural situation, then the notion of a natural body and, indeed, a natural 'sex' seem increasingly suspect. The limits to gender, the range of possibilities for a lived interpretation of a sexually differentiated anatomy, seem less restricted by anatomy than by the weight of the cultural institutions that have conventionally interpreted anatomy. Indeed, it becomes unclear when we take Beauvoir's formulation to its unstated consequences, whether this linkage is itself cultural convention. If gender is a way of existing one's body, and one's body is a situation, a field of cultural possibilities both received and reinterpreted, then both gender and sex seem to be thoroughly cultural affairs. (Butler, 1987: 134)

But if both sex and gender are cultural affairs, what then is the relation between a body as a material reality and different representations of femininity? If we do not believe that femininity can be derived from some physiological fact, or that the relation between sex and gender is a causal one, how do we view it then? If we want to study the body in relation to meanings of femininity without falling into the trap of causality, how do we go about it? Again Judith Butler provides a possible direction.

She criticizes the commonly held idea that femininity and masculinity are the cultural *expressions* of a material fact, namely the female or male body. Instead of a notion of gender as an expressive act she proposes viewing gender as a *performative* one (Butler, 1990b: 279). She develops the notion of gender as a performative act using the phenomenological theory in which acts are how social agents constitute reality. Butler's notion of gender as a performative act can be seen as an elaboration of her earlier thoughts on the body as a situation. In Butler's view, the body and gender are closely connected, but not as a biological facticity nor as the cultural interpretation of that facticity. Rather, the body and gender are connected because,

> gender is instituted through the stylization of the body and, hence, must be understood as the mundane way in which bodily gestures, movements, and enactments of various kinds constitute the illusion of an abiding gendered self. (Butler, 1990b: 270)

The idea of gender 'as *a corporeal style*, an "act", as it were, which is both intentional and performative' (Butler, 1990b: 272, original italics), makes it possible to examine how individuals live their bodies and in this process constitute gender. The body, be it female or male, offers infinite possibilities, albeit within the confines of already existing historical directives.

> As an intentionally organized materiality, the body is always an embodying *of* possibilities both conditioned and circumscribed by historical convention. In other words, the body *is* a historical situation, as Beauvoir has claimed, and is a manner of doing, dramatizing, and *reproducing* a historical situation. (Butler, 1990b: 272, original italics)

Butler emphasizes that her notion of performativity must be understood 'not as a singular or deliberate "act", but, rather, as the reiterative and citational practice by which discourse produces the effect that it names' (1993: 2). The 'citationality' of gender practices lies in the reiteration and reproduction of cultural norms and social inequalities. Butler views the body, in all its aspects, as fully material, but its materiality must be seen as an effect of power relations.

In my view, Butler offers us the foundations of a research agenda that devotes attention to the body in relation to the construction of femininity, while freeing itself from the 'Cartesian ghost' of a separation of mind and body. In her proposal to see gender as a performative act which constitutes reality, Butler breaks away from the popular notion of a distinction between the reality of sex and the appearance of gender. Gender reality is created through a continuation of performances in which the body is stylized to fit existing gender directives and/or produce new ones. In addition, Butler's notion of the body as 'not merely matter but a continual and incessant *materializing* of possibilities' (1990b: 272, original italics) offers possibilities for a new approach to dance, gender and the body.

PERFORMING THE BODY

Lightness can be considered the keyword in ballet. 'Light as weightlessness, light as luminosity: in English the same word serves both meanings' (Jowitt, 1988: 39). Dancers are seen as artists who successfully challenge the law of gravity. This is not only a consequence of the taste and fashion at the time of its origin, but also of the specific characteristics of ballet technique. In ballet the centre of the movement is in the spine. A dancer always keeps his or her body up, letting the arms and legs do most of the work. The basic movement in ballet is upwards, in a constant striving to reach for the immortality of a heavenly creature (Kirstein, 1983). High jumps, legs raised up to the ears, lifts (whereby the male dancer lifts the female dancer and carries her across the stage) and the use of pointe shoes that enable a dancer to stand on the tips of her toes strengthen the illusion of weightlessness.

Ballet has its roots in the French court dances of the fifteenth and sixteenth centuries. In the seventeenth century under the reign of Louis XIV, a true lover of dance, dancing at the court became a real art. It was Louis

XIV who gave an impetus to the development of dance as a profession by founding the Royal Academy of Dance in 1661. In 1670 the king stopped dancing himself. The performance of ballet was removed from the court to the theatre. The basic principles of the ballet technique as we know it go back to that era, written down by the first director of the Royal Academy, Pierre Beauchamps. The first principle in ballet is always the *en-dehors*, the turn-out, where dancers try to turn their legs to make their feet stand at a 180 degree angle. Originally the *en-dehors* was meant to enable dancers to move sidewards on stage, thus looking the audience in the face while they danced. But a good turn-out also enables a dancer to raise the leg higher, move faster, jump further and change directions more rapidly and more fluidly. Derived from the turn-out, five basic positions of the feet are used. The second principle is the mastery of aerial space, as is manifest in the capacity to leap, fly and dance *en pointe*. In the nineteenth century the extensive use of jumps, originating in the elevated dance ('*danse haute*') of the courts, was developed further. Jumps become higher and more frequent, spectacular pirouettes and innovating lifts become part of the standard technique. Finally, ever since Marie Taglioni rose to the points of her feet in 1832, there has been the perfection of pointe work for female dancers.

All these techniques require a strong control of the body by the dancer. Years of training are needed to learn the right technique and to master it. In the Netherlands girls who want to pursue a career in ballet have to start early in life, definitely before they are 10 years old. Training is hard and time-consuming. It is not uncommon for a 12-year-old to leave the house before dawn and not come back before nine o'clock at night. Days are filled with early dance classes, then school, and after that more dancing lessons. If asked, young trainees admit to leading a life of work and discipline. Since the demands of the profession are high, the selection process is severe and often cruel. A promising career can be cut short by injuries or physical changes, like the development of breasts that are too large. Some of the female dancers I interviewed referred to their bodies as 'unproblematic', but others suffered enormously during their training years. One dancer told me she had been in constant pain at the academy throughout the first four years, but she 'had become used to that'.

Nobody expects ballet dancers to have 'natural' bodies. As a consequence of the 'unnaturalness' of Western ballet, unlike the 'naturalness' of German modern dance at the beginning of this century, dancers are required to sculpt their bodies into a cultural form. Following Butler, this training process is a 'reiterative and citational practice' by which particular ballet bodies are created. This performing of the body is highly gendered. Whoever has witnessed ballet training in the Netherlands has seen that men and women do the same exercises and execute the same movements. However, the physical demands that are made on them are different.

In an interview, American dancer Bruce Marks recounted how back in the 1950s, the technique of male dancers clearly differed from that of female ones. Men were not expected to lift their leg any higher than their hip. It simply was not done. At the time, seeing French male dancers lift their legs way up into the air merely made Americans laugh (Newman, 1982: 223). Moreover, it was believed that doing a split was detrimental to men's ability to jump (Newman, 1982: 206). Since then, male dancers have been stretching their legs as high and far as they can. Their female colleagues, however, are expected to lift their legs even higher. Women also excel in tiny, rapid movements such as swift pirouettes *en pointe*, in which case they are often supported by their partners, fast little jumps similarly on the tips of their toes, and tiny little steps. Men show off their technical mastery in larger leaps and impressive turns. To make their leaps as long as possible, they use their arms to add extra force. Women don't do that. Nor should they, as a matter of fact, according to today's conventions. According to Sayers:

> A central ideal of the classical technique is the masking of the technique and strength, particularly so in the case of the ballerina where a display of strength would be inappropriate to the ideology that informs it. (1993: 170)

Female dancers generally make smaller movements, showing less strength than male dancers. Their leaps are primarily supposed to be supple and ornamental or tiny and rapid, like the *sissonne*, a little jump the *willis* in *Giselle* often use. A young female dancer told me that when she was a student her instructors would always tell her she 'jumped like a man'. They told her not to make such strong movements with her arms. Once she obeyed she noticed she wasn't jumping nearly as high or as far any more.

How are dancers successful in mastering the required technique and using it? Or, using Butler's terminology, how is the dancer's body stylized to constitute the illusion of the carefree village girl who turns into a *willi*? How does the performative act of a *willi* relate to the material reality of the dancer's body? A good turn-out is basic in ballet, and since the eighteenth century dancers have gone to extremes to accomplish it. Because it goes against the natural movements of the human body (human feet do not stand out in a 180 degree angle), the training process is long and arduous. In the nineteenth century dancers at the beginning of their training were sometimes put in a box with braces that could be adjusted via a series of grooves. As an anonymous dancer recounted: 'There, heel to heel, with my knees pointing outwards, my martyred feet became used to remaining in a parallel line by themselves' (quoted in Adair, 1992: 87). To increase their turn-out many dancers had their maids or colleagues stand on their hips and Carlotta Grisi 'said sourly that those times Jules Perrot stood on her hips while she lay face down on the floor with legs spread were the erotic high points of their liaison' (quoted in Jowitt, 1988: 43).

Nowadays a good turn-out is attained through extensive training, starting at as early an age as possible. William Hamilton, orthopedist and former doctor of the New York City Ballet, stated that there 'are few, if any, *absolute contraindications* to dancing. If pressed, I would say that very poor turn-out of the hips precludes a ballet career' (1982: 83, original italics). This opinion was also voiced by a physical therapist I interviewed at the ballet academy in Amsterdam: an auditioning student can be extremely talented, but without the required turn-out she will not be admitted. I interviewed a young trainee who had passed all the auditions at both ballet academies in the Netherlands, but was sent away because her turn-out wasn't good enough. She tried again a year later. Unfortunately, her body had not improved. Now she specializes in modern dance.

Although the human body can be moulded into many forms, the basic material of a dancer has to be there. Ballet academies select their students on the basis of physical qualities. Apart from a good turn-out, certain body proportions are absolutely necessary for dancers who aspire to a career in classical ballet. For female dancers, having the right proportions means having long legs, a slim body and no hips. A combination of a long trunk and short legs is not acceptable for women in ballet and even the most talented and hard-working dancer cannot change that. On the other hand, the extent to which a dancer is thought to have the right proportions also depends on fashion and taste. The proportions of female dancers in American and Western European major companies nowadays are clearly influenced by a general preference for extremely slim bodies with long legs, a short torso, a long neck and a small head. As the American dancer Violette Verdy once said: 'These days everybody's a greyhound' (quoted in Jowitt, 1988: 268). Looking at the body of the present-day dancer, one is reminded of the words of the French nineteenth-century writer and ballet lover Stéphane Mallarmé: 'The main point is that the ballerina is not a woman who dances' (quoted in Klein, 1992: 121). A body with curves at the hips, buttocks and breasts is definitely not considered well proportioned for present-day ballet. Nowadays in ballet, beauty and grace for women are equated with excessive thinness.

Weight has been an issue in ballet since lifts became part of the standard repertoire. If one is familiar with the number of times male dancers in *Giselle* have to lift their female colleagues and carry them around the stage, it is easy to see why this is so. On the other hand, the contact improvisation dancers of the 1960s demonstrated that weight is not the determining factor when trying to lift someone (Adair, 1992: 148). Weight is obviously important, but the emphasis on thinness for female dancers has more to do with fashion and taste than with any technical demands of the profession. Portraits and photographs of nineteenth-century female dancers show that dancers were heavier then, and poor nineteenth-century dancer Madeleine Guimard 'was nicknamed the "Skeleton of the Graces" because her scrawny figure lacked the voluptuous curves of her rivals' (McConnell, 1977: 19). Even a comparison with dancers of a more recent past makes it clear that, while the physical demands have become greater, the bodies of female dancers tend to be thinner. In my conversations with female dancers in the Netherlands, the enormous pressure on female dancers to be thin often came up. Female dancers are constantly told to watch their weight by teachers, ballet masters, choreographers and directors. Many dancers experience a permanent struggle against food and the autobiographies of some present-day dancers can be read as accounts of this struggle (Bentley, 1982; Kirkland and Lawrence, 1986). The aesthetic ideal of the present-day ballet world has therefore been the subject of much feminist criticism (Gordon, 1983: 134–63; Adair, 1992: 60–1; Novack, 1993) and the cause of misery in many dancers' lives (Brady, 1982; Kirkland and Lawrence, 1986).

The preoccupation with weight starts at the schools where young girls on the verge of puberty are scrutinized for the first physical signs of femininity. Any signs of feminine curves are met with disapproval, both at school and in the company. Journalist Suzanne Gordon spent more than a year at some prominent ballet schools in the United States. She described how contagious the panic about gaining weight was among ballet students. As a result of comments by their teachers and the conduct of their fellow students, even girls who had no weight problems were soon talked into them. The same picture emerged in my own talks with female dancers. A 20-year-old ex-dancer told me how she had never been at all concerned about her weight in the first years of her training and had always been 'nice and slim'. In her senior year this changed and she suddenly began compulsive dieting. Her weight started to yoyo. In the end, her eating disorder was the reason she dropped out of the school. A limited survey among ballet students has shown that they systematically eat meals that fail to provide adequate nourishment and do not compensate for the shortage of calories with extra vitamins (Bonbridge, 1989). Gordon estimated that at least 15 percent of the girls at the American ballet schools suffer from anorexia nervosa and many more have eating disorders (1983: 140). On the other hand, the physical demands do not lead to eating disorders for all dancers. Some of them are built slim; others perceive the need for a constant bodily control not as a threat, but as a challenge (Bentley, 1982).

Research on the body composition of dancers has shown how the often very low intake of calories, in combination with the daily physical training, leads to strikingly low percentages of body fat in female dance students and professional dancers (Evans et al., 1985; Freedson, 1988; Lichtenbelt et al., 1995). A recent survey at a ballet academy in Amsterdam indicated that the majority of the trainees had a lower weight than was normal for their age group, but 44 percent thought that losing weight would improve their dancing and 70 percent constantly watched their weight (Procee, 1991). The lack of body fat often results in a delayed menarche and amenorrhea (Warren, 1988). Ex-dancer and physician Lawrence Vincent described how the extreme thinness of young dancers can delay the onset of menstruation and keep them in what he called a 'puberty holding pattern' (Vincent, 1979: 99). As a consequence of low body fat that causes a lack of œstrogen and other hormones, these girls preserve the body configuration of an adolescent (Vincent, 1979: 77–107). Thus he states that:

> The claims of ballet mistresses that they can pick out a future ballet body are false; they're simply selecting late developers and, with the help of poor nutrition, keeping them that way. It's almost as if ballet had created a new species of woman: low estrogen and androgynous (quoted in Gordon, 1983: 153–4).

In the Amsterdam survey, 40 percent of the female students menstruated irregularly (Procee, 1991). Systematic research among adult professional dancers, however, remains to be conducted.

The use of pointe shoes also contributes to the swiftness and the impression of weightlessness of the female dancer. Pointe shoes are used exclusively by female dancers; they materially underline the difference between female and male dancers. Nowadays dancers use blocked and stiffened pointe shoes that make it possible to stand on the very tip of the toes. The nineteenth-century dancer had nothing but her toe pads and the only way she could stay on tiptoe was by exerting all her leg muscle and a tremendous lift in her body (Terry, 1962). Obviously, the tips of human toes are not made to walk on and the feet of female dancers are therefore susceptible to injuries. Still, pointe shoes are used, not only in the choreographies of the nineteenth-century repertoire, but also in the neo-classical works of George Balanchine and the post-modern choreographies by William Forsyth. Good pointe work demands years of training and constant practice, and even then it is never easy. But it does have its merits; a dancer moves faster and turns more easily on pointe and, as one dancer told me, 'it is the closest to flying a human being can ever get'.

Using Judith Butler's notion of gender as a performative act, masculinity and femininity can be seen as enacted through the bodies of male and female dancers, and the schools and companies reiterate and reproduce these cultural norms in the training process. For female ballet dancers, these practices result in a specific materiality: a super-slim body without feminine curves. The masculinity of the male dancer is created in his big jumps and his strong, supportive arms. The femininity of the female dancer is expressed in her tiny, rapid movements on pointe, her high legs and the graceful movements of her arms. Male dancers have to possess strength, while light and fragile female dancers must move as if they are nearly flying.

CREATING CULTURE

I shall now look at the dancer's body in relation to *Giselle*'s representations of femininity, taking Judith Butler's notion of the body as a historical situation as my starting point. Having shown how the dancer's body is stylized by the specific bodily practices of ballet training as well as how

FIGURE 1
Creating culture

historical conventions condition and circumscribe the body of both male and female dancers, how can we relate these corporeal practices to the performance of femininity on stage?

In *Giselle*, the specific technique of ballet can be seen in its purest form. The leading role of Giselle demands very strong technical skills and

> in addition to that a great range of expression. She starts as a carefree village girl, fond of dancing and very much in love. Next we see her betrayed and driven mad, until she dies a suicide. Then, in the following act, she is a spirit who must impress upon us the fact that she is lightness itself and so make a vivid contrast with the red-cheeked villager of the first act. (Haskell, 1955: 139–41)

The part of Giselle is considered the touchstone for the real ballerina. Female students at ballet academies in the Netherlands are trained to dance this role or one of the other principal roles of the nineteenth century. *Giselle* can be seen as the highlight of Romantic ballet not only in its

artistic qualities, but in its theme. The confrontation between the immoral-
ity and decadence of the aristocracy, embodied in Albrecht, and the purity
of ordinary village people like Giselle is typical of nineteenth-century
Romanticism. Emotion abounds: passion, death and magical revenge by
the *willis*, and finally Giselle's pure love that conquers the evil forces of
Queen Myrtha and death. *Giselle* can also be viewed as the representation
of a wide range of femininities (Jowitt, 1988; Adair, 1992). As a girl carried
away by dance and love, in the first act Giselle is the embodiment of the
erotic, sexually active woman. In the second act she changes into a super-
natural creature and joins forces with the *willis*. Unlike the other *willis*,
however, she is not driven by a desire for revenge. Instead she does her
best to save Albrecht. Thus she also represents the benevolence of love,
true but unconsummated. Giselle remains inaccessible in her spiritual virginity.

The Ann Daly once called classical ballet 'a discourse of difference'
(1987/88). In the way women and men are represented in ballet, difference
is central. Women are passive, ethereal and delicate, men are dynamic,
active and take up a lot of space. The representations of femininity presented in *Giselle* contain contradictions that can only be comprehended
against the background of the era from which the ballet comes. Nineteenth-century Romantics venerated women because they felt they were
more natural than men. Women were seen as beings who were closer to
their feelings; they symbolized the emotionality to which the Romantics
aspired. The Romantics were also preoccupied with the dichotomy of
body and mind. The body and the mind or soul were viewed as opposites,
with the body being inferior. Since women were thought to be closer to
nature, they were associated with the inferior body. For this reason femininity was presented in ballet as disembodied and incorporeal. Writing in
the early twentieth century, ballet critic Rayner Heppenstall described this
femininity in the following way:

> a woman on her points, 'because of change in significant line and stress and
> action, ceases to be significantly a woman. She becomes an idealised and
> stylised creature of the Theatre.' And there is a kind of eternal virginity about
> her. She is inaccessible. She remains unravished. (1983: 274)

When dancing Giselle, the female dancer embodies a nineteenth-century
ideal of femininity. Giselle is the unattainable woman, whose feet never
touch the ground; her virginity is eternal.

The symbolism of *Giselle*, which is so typical of nineteenth-century
Romanticism, brings me back to the paradox I pointed out earlier. How is
it possible that I, a twentieth-century feminist with an awareness of the
nineteenth-century images of femininity on stage and the unhealthy practices behind it, can enjoy a performance of this ballet? Why am I (still?)
susceptible to the aesthetics of the ballet, given the disembodied femininity Giselle represents and my knowledge of the rigorous bodily discipline
that is necessary to perform it? Maybe my pleasure stems from an ability

to admire the aesthetic and technical skills of the performers. The fact that I danced for many years and my body knows the requirements of the technique undoubtedly makes me receptive to the display of technique and virtuosity. Since my body knows what it feels like to dance ballet, this feeling is activated whenever I see people doing it, perhaps accounting for the admiration and awe. But there is also another possibility. Maybe the pleasure I derive from a ballet performance like *Giselle* stems from my own acquiescence, either conscious or unconscious, to the dominant cultural codes of my society.

If ballet is a form of ethnic dance, then classical ballet can indeed be viewed as a reflection of typical nineteenth-century values that are still in effect today. The themes, the setting, the costumes, the stories – and in neo-classical ballet even more so the absence of stories – make ballet most notably a form of ethnic dance. Western aesthetic values are shown in the long line of slender lifted bodies, in the total exposure of legs and in the principle of verticality. Western body politics are reflected in the standardization of the technique and in the belief that the body is an object, a thing that can be moulded and shaped. As a viewer I can appreciate all these aspects in the performance of *Giselle*. I am touched by the tragic story of the impossible love affair between Albrecht and Giselle, while I enjoy the beauty of the dancers' bodies and their movements, and I admire their technical virtuosity. It is possible that with my joy and admiration I subtly but powerfully subscribe to a specific social order, including the gender relations it creates (Alderson, 1987; Novack, 1993).

The bodies of ballet dancers are clearly cultural bodies. In other words, female and male dancers take up the cultural definitions of femininity and masculinity that ballet, with its Western aesthetics, offers them. In order to render these representations on stage, what is required is 'a sculpting of the original body into a cultural form'. Put in Butler's terminology, the physical practices of dancers are 'reiterative and citational practices' which evoke and reproduce nineteenth-century images of femininity and masculinity. Through their bodies dancers creatively explore its possibilities. The body is not only the materialization of cultural norms, but also materializes the dancers' interpretation of them. Within the dance world, bodies are seen as extremely malleable, subjected to a superior mind. There is a shared belief in the pliability of the body. This belief stems from a typically Western, Cartesian split between body and mind in which the mind rules the body. Because ballet masters, teachers and choreographers uphold this premise, dancers are trained to control their bodies to the extreme. They control their muscles and their appetites; they are told to dance through pain and exhaustion.

But a discourse that views female dancers as nothing more than the passive recipients and unquestioning transmitters of the cultural meanings of femininity is too limited. While the world of classical ballet is clearly permeated with gender stereotypes and power inequalities, if the life of a female dancer is as unbearable as is sometimes suggested, why would any woman ever aspire to become a professional dancer? And how is it possible that I have met so many dancers who, while suffering from the bodily demands made of them, clearly enjoyed their profession? Are these demands experienced as oppressive or maybe as a continual challenge?

To enable the answering of questions like these, one has to abandon the woman-as-victim model and devote more attention to the stories of female dancers. Ex-dancer and choreographer Agnes de Mille suggested in her autobiography that the specific demands made by the technique were precisely what attracted women to classical ballet.

> The very physical stresses, the strengthening and bracing and tautening of her back and leg supply such a sense of driving power as to give her the illusion of male potency. The plunging leg, the arched, vital foot, the delicate mechanism of equilibrium and balancing with their attendant hypnotic reflection in the audience suspend her in a state of continuing power. (de Mille, 1951: 60–1)

The combination of 'feminine' beauty and 'masculine' strength may give female dancers a special feeling of gratification (Dyer 1992: 41–2).

In conclusion, I have shown how female dancers' bodies are moulded to conform to the cultural norms of dance. The dancers' stories sketch a depressing picture of the practices that make their bodies fit to represent the nineteenth-century ideal of a disembodied femininity. But their stories also may make us aware of the challenging and power-generating aspects that ballet has to offer women in channelling their agency towards achieving perfection. This depends, however, on the extent to which female dancers are able to perceive their bodies as more than just matter. The bodily practices of ballet could then become a continual materializing of possibilities rather than an enactment of cultural norms.

NOTE

I would like to express my gratitude to Kathy Davis for stimulating comments and superb editing. Her faith in my abilities was indispensable as I wrote this article.

REFERENCES

Adair, Christy (1992) *Women and Dance: Sylphs and Sirens*. London: Macmillan Press.

Alderson, Evan (1987) 'Ballet as Ideology: *Giselle*, Act II', *Dance Chronicle* 10(3): 290–304.

Bentley, Toni (1982) *Winter Season. A Dancer's Journal*. New York: Random House.

Birke, Lynda (1986) *Women, Femininism and Biology. The Feminist Challenge*. Brighton: Wheatsheaf Books Ltd.

Bonbridge, Jane M. (1989) 'The Nutritional Status of Female Ballet Dancers 15–18 Years of Age', *Dancer Research Journal* 21(2): 9–15.

Bordo, Susan (1993) *Unbearable Weight. Feminism, Western Culture, and the Body.* Berkeley: University of California Press.

Brady, Joan (1982) *The Unmaking of a Dancer. An Unconventional Life.* Washington: Washington Square Press.

Butler, Judith (1987) 'Variations on Sex and Gender. Beauvoir, Wittig and Foucault', pp. 128–43 in Seyla Benhabib and Drucilla Cornell (eds) *Feminism as Critique. Essays on the Politics of Gender in Late-Capitalist Societies.* Cambridge: Polity Press.

Butler, Judith (1990a) *Gender Trouble. Feminism and the Subversion of Identity.* London: Routledge.

Butler, Judith (1990b) 'Performative Acts and Gender Constitution', pp. 270–83 in Sue-Ellen Case (ed.), *Performing Feminisms. Feminist Critical Theory and Theatre.* Baltimore: Johns Hopkins University Press.

Butler, Judith (1993) *Bodies that Matter. On the Discursive Limits of Sex.* New York: Routledge.

Cowan, Jane K. (1990) *Dance and the Body Politic in Northern Greece.* New Jersey: Princeton University Press.

Daly, Ann (1987/88) 'Classical Ballet: A Discourse of Difference', *Women & Performance. A Journal of Feminist Theory* 3(2): 57–67.

de Beauvoir, Simone (1972) *The Second Sex.* Harmondsworth: Penguin.

de Mille, Agnes (1951) *Dance to the Piper: Memoirs of the Ballet.* London: Hamish Hamilton.

Dyer, Richard (1992) 'Classical Ballet: a Bit of an Uplift', pp. 41–5 in *Only Entertainment.* London & New York: Routledge.

Evans, Blanche W., Antoinette Tiburzi and Candace Norton (1985) 'Body Composition and Body Type of Female Dance Majors', *Dance Research Journal* 17(1): 17–21.

Flett, Una (1981) *Falling from Grace. My Early Years In Ballet.* Edinburgh: Canongate.

Foster, Susan Leigh (1996) 'The Ballerina's Phallic Pointe', pp. 1–25 in S.L. Foster (ed.), *Corporealities. Dancing Knowledge, Culture and Power.* New York: Routledge.

Freedson, Patty (1988) 'Body Composition Characteristics of Female Ballet Dancers', pp. 109–25 in P. Clarkson and M. Skrinar (eds) *Science of Dance Training.* Champaign: Human Kinetics Books.

Gordon, Suzanne (1983) *Off Balance. the Real World of Ballet.* New York: Pantheon Books.

Hamilton, William (1982) 'Nature's Choice: The Best Body for Ballet', *Dance Magazine,* October: 82–3.

Hanna, Judith L. (1988) *Dance, Sex and Gender; Signs of Identity, Dominance, Defiance, and Desire.* Chicago. University of Chicago Press.

Haskell, Arnold (1955) *Ballet.* Harmondsworth: Penguin Books.

Haug, Frigga (eds) (1987) *Female Sexualisation. A Collective Work of Memory.* London: Verso.

Heppenstall, Rayner (1983) 'The Sexual Idiom', pp. 267–89 in Roger Copeland and Marshall Cohen (eds) *What is Dance? Readings in Theory and Criticism.* Oxford: Oxford University Press (originally published 1936).

Jacobus, Mary, Evelyn Fox Keller and Sally Shuttleworth (1990) *Body/Politics. Women and the Discourses of Science.* New York: Routledge.

Jowitt, Deborah (1988) *Time and the Dancing Image.* New York: William Morrow and Co.

Kealiinohomoku, Joann (1983) 'An Anthropologist Looks at Ballet as a Form of Ethnic Dance', pp. 533–50 in R. Copeland and M. Cohen (eds), *What is Dance? Readings in Theory and Criticism.* Oxford: Oxford University Press.

Kirkland, Gelsey and Greg Lawrence (1986) *Dancing on my Grave.* New York: Doubleday.

Kirstein, Lincoln (1983) 'Classic Ballet: Aria of the Aerial', pp. 238–44 in R.
     Copeland and M. Cohen (eds) *What is Dance? Readings in Theory and Criticism.*
     Oxford: Oxford University Press.
Klein, Gabriele (1992) *Frauen Körper Tanz. Eine Zivilisationsgeschichte des Tanzes.*
     Berlin: Quadriga.
Lichtenbelt, Wouter van Marken, Mikael Fogelholm, Ramon Offenheim and Klaas
     Westerterp (1995) 'Physical Activity, Body Composition and Bone Density in
     Ballet Dancers', *British Journal of Nutrition* 74: 439–51.
McConnell, Joan (1977) *Ballet as Body Language.* New York: Harper & Row.
Martin, Emily (1987) *The Woman in the Body. A Cultural Analysis of Reproduction.*
     Boston: Beacon Press.
Mazo, Joseph H. (1974) *Dance is a Contact Sport.* New York: Da Capo Press.
Newman, Barbara (1982) *Striking a Balance. Dancers Talk About Dancing.* Boston:
     Houghton Mifflin Co.
Novack, Cynthia J. (1990) *Sharing the Dance: Contact Improvisation and American
     Culture.* Madison: University of Wisconsin Press.
Novack, Cynthia J. (1993) 'Ballet, Gender and Cultural Power', pp. 34–49 in H.
     Thomas (ed.) *Dance, Gender and Culture.* London: Macmillan Press.
Polhemus, Ted (1993) 'Dance, Gender and Culture', pp. 3–16 in H. Thomas (ed.),
     Dance, Gender and Culture. London: Macmillan Press.
Procee, Gea (1991) 'Eetproblemen. De docent-dansopleiding als risicogebied'.
     mimeo Amsterdam: opleiding docent klassieke dans, scriptie pedagogiek.
     Unpublished MA thesis.
Sayers, Lesley-Anne (1993) ' "She Might Pirouette on a Daisy and it Would Not
     Bend": Images of Femininity and Dance', pp. 164–84 in H. Thomas (ed.)
     Dance, Gender and Culture. London: Macmillan Press.
Terry, Walter (1962) *On Pointe! The Story of Dancing and Dancers on Toe.* New York:
     Dodd, Mead & Co.
Vincent, Lawrence M. (1979) *Competing with the Sylph: Dancers and the Pursuit of the
     Ideal Body Form.* New York: Andrews & McMeel Inc.
Warren, Michelle P. (1988) 'Menstrual Effects of Dance Training', pp. 209–23 in P.
     Clarkson and M. Skrinar (eds), *Science of Dance Training.* Champaign: Human
     Kinetics Books.
Wijngaard, Marianne van den (1991) *Reinventing the Sexes. Feminism and Biomedical
     Construction of Femininity and Masculinity 1959–1985.* Delft: Eburon.

4 Female Bodies and Brittle Bones

Medical Interventions in Osteoporosis

Ineke Klinge

It has long been held that the body as object of research can be 'discovered' by biomedical research. According to the positivist paradigm of the life sciences, much can be learned about the body through descriptive and experimental research. The mysteries of nature and life can be explored at an ever-deeper level. It seems the privileged way to obtain knowledge on life processes, for instance on ageing of the body. However, science and technology studies have criticized the concept of 'discovering' the body (and nature) (Latour, 1987). The claim is made that biomedical knowledge cannot directly 'mirror' natural reality. On the contrary, the production of scientific knowledge is a human enterprise and in accordance with operative norms and values – in short, with social-cultural conditions. Consequently, scientific knowledge has to be considered as historical and local.

Analysing the body poses a particular challenge to feminists. As daughters of the heritage which Simone de Beauvoir spelled out in *The Second Sex*, we have become 'conditioned' to regard the body and biology with suspicion. As a result, the separation between sex and gender as introduced by Oakley (1972), was wholeheartedly welcomed by lots of feminists. By putting the 'social' gender as a new topic on the research agenda, feminists could afford to care less about biology and biomedical knowledge. When the body returned to their agenda, it was in the manifestation of women's embodied experience – an intriguing object of research (see the call for proposals for this issue). What remained unexplored, however, was 'biological' sex or the body as 'material resource'. Because the body in biology and medicine remained unquestioned, it could still be regarded as 'natural' and keep its capacity to – unexpectedly and in new contexts – pin women down to their bodies again. Fortunately, the challenge of the material body was taken up by feminist biologists. How did they tackle this difficult question?

Feminist biologists turned to social studies of science and technology because these analytical frameworks offered several possibilities. It enabled analysis of the role of gender in biomedical discourse on the body (Fausto-Sterling, 1985; Birke, 1986; Hubbard et al., 1982; Bleier, 1988; Keller, 1986). By a detailed focus on various knowledge practices, one could catch a glimpse of the historicity of the body. It seemed an opportunity to 'escape' the 'one and only natural body'. Since then many authors have given examples of the production of bodies by biomedical discourse and have focused on the variety of (f)actors involved in these productions (see Laqueur, 1990; Mol, 1989; Oudshoorn, 1994; Wijngaard, 1991). Such studies emphasize that the 'biological body' is never ahistorical, but bears the marks of time and place of production.[1] Philosopher of science Annemarie Mol has pointed to the disciplinary background of researchers to find an answer to the question 'Who knows what a woman is?' Anatomists tend to answer this question in terms of absence or presence of internal or external organs. Endocrinologists, however, describe women and men in terms of blood levels of sex hormones. And geneticists focus on chromosomes and more recently on genes. Mol draws our attention to the fact that the bodies that emerge in these discourses do not need to coincide: in an 'anatomical' female body not so 'feminine' levels of oestrogens (female sex hormones) may be present. This implies that the 'biological body' cannot easily be known, nor that we can speak of 'the female body'. Instead we have to analyse which female body is being produced by specific discursive practices. Moreover, a detailed study of the many different practices seems justified because in medical practice each 'body' can be a focus of intervention. Organs can be removed from the 'anatomical body' (as with womb removals), or added to it (like in organ transplantations); high hormone levels in the 'endocrinological body' can be modulated and low levels can be supplemented, and the 'genetic' body in the future will have to face interventions like gene therapy. Among the feminists inspired by a social studies of science and technology perspective, Donna Haraway (1988, 1989) occupies a prominent place. She has elaborated the metaphor of production and describes how, for instance, 'immunological bodies' are the result of what she has called the *apparatus of bodily production* in which immunological discourse, technology, matter and language are knotted together. Haraway has stressed another aspect of the bodies thus produced: she points to their power in determining how both medicine and we ourselves deal with our bodies.

In this article I address a particular biomedical discourse on the female body in relation to a condition which is presented to us as a major health problem. Ageing for women in our society has become an issue which deserves serious attention. Menopause and brittle bones loom on the horizon. Gone are the days when 'the change' or ageing could mean a relatively relaxed and simple phase in life of not having periods or pregnancies anymore. On the contrary, women are all of a sudden 'perimenopausal' and confronted with a body that requires all their attention. They have to anticipate the 'postmenopause' and its phenomena. Although osteoporosis or the process of bones becoming brittle is an ageing process occurring in men and women, it is presented as a serious health problem for women.[2] In looking at osteoporosis from the perspective of social studies of science, one can see that many actors are involved. Medical professionals are negotiating the definition of the condition and the design of clinical studies, stimulating prevention and applying therapeutical solutions. Entrepreneurs are engaged in application and dissemination of new medical technologies in this particular field like densitometry, a technology to measure bone mass; scientists participate in advice to the government regarding future policies with respect to osteoporosis. Still another set of actors can be found in education and communication on osteoporosis. Many materials are produced, from a wide range of viewpoints, some of them explicitly addressing the issue of prevention of osteoporosis, others merely drifting along with the public upsurge of the osteoporosis issue.[3] Women too, in many different roles, are enrolled in the discourse on osteoporosis.

My aim is to take a closer look at *intervention practices* concerning osteoporosis,[4] where both preventive strategies and therapeutic regimes come to the fore. My material consists of consensus texts,[5] local clinic protocols and doctor–patient consultations. Analysis of the production of the female body in this clinical setting and exposure of the material and technological conditions for its production is central. Which body emerges and what are its effects? And why should feminists bother? Let me start by focusing on the bony materiality of bodies.

BIOMEDICAL RESEARCH ON OSTEOPOROSIS

The biomedical literature on osteoporosis in women can be characterized as dominated by two competing theories on the primary causal event in the process of osteoporosis. Research traditions evolving from early epidemiological observations have developed a hormonal concept of osteoporosis and a mineral concept of osteoporosis. One theory holds a lack of oestrogen responsible for the decrease of bone mass and the other maintains that a lack of calcium is triggering the pathophysiological process (Albright et al., 1941; Nordin, 1960).[6] In the two research traditions, different conceptualizations of the female body emerge. The female body is either represented as a 'hormonal body', thereby linking the process of osteoporosis to menopause. In research focusing on the role of calcium, the female body is represented as a 'mineral body' and the process of osteoporosis is therefore part of an ageing process. The two traditions suggest different solutions for the problem of osteoporosis: hormones or calcium.

Both research traditions are *in dialogue* with each other and mutually accommodate or incorporate each other's theoretical points. They, nevertheless, remain true to their own pathophysiological principle and by enlarging their respective actor networks emphasize different aspects as worthy of research. Researchers of the mineral tradition extend their research focus to the role of calcium in the first three decades of life thus moving possible evolving preventive activities to an earlier phase in life. Research within the hormonal tradition started to explore the benefits of long-term oestrogen therapy in reducing cardiovascular risks and overall death rate (Henderson et al., 1991), thus integrating osteoporosis prevention into a lifelong hormonal preventive activity, starting at menopause. The present-day relationship between the two traditions can best be described as an ongoing polemic.

FROM LAB TO CLINIC

If contemporary research on osteoporosis is still fuelled by the two competing theories, what about clinical practice? Clinicians face the task of offering a solution to the problem of osteoporosis, and are less interested in a debate over the primary event in causing osteoporosis than in finding an adequate solution. But how do they handle the divergent knowledge fragments from research practices pointing to different solutions? What are the ultimate factors operating in or guiding local clinical practice in the approach of osteoporosis?

To tackle this question, as a first step, I analyse the process of consensus development. In biomedical practice in general a process of consensus development is started when a controversial issue needs to be resolved. Controversial issues in biomedical practice are characterized by the existence of a debate on the scientific value of research results or when actual practice does not correspond to scientific standards, resulting in large differences between local practices. As such, osteoporosis met the requirements for starting a process of consensus development. Consensus development can be seen as the transformation of research knowledge into a temporary pacification of available knowledge, yielding guidelines for medical practice. This endeavour was first undertaken in the USA in 1984 (Anonymous, 1984). Soon other countries followed. In the Netherlands consensus development took place in 1985 and 1992 (Bijvoet, 1986; Lockefeer, 1992). During the interval at least two international/European consensus development conferences were held.

THE DUTCH CONSENSUS DEVELOPMENT ON OSTEOPOROSIS

The outcome, 'Consensus Osteoporose', of the first Dutch consensus development conference consisted of 33 statements on diagnosis, prevention and treatment of osteoporosis and was published in the leading Dutch scientific medical journal *Nederlands Tijdschrift voor Geneeskunde*. In this text prepared by a select company of medical professionals, the multifactorial aetiology of osteoporosis is acknowledged. Next to the two factors representing primary pathophysiological principles (oestrogen and calcium), factors like heredity, race, immobilization, endocrine disorders, absorption disorders and the use of glucocorticosteroids are incorporated into the proposed approach to the phenomenon. Concerning the relationship between the two research traditions, a certain *division of ground* becomes visible in the resulting guidelines. Primary prevention is allocated to the mineral tradition where the importance of adequate calcium intake is stressed and moved to a younger phase of life (0–30 years). The field of secondary prevention – that is, preventive measures taken by persons 'at risk' – is colonized by the hormonal tradition, at the cost of the mineral tradition. Although the 'mineral solution' for the phase of life around menopause has come under pressure from the 'hormonal solution', it has kept a certain place by profiling itself against the 'hormonal solution'. This has been achieved by stressing that a therapy with calcium is riskless, has no side-effects, is easy and cheap and makes intensive medical monitoring redundant. In the domain of tertiary prevention (i.e. treatment), the relationship and observed hierarchy between the hormonal tradition and mineral tradition is less prominent (or absent). In treating patients a lot of other treatment modalities have made their appearance, broadly divided into regimens which suppress bone resorption or stimulate bone formation (Riggs and Melton, 1992).

There are several characteristic elements in the Dutch consensus development (concerning content, not process of consensus development). First, the chair of the group of medical specialists who prepared the 'Consensus Osteoporose', added several personal accents to the discussion.[7] He made a case of the need to bring about a change in women's attitude towards use of oestrogens after menopause. The 'common' knowledge on hormones is connected to debates on side-effects of oral contraceptives and still carries a negative image. This chair expected that if more were published on the beneficial psychological (well-being) and biological effects of oestrogen, this attitude would change. At the same time he emphasized the seriousness of the osteoporosis condition and refuted potential risks of developing endometrial cancer by confirming that this problem was adequately solved by the addition of progestogens to oestrogen therapy. Second, the input from Dutch research results evolving from the mineral tradition can be seen to have had an impact on the formulations in the consensus document. The results of a long-term (ten-year) research into dairy calcium intake combined with bone mass measurements performed among healthy women by Beresteijn (Beresteijn, 1989) are traceable in the negotiations on the final text, the result being the above-mentioned division of ground and profile of calcium. In comparison to the international consensus of 1987 held in Aalborg, Denmark (Anonymous, 1987), the Dutch consensus has paid explicit attention to the design of a table of risk factors for osteoporosis combined with an assessment of the relative weight of these factors. The first Dutch consensus is more restrictive than the American one (Anonymous, 1984) on the use of oestrogens: they should only be given to women at risk, cyclically and always combined with progestogens, except if the woman does not have her uterus anymore; the US consensus recommended oestrogens for all women. In comparison to the European one (Anonymous, 1987), the Dutch consensus is also more restrictive on the use of treatment modalities like fluoride, anabolic steroids and calcitonine.

Between publication of the Dutch consensus (1986) and its revision in 1992, a committee of the Dutch Health Council also studied the osteoporosis issue. After an assessment of available literature, they proposed in their report 'Prevention of Osteoporosis' to the Ministries of Welfare, Health and Cultural Affairs (WVC) and Science and Education (O&W) to offer perimenopausal women a screening of their bone mass by densitometry in order to *target* secondary prevention. This secondary prevention should consist of oestrogens, combined, if necessary, with progestogens (Gezondheidsraad, 1991). They recommend that this screening should be preceded by a pilot study to assess the feasibility (attitude of women and costs) of such a screening. Other striking features of this document are the explicit attention to physical activity (resulting in recommendations to the Minister of Science and Education to maintain the hours for physical education in secondary and high schools) and to calcium intake during youth and adolescence, to be accomplished by offering school milk and by disseminating information in places frequented by adolescents, like discos. However the State Secretary of WVC, Simons, did not implement the screening proposal or the pilot study, arguing that the scientific issues were not adequately resolved. This same argument was put forward by the College of General Practitioners (NHG) working party for clinical guidelines: that it was too early to design a standard for general practitioners on osteoporosis (Wiersma and Lagro-Jansen, 1992). So in the Netherlands we are confronted with the situation that views on the desirability of developing guidelines on the issue of osteoporosis differ considerably between organizations of medical specialists and organizations of general physicians. According to the 'Consensus Osteoporose', developed by the first, GPs should play a role in bringing the issue of osteoporosis to the attention of their female patients in their mid-40s. General practitioners are thus confronted with a considerable dilemma in their everyday practice.

In 1992 the Revision of 'Consensus Osteoporose' appeared. This document bears the marks of the Health Council's report. The screening issue is incorporated into the text which means that the assessment of the many possible risk factors (according to the table of risk factors in 1986) is replaced by a plea for screening of bone mass at perimenopausal age as this is said to yield a better prediction of future osteoporosis. However, in critical comments on the Revision in medical journals, the value of a single bone mass measurement for the prediction of individual fracture rates was intensively discussed. The ongoing difference in attitude regarding bone mass screening and concomitant hormone therapy between specialists and general physicians became very explicit to the Dutch population because of an incident in the autumn of 1994. An insurance company launched an initiative directly targeted at perimenopausal women. They received by mail an application form for a bone mass measurement, which only needed the signature of their GP. Both Dutch associations of GPs (NHG and LHV) protested against this initiative. Insurance companies should not try to take over the pivotal role of GPs in the Dutch health care system. The incident urged the NHG to publish once more the provisional NHG standpoint ('no standard needed yet'). They informed the Dutch Association of Obstetricians and Gynaecologists of their intention to publish. The latter responded with an angry letter, accusing the GPs of an unbalanced and undocumented reporting resulting in confusion among women and jeopardizing the consensus guidelines. By going to court they tried repeatedly to inhibit publication of the NHG standpoint, but they lost their case. In the aftermath, editorials on this event appeared in several journals. In a journal aimed at gynaecologists the value of bone mass measurement and of hormone therapy was re-explained (Kenemans, 1994; Barentsen, 1995). In another journal aimed at nutrition specialists and GPs, the author cites the NHG standpoint, that still questions the predictive value of bone mass measurement for fractures occurring so much later in life and in which the 'hormonal solution' is criticized because of the accompanying risk of breast cancer. According to the NHG standpoint a GP's answer to a woman who consults her or him on prevention of osteoporosis should be: 'ensure a healthy lifestyle, with adequate physical exercise and ample dairy products' (Blom, 1994).

THE LOCAL CLINIC PROTOCOL

We now move our attention to local settings and the transformation of a national consensus text into a local clinic protocol. Is the consensus pacification transferred in the same way to local settings, or can we identify specific local practices? I conducted my ethnographic fieldwork in the outpatient clinic for bone metabolism of the Academic Hospital in Utrecht. This clinic is connected to a geriatric ward where the staff has been involved for more than 25 years in bone research. They are engaged in fundamental research on the influence of oestrogens and progestogens on cultivated bone cells and have participated in clinical trials. The head of this clinic has launched a theory on the influence of oestrogens on bone mass (Duursma et al., 1991). They have a lot of experience in treating patients with the compound fluoride, a stimulator of bone formation. The majority of patients frequenting the Utrecht clinic have entered the clinic via their GP. Subsequently they are diagnosed to *have* osteoporosis and receive treatment, according to the clinic's protocol.[8] Because of the clinic's reputation and its densitometry equipment, patients sometimes enter on their own initiative, for an assessment of bone mass and a diagnosis of osteoporosis. Medical sociological studies have drawn our attention to the fact that medical action in clinical settings is not only guided by scientific (consensus) knowledge, but also by 'locally situated routines' (Berg, 1992). These routines are the outcome of specific interests of the specialists, participation in scientific research and clinical trials and characteristics of a particular hospital ward such as the technological-material equipment. Analysis of the Utrecht protocol and observations made during my fieldwork on doctor–patient consultations, allow for the conclusion that this local practice is a *specific mix of consensus knowledge and locally situated routines*.[9] The local solution for osteoporosis that results is the following: treatment of choice for osteoporosis in Utrecht is fluoride. Severe osteoporosis is treated with fluoride and oestrogen/progestogen or bisphosphonates (inhibitor of bone resorption). Less severe forms can be treated with bisphosphonates alone. Following from the consensus text, calcium is absent as a treatment option. However, it is present as a necessary adjuvant (together with vitamin D) to fluoride therapy (Raymakers, 1994).

FEMALE BODIES AT THE CLINIC

Let us now take a look at bodies in clinical practices. In research practices the female body emerged either as a 'hormonal body' or a 'mineral body'; in consensus texts as a 'body at risk' and a 'body in need of treatment'. On entry to the clinic a lot of measurements of the body are taken. Height, weight, laboratory investigations of blood and urine, X-rays of the lumbar spine and bone mass measurement by DEXA densitometry. During the first conversation, the medical specialist has asked the general anamnestic questions, with special attention to dairy intake and physical exercise, and has conducted a standard physical examination in which stature and possible vertebral pains can be assessed. In a second encounter between a woman and her doctor she is confronted with the results of the above investigations which are read to her by the specialist:

> These results are fine. The electrolytes are normal as is the gamma GT. Alkaline phosphatase is nice; this value is increased in case of bone resorption.

On receiving this message the woman nods as if understanding that the value of alkaline phosphatase is the value that matters. Subsequently, the specialist shows her the X-ray pictures of her spine.

> Look, this is a normal vertebra and this is a wedge-shaped one. The sides are different in height which means that these are crushed. And you have five of these. You should stop carrying heavy purchases or pushing a wheelbarrow!

She now has to think of her body in terms of crushed vertebrae and receives at the same time a message to change her lifestyle. The lab values and X-ray pictures are instrumental in drawing her attention to the skeleton. Today's bone mass measurement through the technology of densitometry has replaced the weighed estimation of risks. The female body is represented by the figure for her bone mineral density expressed in grams per square centimetre, say 0.841 g/m^2, often pronounced by the physician in round numbers: 'there was an increase of 82 to 84'. Any individual bone density is compared to a standard. It depends on local decision-making how the threshold for intervention is constructed. This so called 'fracture threshold' can be viewed as crossed if the value differs more than 2 (or 3) standard deviations from the mean value for her sex. An individual bone mass can also be compared to mean female peak bone mass at the age of 35. The female body that thus emerges through this diagnostic procedure is a 'bone mass body'. Bone mass measurement and the 'bone mass body' are of pivotal importance in the clinic and have multiple effects: they are central *to start intervention* regimes but are also used *to increase a woman's motivation* to continue her (heavy) therapy. Consider the following example on starting intervention.

In opening the conversation on a possible therapy, the specialists in Utrecht start by explaining the phenomenon of osteoporosis. The usual sequence is a description of hormonal events at menopause, followed by the 'hormonal solution' in which risks and benefits are given a place. The sequence and way of talking of these issues varied enormously between individual members of staff. This influenced the counter-questions asked by the patients. If the doctor was a woman, she could often expect the question, 'What would you do?' After the 'hormonal solution', other solutions were explained. The final decision, however, is left to the woman. A statement I frequently heard from women was: 'What is best for my bones?' A choice for the 'hormonal solution' implies that organs like the uterus and breasts, which become subjected to risks due to the chosen treatment, are subordinated to the skeleton.

And consider this example on motivation. A woman has told her specialist that she still has a painful chest although she is practising her therapeutic exercises. She has become afraid of the pain. She asks:

> Have the hormones been working? Because, things have not been easy with hormones. I have been bleeding, waking up in a puddle of blood, feeling dizzy. I also have painful breasts, I have come to dislike my body.

In answering this woman, the doctor tells her that her bone density has improved (from 77 to 82), so the hormones must have been acting on her bones and she announces the next measurement in six months. Thus, when a patient does not *feel* any improvement, she is made to *trust* the bone mass values and she has to stay optimistic.

I argue that the representation of the female body as a 'bone mass body', expressed in laboratory findings and bone mass measurements, is the most important representation in the clinical setting. The 'hormonal body' and the 'mineral body' only reappear in the 'hormonal solution' and the 'mineral adjuvant solution'.

OSTEOPOROSIS THERAPY AND WOMEN: A DISCIPLINARY PRACTICE?

Having encountered a variety of bodies in this analysis of biomedical discourse on osteoporosis I have illustrated that we cannot speak of *the* biological body or *the* body in biomedicine as this body is not one (body). We have to take a look at the technical-material apparatus at work in practices of knowledge production, be it research, treatment or information. The exposure of these different bodies is not, however, a sheer exercise in describing as many bodies as possible which could be regarded as a contribution in itself to the deconstruction of the 'natural body' in biology and medicine; above all it is instrumental in analysing the *power* of the bodies produced.[10]

Elaborating on these power effects, I want to draw your attention to the following. We have seen that a local therapeutic practice is a complex one, many combinations of treatment modalities are possible and pluriform therapeutic proposals may result. I suggest considering therapy proposals for the 'bone mass body' as subject positions offered to women.[11] In discussing a possible therapy the woman is defined as intelligent, skilled in the interpretation of X-ray pictures and responsible for the choice of therapy. In practising the therapy in daily life she is constituted as very well organized (in the case of a combined therapy of fluoride with hormones she has to take five different pills during the day, some of which cannot go together and others have to be spaced two hours apart) and capable of planning (a visit to the clinic requires special collection of urine for 24 hours, a visit to the nuclear ward for her densitometry and omission of fluoride intake on the day of her visit to the clinic, because of interference with the measurement). She has to be attentive to possible side-effects (irregular bleeding, pointing to a possible malignant transformation), and last but not least, she has to have a firm attitude, actively managing her pain. This disciplining of her body deeply invades her personal life. Inspired by Sawicki's feminist assessment of Foucault's theory on disciplinary practices (Sawicki, 1991), I propose to view these subject positions not as the mere constitution of women in this discourse, but as themes they will have to relate themselves to, thus leaving room for contestation and action. This issue is discussed in greater detail elsewhere drawing on analysis of subject positions in information practices on osteoporosis and on interviews with women (see Wingerden, 1996). Subject positions have to be understood as two things: they have an element of being subjected to representation, but there is at the same time the aspect of the subject being the subject of her own story. Both aspects are essential and inseparable and allow for an articulation of agency and of differences between women (Braidotti, 1994).[12]

In my opinion, one theme in the offered subject positions is very conspicuous in the Dutch context and that is the theme of an individual woman's responsibility in contributing to a reduction in the ever-rising costs of public health care. Due to the debate on 'Choices in Health Care', public awareness of the unmanageable costs of health care has increased enormously in the Netherlands.[13] The media representation of the issue of osteoporosis is always accompanied by numbers of future hip fractures and calculations of costs for care and physical rehabilitation. So the appeal to women to take preventive measures, sold as improving the quality of her life, serves another agenda: that of savings in health care expenditures. To this end women will just have to be prepared for a life of body management.

NOTES

I wish to thank participants in the graduate seminar in Women's Studies, chaired by Professor Rosi Braidotti, for their stimulating discussion of this part of my research. This article is based on a paper delivered at the Second Feminist Research Conference, held in Graz, Austria in 1994.

1. In the past immunological discourse has very much drawn on war metaphors in describing bodies in immunology and in explaining immunological processes (see Martin, 1993). Martin states that characteristics of our society pervade immunological theories. In *Flexible Bodies* she illustrates how our present-day information society where things become obsolete and are replaced at high speed, again is reflected in immunological theory where the immunological response is now described in terms of agility and flexibility (Martin, 1994).
2. This is truly a matter of representation. If osteoporosis is represented graphically in terms of bone mass of men and women plotted against time then we see two lines. Bone mass in men is always higher than in women and the decline over time is very gradual. Bone mass in women is always lower than in men and there is a steep decrease around menopause. This is a serious looking picture of osteoporosis for women. If, however, the actual number of hip fractures is plotted against time, then we see a similar (pretty steep) rise in the number of hip fractures in men and women, be it somewhat later in life in men. One could read this picture as 'osteoporosis: a serious health problem resulting in hip fractures in both sexes'.
3. In an interview, a PR manager in the dairy industry explained the introduction to the market of their new product, skimmed milk with a double amount of calcium, in the following way, 'Of course osteoporosis prevention is not our task; we simply profit from the raised consciousness for the issue of brittle bones.'
4. My research as a whole addresses three practices concerning osteoporosis: research practices, intervention practices and communication and educational practices. Furthermore, women's relationship to these practices is explored through analysing an Internet discussion on menopause and osteoporosis and by interviewing women receiving treatment (see Klinge, forthcoming).
5. A consensus text is a scientific publication on the outcome of a consensus development conference (see paragraph on the Dutch consensus development on osteoporosis).

6.   The material conditions which allowed for these conceptualizations to come into existence and the relationship between the two theories have been analysed in detail (Wingerden, 1993).

7.   I could gather this non-official information by studying the preparatory trajectory of both consensus texts in the archives of the CBO (Central Organ for Consensus Development in the Netherlands) thanks to the courtesy of Dr J. J. E. van Everdingen.

8.   The definition of osteoporosis has shifted considerably over time. With X-ray technology available, osteoporosis could only be diagnosed *after* a fracture, and histological examination of a bone biopsy had to confirm that it was an osteoporotic fracture. With the technology of densitometry it becomes feasible to assess small losses in bone mass before fractures have occurred. The condition 'osteoporosis' thus became redefined several times. In the Utrecht protocol operative at the time of my fieldwork osteoporosis was defined as 'a situation with existing spinal fractures together with a low bone mineral density, in the absence of other causes of fractures or bone mineral loss'. Persons having a bone mineral density of more than 3 standard deviations from the value for 'young-normal' are regarded as having osteoporosis too (in the latter case fractures are absent).

9.   In this article my focus is on transformations from consensus to local protocols. This should not be regarded as a unidirectional process. New 'clinical knowledge' in its turn influences the next consensus development. For reasons of brevity, I do not go into this part of the dynamics of consensus development here.

10.   For feminist scholars this kind of analysis of biomedical practices can be viewed as an enrichment to textual analyses of the body. It can be regarded as a plea for extensive interference with biology and medicine. It also exposes the material limits of the bodies produced.

11.   Compare Armstrong (1982) who has argued that doctor–patient interactions can be viewed as constituting both doctor and patient.

12.   In her book *Reshaping the Female Body* (1995), Kathy Davis also explicitly addresses the issue of agency. Cosmetic surgery can be viewed as 'an impetus to move away from a passive acceptance of herself as nothing but a body to the position of a subject who acts upon the world in and through her body'. In my research I do have indications of the active negotiations women make concerning for example the 'bone mass body'. They make their own assessment of risk and quality of life (see Wingerden, 1996).

13.   A government committee has written the report 'Choices in Healthcare' (1992), aimed at raising public consciousness of the issue that choices will have to be made for financial reasons. At the same time the committee developed an instrument to be used in the implementation of such choices. The report and the instruments have been discussed in a three-year long public discussion of this report with a variety of groups in society (e.g. women's health organizations) and in very different ways (lectures, workshops, TV programmes, expert meetings).

REFERENCES

Albright, F., P. H. Smith and A. M. Richardson (1941) 'Postmenopausal Osteoporosis: Its Clinical Features', *Journal of the American Medical Association* 116(22): 2465–74.

Anonymous (1984) 'Consensus Conference Osteoporosis', *Journal of the American Medical Association* 252(6): 799–802.

Anonymous (1987) 'Consensus Development Conference: Prophylaxis and Treatment of Osteoporosis', *British Medical Journal* 295: 914–15.

Armstrong, D. (1982) 'The Doctor–Patient Relationship 1930–1980', pp. 109–22 in P. Wright and A. Treacher (eds) *The Problem of Medical Knowledge*. Edinburgh: Edinburgh University Press.

Barentsen, R. (1995) 'Botdichtheidsmeting: wat doen we ermee?', *Tijdschrift voor Climacterium en Postmenopauze* 9: 3.

Beresteijn, E. H. C. (1989) 'Nutritional Calcium and Postmenopausal Osteoporosis: A Ten Year Longitudinal Study', NIZO verslag V297, Ede.

Berg, M. (1992) 'The Construction of Medical Disposals: Medical Sociology and Medical Problem Solving in Clinical Practice', *Sociology of Health and Illness* 14(2): 151–80.

Bijvoet, O. L. M. (1986) 'Consensus Osteoporose', *Nederlands Tijdschrift voor Geneeskunde* 130(13): 584–90.

Birke, L. (1986) *Women, Feminism, and Biology: The Feminist Challenge*. Brighton: Wheatsheaf/Harvester.

Bleier, R. (1988) 'A Decade of Feminist Critiques in the Natural Sciences', *Signs* 14(1): 186–95.

Blom, J. (1994) 'NHG Rapport: Wat te doen bij osteoporose. Huisarts dient zuivel en beweging te adviseren', *Voedingsmagazine* 6: 6–7.

Braidotti, R. (1994) 'Sexual Difference as a Nomadic Political Project', in *Nomadic Subjects: Embodiment and Sexual Difference in Contemporary Feminist Theory*. New York: Columbia University Press.

Davis, K. (1995) *Reshaping the Female Body: The Dilemma of Cosmetic Surgery*. New York and London: Routledge.

Duursma, S. A., J. A. Raymakers, F. T. J. Boereboom and B. A. A. Scheven (1991) 'Estrogen and Bone Metabolism', *Obstetrical and Gynaecological Survey* 47(1): 38–44.

Fausto-Sterling, A. (1985) *Myths of Gender: Biological Theories about Women and Men*. New York: Basic Books.

Gezondheidsraad (Health Council) (1991) *Preventie van osteoporose* No. 91/21.

Haraway, D. (1988) 'Situated Knowledges: The Science Question in Feminism and the Privilege of Partial Perspective', *Feminist Studies* 14(3): 575–99.

Haraway, D. (1989) 'The Biopolitics of Postmodern Bodies: Determinations of Self in Immune System Discourse', *Differences* 1(1): 3–43.

Henderson, B. E., A. Paganini-Hill and R. K. Ross (1991) 'Decreased Mortality in Users of Estrogen Replacement Therapy', *Archives of Internal Medicine* 151: 75–8.

Hubbard, R., M. S. Henifin and B. Fried (1982) *Biological Women – The Convenient Myth*. Cambridge, MA: Schenkman Publishing.

Keller, E. Fox (1986) 'Making Gender Visible in the Pursuit of Nature's Secrets', pp. 67–77 in T. de Lauretis (ed.) *Feminist Studies, Critical Studies*. Bloomington: Indiana University Press.

Kenemans, P. (1994) 'Top op het broze bot', *Tijdschrift voor Climacterium en Postmenopauze* 8: 3.

Klinge, I. (forthcoming) 'Bones and Gender: The Female Body and the Debate on Osteoporosis', PhD thesis, Utrecht University.

Laqueur, T. (1990) *Making Sex: Body and Gender from the Greeks to Freud*. Cambridge, MA: Harvard University Press.

Latour, B. (1987) *Science in Action: How to Follow Scientists and Engineers through Society*. Cambridge, MA: Harvard University Press.

Lockefeer, J. H. M. (1992) 'Herziening consensus osteoporose', *Nederlands Tijdschrift voor Geneeskunde* 136(25): 1204–6.

Martin, E. (1993) 'Histories of Immune Systems', *Culture, Medicine and Psychiatry* 17: 67–76.

Martin, E. (1994) *Flexible Bodies: Tracking Immunity in American Culture from the Days of Polio to the Age of AIDS*. Boston, MA: Beacon Press.

Mol, A. (1989) 'Sekse en Wetenschap: een vergelijking met twee onbekenden', pp. 97–107 in L. Boon and E. de Vries (eds) *Wetenschapstheorie, de empirische wending*. Groningen: Wolters Noordhof.

Nordin, B. E. C. (1960) 'Osteomalacia, Osteoporosis and Calcium Deficiency', *Clinical Orthopaedia and Related Research* 17: 235–57.

Oakley, A. (1972) *Sex, Gender, Society*. London: Maurice Temple Smith.

Oudshoorn, N. (1994) *Beyond the Natural Body: An Archeology of Sex Hormones*. London: Routledge.

Raymakers, J. A. (1994) 'Osteoporose: welke therapieën voor welke patiënt?', pp. 89–102 in S. A. Duursma, P. A. F. Jansen and J. A. Raymakers (eds) *Osteoporose en heupfracturen bij ouderen*. Utrecht: Universiteit Utrecht, Fakulteit Geneeskunde.

Riggs, B. L. and L. J. Melton (1992) 'The Prevention and Treatment of Osteoporosis', *New England Journal of Medicine* 327(9): 620–7.

Sawicki, J. (1991) *Disciplining Foucault: Feminism, Power and the Body*. New York: Routledge.

Wiersma, T. and A. L. M. Lagro-Jansen (1992) 'Preventie van osteoporose. Voorlopig te broos voor een NHG-standaard', *Huisarts en Wetenschap* 35(11): 428–9.

Wijngaard, M. van (1991) *Reinventing the Sexes: Feminism and the Biomedical Construction of Feminity and Masculinity, 1923–1940*. Amsterdam:

Wingerden, I. van (1993) 'Hormonaal of mineraal? Osteoporose en het vrouwenlichaam', *Tijdschrift voor Vrouwenstudies* 14(2): 149–71.

Wingerden, I. van (1996) 'Postmodern Visions on the Menopausal Body: The Apparatus of Bodily Production and the Case of Brittle Bones', pp. 192–206 in N. Lykke and R. Braidotti (eds) *Between Monsters, Goddesses and Cyborgs. Feminist Confrontations with Science, Medicine and Cyberspace*. London: ZED Books.

5   The Body of Gender Difference

Gesa Lindemann

Body and gender difference are two closely related subjects within feminist discourse. The body – that is, our everyday understanding of it as well as how it is seen by biomedical research and within a broad base of feminist theory – is considered the ultimate point of reference for a distinction of gender that precedes social forms and practices. When ethnomethodologists and deconstructivists break down the assumption that sex difference is not socially determined, this inevitably leads to the view that bodies differ in gender as a result of social practices.[1] This also raises the question whether or not the material conditions of the body are to be comprehended entirely as a socially created reality.

In this article, I take up this hypothesis by attempting a seemingly paradoxical experiment. On the one hand, I regard it as untenable to assume a natural gendered body; on the other hand, it seems to me just as imperative to recognize an inherent logic of the body and the sensory reference of bodies to their environment. Based on this, my thesis is as follows: gender difference must be fundamentally understood as a social form, the local realization of which is broken down by the inherent logic of that which is physical or sensory. In order to develop this line of reasoning, I proceed in two steps. We must first determine how gender difference can be viewed as a variable social form that regulates the distinction between genders. In this way, the gender form of distinction also becomes a condition for the distinction between bodies, insofar as they are experienced and treated as gender-defined bodies. Consequently, gender-different bodies exist only within the framework of historically variable forms of gender distinction. Since the form of distinction only exists when it occurs locally, however, it becomes possible, if not imperative, to examine the events of distinction in terms of its physical and sensory constitution. In order to do this, it is helpful to refrain from making sweeping reference to 'the body'. If a body is seen as a gendered body, for example, it is important to see how the gender form of distinction functions within the framework of the inherent logic of the visual perception of gestalt. If, on the other hand, one's own body is felt as painfully or pleasurably gender significant, such as during menstruation or sexual arousal, the inherent logic of feeling is indeed different from that of perception of gestalt. Gender difference as a physical phenomenon is manifested so differently that I feel it is necessary to abandon any uniform reference to 'the body' and replace it with a more differentiated concept.

GENDER AS SOCIAL FORM

The central aspect of the thesis that gender is a social form is the establishment of a novel concept of gender. The point is no longer to prove that 'sex' is irrelevant in determining 'gender', but to examine how two genders are distinguished at different levels. Differentiating between 'sex' and 'gender' makes this perspective impossible, since within this framework the fact of two genders is nevertheless always presupposed. This arises from the biological point of view that there are two genders, and social scientists merely receive the task of determining how genders that already exist at the 'sex' level can be interpreted within a 'gender relationship' that is understood exclusively in social terms. However, this overlooks the fact that only to a certain degree do biologists in their laboratories act differently than do people in their everyday lives; biologists, namely, also distinguish between two genders. Even if the methods they utilize differ in character from everyday methods, they basically follow the same obsession as sociologists or visitors at a public swimming pool: they distinguish between two genders and rule out a third. Kessler and McKenna (1978), taking up the ideas of Garfinkel (1967), already said this in 1978, and, using very confusing terminology, they gave the name 'gender' to the new concept they came up with that no longer distinguished between 'sex' and 'gender'. Whenever I speak of 'gender' in the following, I mean 'gender' in this comprehensive sense as formulated by Kessler and McKenna.

This view of gender difference is familiar under the aspects of construction and deconstruction of gender. I do not discuss whether these labels are an appropriate choice or not. In terms of content it is more significant that this perspective serves to dissolve firm entities such as 'man' and 'woman' into a process, that is, they are referred to in relative terms along a process that creates and fixes them.[2] This, however, leaves a particular problem largely unconsidered: what are the implications of focusing on the distinction? Differentiating between ways in which genders are distinguished means much more than merely taking note of the fact that two conditions are different. If that were the case, there would be no difference between the man–woman distinction and a man–gorilla distinction. Although mistakes are rarely made in either of these two examples, the man–woman distinction entails something specific in that it is structured as a polar contrast, that is, the two aspects are opposites. Opposites are defined such that one of the poles cannot exist without implying the existence of the other. This is true of the man–woman distinction, but not the man–gorilla distinction. In determining what 'man' is, not everything that differs from a man is significant (canaries, computers, etc.). The only relevant information is the fact that 'man' and 'woman' differ, and the ways in which that difference is manifested. Everything that distinguishes man and woman from each other is – through that very distinction – brought together as two halves of that contrast. The distinction, and only the distinction, is what implicitly proves the copresence of one half of the relation when the other half is mentioned.

At this point, the theory that gender is a social form goes beyond concepts of construction or deconstruction of gender that have been developed up to now. If the unit of the contrast links the two poles, a new question can be posed: how is the unit itself comprised and what kind of relationship between the poles is established by linking them into a unit of a contrast? And are there different forms of contrast that constitute formally different relationships between the two poles? It is no longer important to perceive genders as fixed entities that are relative along a process in which they are created as distinctive; instead, it is important, beyond that, to determine how the unit of their distinction is produced.

The Centric Form of Gender Distinction

The problem of such a distinction can be described loosely in terms of Luhmann's (1988) assumption of the 'Laws of Form' (Spencer Brown, 1969). If the poles of the distinction are not presupposed, but rather created in making the distinction itself, two poles will be differentiated by distinguishing one of them and indicating it as such. In doing this, it is contrasted with that which is not indicated. The result is two poles that are distinguished from one another by the distinction and their particular relationship – the distinction – which links them. Because of this, distinguishing and indicating one pole implies both the distinction of the two poles as opposites, and the distinction of each pole from the distinction itself. This is the basic precondition for distinguishing different forms of the distinction.

When considering historical developments in Europe from Greek antiquity to the present day, at least two forms of gender distinction become apparent. With respect to the problem of the unit of distinction, these forms can be described as centric and acentric gender distinction. Centric gender distinction, which predominated until into the eighteenth century, formed the unit of difference by distinguishing between the two aspects 'man' and 'woman', whereby one aspect of the distinction, the male, was indicated not only in terms of gender but as the generic as well, forming the unit of the distinction. Within this framework, the male pole thus stands for one aspect as well as for the whole, the unit of the distinction. Woman does not mean something qualitatively different, but a gradation relative to the male. Laqueur (1992) showed how this form of distinction also regulates how gendered bodies are distinguished. He referred to this as the 'one-sex model', which views the male body as the fully developed human body. According to this form of distinction, the female body is fundamentally isomorphic with the male body, though simply not fully developed. This clearly points to the consequence whenever a generic, the whole of a distinction, is identified with one pole. There can be no qualitative differences, but merely gradations along a continuum, the quality of which is determined by one pole. In logical terms, this distinction is made according to a polar relation of opposites: there are two poles with a continuum of gradations between them.

In a form of distinction in which the unit of distinction is formed such that the pole indicated as the unit of the distinction is at the same time indicated in gender terms, then this form of distinction has a gender-defined centre. For this reason, the equivalence of the genders within the framework of a centric gender distinction is virtually inconceivable; it is ruled out through the form of the distinction itself. Equivalence could only mean that women, too, are complete in the same way as men are, and are thus men. A centric gender distinction, through the mere act of distinguishing between genders, thus stabilizes the domination of the gender that forms the centre of the unit of distinction.

The Acentric Form of Gender Distinction

Within the context of social change that led to modern bourgeois society, obviously hierarchical distinctions became problematic. The assumption that all humans are equal made it necessary to recreate the unit of contrast in gender distinction. Consequently, gender distinction took on an acentric form. This was essentially an innovative way of resolving the problem of indication. In the process of distinction, it is no longer the general, the whole – the unit of distinction – that is indicated, but the other pole. That which is not generic is defined in gender terms. In this way, the unit of distinction becomes something that is not defined in gender terms.

This form of distinction corresponds to what Jakobson (1971: 15ff.) described as the contrast between marked and unmarked.[3] Let us illustrate this using the German words *Professor* and *Professorin*. The word *Professor* can be used either to refer generically to a person who holds a university position – without any reference to the gender of the person – or it can refer to the fact that the person holding the position is male. In contrast to this, the word *Professorin* always signals that the person holding the university position is a woman. The term *Professor* is unmarked in this contrast of opposites, that is, it does not mark the gender, whereas *Professorin* is marked.

In order to describe the logical relationship that exists between the generic professor and a male professor, the concept of 'chaotic-manifold' (Schmitz, 1964) seems most appropriate to me, as the boundary between the two is hardly perceivable. Although *Professor* never exclusively refers to a male professor unless an explicit contextual or other type of specification is added, the two meanings are so similar that there is always a tendency to perceive the word *Professor* as referring to a male. As a result, the generic and the male professor are related to each other such that it is left open whether this relationship is one of identity or difference. The type of relationship between two moments (i.e. manifold) that display this type of openness is referred to as chaotic.

Now we can comprehend more precisely how gender distinction on the basis of a marked–unmarked contrast can resolve the identity of human and male by shifting the indication when making the distinction. Centric gender distinction determines the male pole as positive – it is indicated and simultaneously forms the unit of distinction; it represents the whole, the generic human. The female pole, on the other hand, is not specifically indicated, merely representing the deviation from human-male. As regards the marked–unmarked contrast, however, it is not the generic that is indicated in gender terms, but, first of all, only the female. The other, non-indicated pole, breaks down into two moments: the generic as the unit of distinction, and the male as the gender opposite to the female pole. By shifting the indication to the non-generic, the identity of human and male is thereby dissolved, whereby the distinction can make reference to a centre that is not defined in gender terms.[4]

The Choreography of the Transsexual Gender Change

Transsexual gender change provides further empirical verification of the theory that the modern form of gender distinction is acentric, since it proceeds as if choreographed according to the pattern of the marked–unmarked contrast of opposites. My reference to the phenomenon of transsexuality comes from a methodological perspective, i.e. I see transsexuality along the lines of Garfinkel (1967) as a methodological alienation. Because it deviates from the norm, transsexuality makes it possible to see behind what is otherwise seen as the everyday certainty of two genders, whereby every person belongs to one of them for the duration of his or her lifetime. Transsexuality brings into focus that which is otherwise too close and familiar and which, consequently, remains hidden. This notion becomes more precise if transposed on to the idea that gender is a social form of distinction. Since there is hardly any other social phenomenon that offers such an obsessive focus on the form of the gender distinction, it is this aspect that is dissected out, as it were, of transsexuality. This is why it is highly likely that the structural limitations that can be identified within the scope of the phenomenon of transsexuality are essentially due to gender difference. With respect to all other social phenomena, not only must one expect an overlap of various social forms[5] – which also is the case with transsexuality – but, depending on the situation, it is possible that other cultural aspects dominate the gender difference.

In order to analyse the choreography of gender change, it is helpful to go back to the previous example (*Professor–Professorin*) and look at it from the perspective of each of the respective terms. In other words, how does the term *Professor* differ from the term *Professorin* and what must happen for a 'him' to become a 'her' and vice versa. A *Professorin* is a generic professor and, on top of that, a female one. In order to become a male *Professor*, the female term merely has to insist stubbornly on the generic description, such that this is separated, so to speak, from its 'female aspects' and can thus enter into a chaotic relationship with 'male'. Asserting its generic description, the female term could gradually and smoothly slide into maleness. A *Professor*, on the other hand, does not have any inherent qualities of femaleness; he is a generic professor and, on top of that, a male one. In order to become a *Professorin*, the *Professor* must cross a qualitative boundary. A smooth transition would at the very best lead to a genderless generic, but never to the female. Consequently, the male term is more clearly and strictly separated from the female than vice versa. The male term is distinguished formally from the female one within the framework of a contradictory contrast and the female is distinguished from the male in an (implicit, hierarchical) polar contrast of opposites. In contrast to Laqueur's two-sex model, this acentric explanation of gender distinction brings together three moments into one form of distinction whose immanent coherence is otherwise hard to comprehend: (1) acentric gender distinction does not have a gender-defined centre, and inasmuch it permits the notion of women gradually attaining the same equality with the generic that men already have;[6] (2) at the same time, the distinction appears from the perspective of the male pole as a qualitative difference; and (3) it remains a hierarchical polar contrast of opposites from the female perspective.

In order to refer meaningfully to a marked–unmarked dichotomy in a non-linguistic context, one must constantly be aware of the structure of the contrast. First of all, it is a matter of the difference itself, and to that extent, both poles refer to each other in a symmetrical fashion. On the other hand, it also concerns reference of a generic – the unit of the distinction – to the two poles in the contrast, by which these are brought together to form the unit of a differential. This reference creates an asymmetry without forming a clear hierarchy, since the generic is not absolutely identical with one of the poles. Consideration of a transsexual gender change against this background yields the following results.[7]

Transsexuality involves a pre-existent gendered subject who, in the process of gender change, undergoes additional subjectification oriented towards the classical notion of an autonomous subject: transsexuals must (1) revolt against their assigned position within gender relations – they are by definition rebellious subjects; (2) they have to convince themselves and others that they recognize and acknowledge themselves as the gender which they originally are not; (3) finally, they must make a commitment to undergo medical and legal procedures and must follow through on that commitment, that is, they must vouch for the truth of their self-knowledge, which then also serves to verify that truth.

The gender of non-transsexuals is free of such additional subjectifica-tion, as it is realized in absent-minded fashion. Transsexuals cannot par-ticipate in this normalcy because it is broken by the three additional subjectifications. This means that, although the new gender must be real-ized in the same way as all others, it is, at the same time, dependent on the reality of an existing, speaking and acting ego, which credibly and reli-ably revolts, recognizes itself, makes a commitment and carries through on it. Since the gender of transsexuals is a reality in this double sense, the transsexual gender change becomes a paradox. The additional subjectifi-cations that make a transsexual gender change possible at the same time rule out a complete and successful change. One could speak of success only if the new gender were indeed just as real as that of everyone else, without any additional subjectification. The more the additional subjectifi-cation can enter into a chaotic relationship with the new gender, the more normal the new gender could be. By the same token, the greater the con-flict between the additional subjectification and the new gender, the more the transsexuality will depict a non-normal way of being the new gender.

This can be clearly illustrated using empirical data. Transsexual men, that is, woman-to-man transsexuals, are far less seriously confronted with the paradox of the transsexuality of their new gender than are transsexual women. This is especially apparent in interviews with psychological evaluators. In Germany, before transsexuals are permitted to change their first name and sex in official records and undergo a surgical body change, a mandatory prerequisite is their being recognized and accepted as a trans-sexual by evaluators.[8] In the interviews I conducted, evaluators almost all spoke of transsexual women as 'he', in formulations such as 'he was totally convincing as a woman', for instance. This contradiction appeared far less frequently in the evaluations regarding transsexual men. There were also numerous examples mentioned in which it did not appear at all: 'Actually, I had no trouble perceiving him as a man.' Whereas the first formulation accentuated the transsexuality by retaining the male pronoun for a trans-sexual woman, a woman-to-man change more often reached a neutral position as regards gender. The change was not negated, nor did it create a contrast to the new gender (on this subject, see Lindemann, 1993: Ch. 5).

The three moments of additional subjectification that are a necessary condition of transsexuality, as mentioned above, are not specific for male-ness or femaleness, or for the change from man to woman or woman to man. This additional subjectification forms the unit of both gender changes, to the extent that it distinguishes transsexuals from non-trans-sexuals and indicates them as deviant. With respect to their relation to the generic, transsexual genders differ from one another in that transsexual women are more often included in the indication of deviance, whereas transsexual men experience a more smooth transition, not only from being a woman to being a man, but also from the category of indicated deviation into the realm of non-indicated gender normalcy. This is only possible if the additional subjectification ceases to function as a distinguishing indication and merges into the form of subjectivity of the new gender. The structural limitations of the distinction between the two directions of gender change refer to the structural limitations of the form of subjectivity of non-transsexual genders. The accentuated form of subjectivity in transsexuality contrasts greatly with femaleness, but is able to enter into a chaotic relationship with maleness.

If we turn our attention to a specific interpretation of the body and its relationship to its environment, the problem shifts. Analogous to the linguistic distinction of terms according to the marked–unmarked dichotomy, discussion up to this point has dealt with the relationship between the generic and the different terms. Now we directly analyse how the two poles differ from each other and what differences can be observed. The hypothesis was the following: the male term is strictly contrasted with the female as a contradictory contrast, whereas the female is distinguished from the male within the context of polar opposites that permit a smooth transition. In other words, male bodies differ from female bodies in a different way from how female bodies differ from male bodies.

If this hypothesis can be confirmed it will serve to prove that the social form of acentric gender distinction also regulates the distinction of gendered bodies. The second part of the theory introduced earlier is that this regulation is broken through the inherent logic of the bodies. For this reason, the analysis in the following will take two directions, dealing with both the regulation of the body through the gender form of distinction as well as the inherent logic of the body.

THE INHERENT LOGIC OF THE BODY AND THE FORM OF GENDER DISTINCTION

In order to analyse the inherent logic of the body, it is essential that sweeping reference to 'the body' be avoided. To start, I would like to choose a three-fold differentiation based on the phenomenology of the body (*Leibphänomenologie*) as formulated by Hermann Schmitz (1965). I use the term 'objectified body' to refer to the body as a visible and concrete gestalt. As far as the body conveys a sensory and practical reference to the environment, I speak of 'experiencing body', sight, hearing, taste, touch, etc. are modalities through which the body experiences the environment.[9] From this, in turn, one's own body must be distinguished, to the extent that it is experienced. I thus refer to this as 'experienced body'. This term refers, on the one hand, to special states in which the body is experienced as prickling or having a pronounced heaviness of the limbs, etc., and, on the other hand, to the body which is experienced as an unobtrusive, usually ignored feeling of pressure or weight. If it is not necessary to differentiate between the experiencing body and the experienced body, or if both are intended, I also refer to the 'living body'. In order to explain and develop these concepts, I now outline the difference between living body and objectified body. As a second step, I specify the relationship between living body and objectified body, as it is of utmost significance for the construction of the modern living body.

Living Body and Objectified Body

An essential difference between living body and objectified body lies in the different spatial realms they occupy. In this context, three differences are especially important: (1) relative and absolute location; (2) centredness and non-centredness; (3) divisible and non-divisible extension.

The location of an objectified body is determined through its relationship to other locations. A table is in front of a window; its legs have a definite angle in relation to the tabletop, which is above the floor, etc. Objectified bodies are incorporated into a system of spatial relations and relative distances. All locations in this system are determined solely on the basis of mutual references to one another. This also implies that objectified bodies can never coexist at the same time in the same place. If this were the case, they would be absolutely identical with one another, that is, indistinguishable.

The living body, on the other hand, is determined through absolute location. In order to know where my living body is located, I do not need to place it within the system of spatial relations and relative distances. Without knowing the relative location of the objectified body, which I have, I know that my living body, which I am, is 'here'. If I feel pain, I do not need first to locate the site of the pain in the sense of above, under, approximately within the outline of my objectified body. The location of the living body is accessible, even without these relative spatial specifications. It spontaneously stands out, as from a background, and is spatially defined in an ad hoc manner. In other words, absolute location denotes how the living body differentiates itself from its environment.

The space in which objectified bodies exist does not inherently denote a centre: objectified bodies define themselves in their spatial determinedness in a reciprocal manner and as such, they make regular, mutual reference to one another. The living body, on the other hand, provides evidence that the experiential space is centred, since space is structured according to the practical demands of the living body's relationship to the environment. For the relative spatial determinedness of 'chair' and 'wall', for instance, it is irrelevant which side of the wall the chair is on. For the practical demands of global references of an experiencing body, on the other hand, it is significant whether the body must first go into the next room to sit in the chair or if it can sit down immediately. For us – and for most phenomenologists as well – it seems a neat theory that one's own body always forms the centre of the corresponding experiential space, but that need not always be the case. Bateson (1985: 168) offers the example of Balinese dancers who become unable to dance, or even totally unable to move, whenever they lose their reference to important orientation points (such as the highest mountain) after a drive along a very curvy road. Not until they are able to reorient their living bodies to these points and structure space relative to them do they fully regain freedom of movement.

The third difference concerns the type of extension. Human objectified bodies are divisible and they extend continuously, that is, the head is connected directly to the neck – without any space in between – which is connected to the torso, etc. The contours of the objectified body are continuous. Furthermore, objectified bodies are endlessly divisible. They can be cut open, divided into organs and organ systems, which are in turn made up of cells with isolable cell nuclei. The only limits to its divisibility are technical ones. Isolating certain DNA segments requires different techniques to removing an organ. Research on how the body is constructed by science almost exclusively concerns the objectified body. It focuses on the process of dissecting the objectified body and ways of recombining the resulting elements. Dividing the objectified body into cells and various cell types makes it possible, for example, to recombine them as different systems. Some examples are the nervous system comprised of nerve cells, or the immune system (see Haraway, 1995).

The experienced body is experienced, or felt, without conveying a sensory perception. In this way it differs from the objectified body, which can be seen or touched. It can be phenomenologically shown by describing the present state of an experienced body that this body extends non-continuously: the area of the soles of the feet: an oval, slightly shivering surface; above that, starting at the calf, an elongated surface of extended prickling; somewhat behind that, two strongly felt points that extend over the area of what, from the perspective of the objectified body, would belong to the chair upon which I am sitting. The back can be described in the same way; it comprises, as an experienced body, two knotty forms perceived as tender. One is closer to the two points that extend into the area of the chair (as an objectified body). The other knotty form is located a bit above this one.

The above description illustrates, first of all, the non-continuous extension, since there is a certain distance between the regions felt in this way; in other words, the regions are not all tangential to one another. In addition, the extension of the experienced body does not remain within the limits of the objectified body. The two points that correspond, at the objectified body level, to the place where the buttocks touch the surface of the chair can extend further as an experienced body than the objectified body does.

This description appears to contradict the theory of the absolute location of the living body, since the individual, perceived regions of the body are located relative to each other: a certain region is above this one and below that one, etc. But in addition to having a position relative to one another, all these regions also have an absolute location. The shivering feet are, on the one hand, immediately accessible, without previously having to be assigned a place in a system of spatial relations and relative distances. On the other hand, they are relative to other felt regions of the experienced body. The fact that individual regions of the experienced body are relative and absolute at the same time shows why they can violate a conclusive law of relative location, according to which there can only be one objectified body at any one place in time. This pertains to the mentioned buttocks and chair as objectified bodies. But as an experienced body, i.e. as an absolute space, the buttocks can also extend into space taken up by the chair. The experienced body represents an absolute location and as such, it can share the same space at the same time with an objectified body.

This can be illustrated using the example of phantom limbs. Phantom limbs are amputated extremities which are felt as though they were still attached. People with phantom limbs normally try to avoid moving in such a way that the phantom limb would collide with anything. If it cannot be avoided, however, and the stump is moved so close to a concrete object – a table, for example – that there would not be enough room for the missing extremity – such as a hand – the phantom hand is felt in the area taken up by the tabletop. The hand is not experienced as anything relating to a table and the table is not experienced as anything belonging to a hand. In a similar way, a phantom limb can be brought into the area of one's own objectified body or experienced body, whereby the area thus penetrated is felt at the same time, without any blending of the two areas of the experienced body. Absolute locations, in this case the extended regions in which the experienced body is felt, can exist in a relative location that is simultaneously taken up by an objectified body. Also, two absolute locations can share a relative location, that is, they can coexist at the same relative location.

The experienced body is indivisibly extended: felt pain, for example, cannot be divided into individual atoms of pain, which can then be recombined in order to rebuild the pain. If I feel my head as nothing but a dulled, hurting mass and the pain begins to segment itself into two regions of pain, a lower one in back and a higher one in front, the original pain has not been divided, but a transformation of the phenomenon as a whole has taken place. The felt pain is not divided; it becomes a different pain.

The Objectified Body as a Modern Artificial Form of the Living Body

Objectified body and living body have assumed an increasingly reflexive relationship in modern times. The cultural formation of the living body orients itself more and more towards the construction of the objectified body, i.e. the processes of dividing the objectified body into elements and their recombination as an organic system. This artificial form of the living body has become so familiar to us that it is hard to imagine it any other way.

Observing the process through which the uteruses of European women became 'fixed' in the course of the seventeenth and eighteenth centuries (see Laqueur, 1992: 130ff.), it can be seen how strongly the objectified body and the living body have assumed a reflexive relationship to one another and how this relationship is becoming intensified.

Anatomy scholars were still despairing well into the seventeenth century that despite all educational efforts, one could still hear nonsense about a migratory uterus. The process was a slow one. Uteruses had already started 'settling down' in the sixteenth century, as anatomical illustrations started becoming more widespread. It was evidently the illustrations that succeeded in calming down the uteruses. Information that already existed in a spoken form did not suffice to modify the physical experience. This leads to the following hypothesis: knowledge – in a concrete or vivid form – about the objectified body and the experienced body have a relationship of reciprocal meaning. The visible and tangible gestalt of the objectified body determines how the living body is experienced, directly and without any reflection or propositional knowledge. To experience one's own body in this way means that a person's objectified body is his or her experienced reality. The experienced body thus carries the meaning and the objectified body is the meaning itself. Conversely, knowledge about the objectified body tells the experienced body which form it should assume. In other words, having knowledge of which objectified body I have means to me that I know how my experienced body is constituted. The reflexive relationship between objectified body and living body is demonstrated to be a normative meaning relationship (see, in more detail, Lindemann, 1996). Experiences that contradict this rule, such as the above-mentioned 'experience of sitting', become marginalized.

At this point it is clearly helpful to distinguish between the location of the objectified body and that of the living body. The space that encompasses relative locations is also determined such that only one object can fill one spatial, temporal position. Anatomists' insistence that there was no space in a human objectified body for a migratory uterus owes to this logic. They said the uterus is surrounded by other organs and besides, as was known even to the Greek physician Galen, it is supported by ligaments, which is why it was inconceivable that it should be mobile. On the other hand, it is by all means possible that two or more absolute locations can exist at one relative time–space position. In this sense, that is with respect to the space occupied by the experienced body, a description of a migratory uterus does not pose a problem. But it is problematic for modern living bodies, since they are integrated into a normative meaning relationship: the experienced extension of a modern living body is disciplined by the objectified body's pictorial form.

In interactions, the reflexive meaning relationship between objectified body and living body leads to an intense experience of the body becoming gendered. The following example serves to illustrate this point. A transsexual woman, whom I call Verena, who at the time of this depiction had not yet had genital surgery, described a visit to a women's public toilets:

Verena: I was sitting on the toilet. I was relaxing and about to pee . . . and then another woman came in and I was startled – what'll happen if she notices something? She went into the stall next to me and she was rather loud, the way she was peeing, so I was relieved. Yeah, well, and then – I just went ahead and started peeing too.

Verena is sitting in a cubicle in a public toilet. She cannot be seen by the person who enters – presumably a woman.[10] Verena is startled. Her reaction is immediate and does not come from a fear of being 'exposed as a man' upon leaving. This reaction implies that a relationship must have been established between Verena and the person who entered such that it is immediately clear to Verena that she is out of place in terms of gender. In order to analyse this relationship it is necessary to understand what it means to sit on a toilet in a relaxed manner. You relax, feel in your abdomen the development of a region of the experienced body, the relative location of which overlaps with the urogenital area of the objectified body. As a result of the socialization of the experienced body, it exists in a reflexive meaning relationship to this part of the objectified body. At this moment, the reference context between objectified body and experienced body seems to become temporarily irrelevant. In any case, Verena does not report that she felt inappropriate in terms of gender from the very beginning. As soon as another person/woman enters the toilets, the situation is fundamentally changed. Verena perceives – she hears the other person – and she evidently feels perceived, since she wonders whether the other person notices anything, that is, whether the other person perceives Verena as a man. It is irrelevant that Verena in fact cannot be perceived at all. In order to understand this, we must consider the following: when I am perceived, I never have access to the form in which others see me. I cannot see how and as what others see me. Even if Verena could be seen, she could not know whether the other person would see her as a woman or a man. The experience of being perceived refers only to the ability to be perceived; as a perceived person, one's only point of reference is how one experiences oneself, that is, as an extended, felt form, consisting of the regions of the experienced body that extend non-continuously. This explains why Verena suspects she could be perceived as a man: in the experience of being perceived, the felt region of the experienced body abruptly clicks into a meaning relationship with the objectified body. The genital form of the objectified body, which Verena knows that she has, becomes the intense reality of the felt region of the experienced body, solely on the basis of the spatial referential context. The basic presupposition of this experience is thus the socially generalized reflexive relationship between living body and objectified body as a normative meaning relationship.

To the extent that objectified body and experiencing body click into a reflexive meaning relationship, perception itself becomes gendered, since it is the living body that is felt and that perceives. This is the fundamental presupposition in simultaneously realizing same and different genderedness, since the positions of the perceiver and the perceived must be realized at the same time as gendered positions. If the experience of being perceived existed in isolation, without any notion of the gender of the perceiver, it would be impossible for the perceived to feel a relationship of same and different genderedness. Same and different genderedness cannot exist within the context of 'gender for others', but only in the act of perceiving, since this simultaneously realizes two positions whose gender is accessible: the position of the perceiver and that of the perceived. In this sense, Verena's perception of the person entering is in itself a male-gendered act of perceiving. Her gendered hearing exists throughout the toilet facility, thus establishing a real different-gendered relationship. Verena's experience contrasts two-fold with normative background knowledge about public toilets, as places of same-genderedness. In a certain sense, Verena's presence there is inappropriate in two ways. First, she has a male body and is in a women's toilet (gender for others); second, Verena establishes a different-gender perception relationship to the person entering instead of the prescribed same-gender perception relationship. It is this last relationship that makes it obvious in that moment that her presence there is inappropriate. Verena's perception relationship to the person entering is real, namely, and not fantasized.

The usefulness of such a startled reaction can be determined against this background. On the one hand, the shock causes tension, that is, the relaxed felt region of the experienced body – which is in a gendering reflexive meaning relationship to the objectified body – suddenly ceases to exist. On the other hand, the shock weakens the perceiving reference of the living body to the environment, sometimes totally eliminating it (see Schmitz, 1965: 177). In other words, the shock largely serves to destroy spontaneously the inappropriately gendered living body.

For the everyday reproduction of human gender, a formal dual structure emerges from this analysis: (1) I am a gender in that I am one for others, that is, in that I am perceived as a gender; (2) I am a gender in that others are one for me, that is, in that I perceive others as a gender. Same and different genderedness are realized in that I refer to others through the act of perceiving. These analyses strongly contradict the assumption that gender can be assigned in an interactive process (see Hirschauer, 1993: Ch. 1), since the gender the 'other' perceives the 'ego' to be remains inaccessible to the 'ego'. Instead of receiving something from the 'other', the 'ego' realizes, through the experience of being perceived, solely the gendering meaning relationship of the living body – which the 'ego' is – to the objectified body – which the 'ego' has.

Now it is possible to go into depth regarding the problem of gender difference. Can the theory be upheld that male objectified bodies differ formally from female objectified bodies in a different way than the reverse? A central aspect of the different forms of distinction also often comes up in interaction analysis as well as in analyses of sexual encounters of transsexuals. It was explicitly formulated in a liberal reform of sexual offence laws in the early 1970s in Germany. According to the penal code, only the male objectified body is capable of exhibitionism (see König, 1990: 265, 372). Exhibiting a female objectified body is not exhibitionism according to its legal definition. In such a case, no one is harassed with a desire directed at them. A woman can desire, but this is not symbolized by her objectified body. Consequently, the objectified body does not prescribe her living body to desire (see Lindemann, 1993: 284). The gestalt of the female objectified body is thus defined as desirable, but not as directing itself desiringly at someone. It is important to be very precise here. The point is that the mere display of genitals means desire. This is not the same as showing one's desire through gestures or glances, an action that is open to men and women.

The problem facing non-surgically changed transsexuals in sexual encounters corresponds to the legal codification of their body symbolism. If the female objectified body does not mean directing itself desiringly at someone, this signifies that the clicking in of the reflexive meaning relationship between objectified body and living body does not unequivocally determine the subjective position of desire and thus the position from which same and different genderedness is realized. This makes it easier for woman-to-man transsexuals to have heterosexual relations with women and homosexual relations with men, even before they undergo surgery. Knowing that they have a vulva and clitoris rather than a penis and testicles does not hinder them, since the clitoris can be brought into a polar contrast with the penis, which is characterized as more or less complete, that is, the clitoris can be felt as such as a region of the experienced body. Relating to a female partner with desire is not experienced as homosexual as a result, since the clitoris is experienced as a homologue to the penis, that is, as a not fully developed penis. This also applies to the clitoris that is perceived as a region of the objectified body of the sexual partner. The difference thus assumes the form of a polar contrast, the continuum of which ranges from complete to incomplete.

This homologue relationship does not exist for changes in the other direction. In the interviews I conducted, the penis was not seen as an oversized clitoris, showing that the difference in that direction is one of a contradictory contrast. Correspondingly, man-to-woman transsexuals face greater difficulties having sexual relations. If their experienced body distinctly responds to a situation such that they feel a region that has a reflexive meaning relationship to the penis of the objectified body, this almost inevitably means relating with desire to others from the male position. In this context, only homosexual relations with men and heterosexual relations with women are possible. The only option open to transsexual women is to try to avoid having the penis become a region of the experienced body, or to attempt to neutralize the meaning relationship between the objectified body and the experienced body. This is possible, but precisely the difficulty involved in doing this makes the structural limitation, i.e. the differential difference of the objectified bodies, all the more obvious.[11]

Summarizing the reflexive meaning relationship between the objectified body and the living body, and relating it to the problem of different forms of distinction, the following conclusions can be drawn. Both male and female objectified bodies mean the 'gender for others'. Moreover, male objectified bodies determine the subjective perception and desire position within the context of the reflexive meaning relationship between objectified body and living body. This implies a more pronounced realization of same and different genderedness from the male position. Since the female objectified body does not determine the subjective perception and desire position in the same way, a clitoris, for example, can be understood as a region of the objectified body that is homologous to that of the penis, whereas this homology does not apply for the reverse. The penis/testicles – clitoris/vulva differential is structured from the perspective of the female pole as a polar contrast, involving a more or less obvious expression of one and the same quality; conversely, the difference from the perspective of the male pole is expressed as a contradictory contrast, since the issue is whether or not the penis exists as a significant region of the objectified and the experienced body.

The different meanings of male and female objectified bodies as a result of the different forms of distinction also involves gendering the fluctuating centres of experiential space. The greater ties of the male position to gendering perception implies a tendency for male experiencing bodies to centre experiential space on the basis of themselves, whereby female experiencing bodies usually experience something else as the centre, and their experiencing body orients itself around that centre.[12]

In order to understand the theory of different forms of distinction of male and female objectified or living bodies, it is important to consider the distinction from the respective gender position perspective that arises when a change in gender position of male to female or vice versa takes place. As shown by the 'choreography of transsexual gender change', acentric gender distinction forms the general structural framework of the differential distinction of objectified and living bodies. If this analysis of gender change is valid, it follows that the acentric form of gender distinction regulates the gendered difference of the objectified body and the living body.

CONCLUSIONS

The opening hypothesis was as follows: gender difference is a social form, the local realization of which is irreducibly broken through the inherent logic of the objectified or living body. This implies a more radical historicizing of 'gender difference' than the theory of gender construction has offered up to now, since the reformulation based on the theory of difference no longer concerns gendering per se, i.e. differential determination of qualities. Instead, it deals with historicizing the form of distinction itself. In this sense, gender-defined bodies are themselves historical phenomena, since male and female bodies differ from each other in the specific way that makes it meaningful to speak of gender difference only insofar as they are distinguished by their being linked into a unit of distinction.

In addition to this radicalization, the hypothesis at the outset entails a modification of the theory of gender construction. This generally focuses on the process nature of reproduction of gender, thereby overlooking the fact that gender as a body is a spatial phenomenon.[13] It is this subject matter that has been focused upon here, as well as the diversified inherent logic of the body as an objectified, experiencing and experienced body, which cannot be reduced to social forms.

For this discussion, it is also significant that objectified body and living body can be brought into a reflexive meaning relationship with each other. To that extent, the objectified body also becomes the continuous artificial form of the living body, regulating it in three ways.

1. The non-continuous extension of the experienced body is felt in the same way as the continuous extension of the objectified body. In this way the felt stirrings of the experienced body are brought into the topography of the objectified body. With respect to the example of uteruses becoming stationary, one could speak of a calming fixation of the experienced body.
2. The experienced boundary of the living body coincides with the limits of the objectified body. This implies a strict delimitation from the environment, which immunizes the modern living body, for example, against assuming external action centres that invade it. Opening up the limitedness of the living body only seems possible by joining human objectified bodies to non-human objectified bodies (computers and their networks). Using an analysis of Homer's Iliad, Schmitz (1965) discovered that severely different forms of the living body can also exist. Homer's heroes do not experience their bodies as a unit, but as an 'assemblage of limbs'. There is also no common action centre that would be isolable from the body as the psyche or soul. Much more the individual regions of the experienced body are experienced as more or less self-sufficient masses of movement, the impulses of which might also conflict with each other. The fact that the living body has no action centre to unite its parts also makes it possible for external forces, such as gods, to invade the living body of a hero and cause individual regions of the experienced body to behave in a certain way. Correspondingly, it is not the person as a whole that is given the power and motivation to throw a spear especially far and accurately, but the arm, as part of the experienced body.
3. Since the experienced body is also always an experiencing one, the regulation of the expansion of the living body also includes the way of relating to the environment. In this sense, the objectified body is a vivid

sign showing a living body that it should behave in a particular fashion and perceive in another particular fashion. As regards gender difference, the way the objectified body suggests to the living body that it centre experiential space is of central importance.

The three-fold regulation of the living body through the objectified body can also be described in this way. As the modern living body clicks into a reflexive meaning relationship with the objectified body, the objectified body becomes a vivid, exemplary programme that regulates how the experienced body is felt and is separate from its environment, and how the experiencing body centres its experiential space, perceives and acts.

NOTES

This article was translated from the German by Allison Brown.

1.   For a survey of the discussion in Germany, see Wobbe and Lindemann (1994), Institut für Sozialforschung (1994) and Pasero and Braun (1995).
2.   There are considerable differences regarding interpretations of the complexity of this process. For a comparison between deconstruction and sociological construction, see Lindemann (1994).
3.   Please note that the terms 'marked' and 'unmarked' are not used here in the sense of Spencer Brown.
4.   Luhmann (1988) also assumes that modern gender distinction no longer has a gender-defined centre. However, he prematurely leaps to the conclusion that gender distinction is presently practised as non-distinction. In any case, discourse on equality and difference of the genders (see Honegger, 1991) that immediately followed the acceptance of an acentric form of distinction can hardly serve as evidence of the beginning of the end of the gender difference, but rather for the emergence of a new form of distinction.
5.   For example, differences in ethnicity or social class.
6.   Another starting point for the empirical development of a theory of gender distinction based on a theory of difference is a gender-based division of labour. Within the framework of acentric gender distinction, it can be presumed that only female labour is specifically designated as pertaining to that gender (housework, childrearing), thus being distinguished from non-gendered, generic work. An analysis based on a theory of difference also focuses on the paradox that gradually attained equality and continued exclusion of women from the areas of non-gendered labour are mutually dependent. In addition, the distinction can be repeated in the area of non-gendered labour, whereby here, too, an area designated as female can result: in academia, for example, women's studies is reserved for women. The firm establishment of this field would be in keeping with the logic of modern gender distinction. All in all, such considerations presuppose a specification of the relationship between labour and gender, based on the theory of difference, and that has not yet taken place in the sociology of labour. For a survey of discourse on this subject, see Wetterer (1992).
7.   In these considerations, I refer to the empirical study on transsexual gender change that I conducted between 1987 and 1991 (see Lindemann, 1993).
8.   For a description of institutional controls on gender change, see also Hirschauer (1993).

9. These modalities also have their own regularities, through which social constructs are subjected to irreducible limitations. A history of smell, for example (see Corbin, 1984), does not encounter the problem of the emergence of a central perspective, which is doubtless an important event in the history of seeing.

10. Even on leaving, Verena did not see the person.

11. For detailed interaction analyses, see Lindemann (1993: Ch. 5). A more indepth analysis complicates the matter, since there are three regions of the objectified body and experienced body, that differ from one another in different ways, as described above. It is not always the male objectified body that represents the standard for completeness or what exists. In the pair contrasts 'breast–male chest' and 'vagina–interior of male body', the female objectified body holds the determining position. These regions of the body do not determine as lasting a perceiving reference to the Other; they have primary relevance insofar as they are perceived, that is, they determine the gender I am for others and less the position, from which the perception of same and different genderedness are realized. This is confirmed by the presentation summarized here, which focuses on the 'penis/testicles–clitoris/vulva' difference.

12. In order to confirm these considerations, it would be interesting to investigate how spatial experience and ethical orientation relate to one another. A spatial structure in which one's own living body is not experienced as the centre could, for example, be understood as backing up an ethics of care. On the other hand, centring a space around one's own living body would correspond to a morality concerned primarily with implementing subjective rights, or just a balance between them.

13. The most prominent example of this is Butler's (1993) concept of gender based on 'citationality'. De Lauretis (1987: 41), on the other hand, made early reference to the necessity of including space and the body as a spatial phenomenon in an analysis of gender construction. However, she did not offer any specific suggestions as to what that would entail.

REFERENCES

Bateson, Gregory (1985) *Ökologie des Geistes. Anthropologische, psychologische, biologische und epistemologische Perspektiven.* Frankfurt: Suhrkamp.

Butler, Judith (1993) *Bodies that Matter: On the Discursive Limits of Sex.* New York and London: Routledge.

Corbin, Alain (1984) *Pesthauch und Blütendurft. Ein Geschichte des Geruchs.* Berlin: Wagenbach.

De Lauretis, Teresa (1987) *Technologies of Gender: Essays on Theory, Film, and Fiction.* Basingstoke and London: Macmillan.

Garfinkel, Harold (1967) *Studies in Ethnomethodology.* Englewood Cliffs, NJ: Prentice Hall.

Haraway, Donna (1995) 'Die Biopolitik postmoderner Körper', pp. 160–99 in Donna Haraway (ed.) *Die Neuerfindung der Natur.* Frankfurt and New York: Campus.

Hirschauer, Stefan (1993) *Die soziale Konstruktion der Transsexualität. Über die Medizin und den Geschlechtswechsel.* Frankfurt: Suhrkamp.

Honegger, Claudia (1991) *Die Ordnung der Geschlechter. Die Wissenschaften vom Menschen und das Weib.* Frankfurt and New York: Campus.

Institut für Sozialforschung (ed.) (1994) *Geschlechterverhältnisse und Politik.* Frankfurt: Suhrkamp.

Jakobson, Roman (1971) 'Zur Struktur des russischen Verbums', pp. 3–15 in *Selected Writings, Vol. II: Word and Language*. The Hague: Niehoff.

Kessler, Susan J. and Wendy McKenna (1978) *Gender: An Ethnomethodological Approach*. New York, Chichester, Brisbane and Toronto: Wiley.

König, Oliver (1990) *Nacktheit. Soziale Normierung und Moral*. Opladen: Westdeutscher Verlag.

Laqueur, Thomas (1992) *Auf den Leib geschrieben. Die Inszenierung der Geschlechter von der Antike bis Freud*. Frankfurt and New York: Campus.

Lindemann, Gesa (1993) *Das Paradoxe Geschlecht. Transsexualität im Spannungsfeld von Körper, Leib und Gefühl*. Frankfurt: Fischer.

Lindemann, Gesa (1994) 'Die Konstruktion der Wirklichkeit und die Wirklichkeit der Konstruktion', pp. 115–46 in Theresa Wobbe and Gesa Lindemann (eds) *Denkachsen. Zur theoretischen und institutionellen Rede vom Geschlecht*. Frankfurt: Suhrkamp.

Lindemann, Gesa (1996) 'Zeichentheoretische Überlegungen zum Verhältnis von Körper und Leib', pp. 146–75 in Annette Barkhaus et al. (eds) *Identität, Leiblichkeit, Normativität. Neue Horizonte anthropologischen Denkens*. Frankfurt: Suhrkamp.

Luhmann, Niklas (1988) 'Frauen, Männer und George Spencer Brown', *Zeitschrift für Soziologie* 17: 47–71.

Pasero, Ursula and Friederike Braun (eds) (1995) *Konstruktion von Geschlecht*. Pfaffenweiler: Centaurus.

Schmitz, Hermann (1964) *System der Philosophie, Vol. 1: Die Gegenwart*. Bonn: Bouvier.

Schmitz, Hermann (1965) *System der Philosophie, Vol. 2, Part 1: Der Leib*. Bonn: Bouvier.

Spencer Brown, George (1969) *Laws of Form*. London: Allen and Unwin.

Wetterer, Angelika (ed.) (1992) *Profession und Geschlecht*. Frankfurt and New York: Campus.

Wobbe, Theresa and Gesa Lindemann (eds) (1994) *Denkaschsen. Zur theoretischen und institutionellen Rede vom Geschlecht*. Frankfurt: Suhrkamp.

6 Victims or Offenders?

'Other' Women in French Sexual Politics

Rachel A. Bloul

This chapter focuses on the continuities and contradictions in the place given to 'other women' in French cultural politics. The first section examines how French colonial sexual politics had sharply differentiated Arab/Muslim women from black African women, both in their understanding of the relative status and 'potentialities' of these women and in the actual policies concerning them. The former were seen as unfortunate, but sexy and certainly 'deserving', victims of a backward Muslim patriarchal order. The latter's status as victims was perceived as compromised by their own 'insensitivity' for, and passive acceptance of, their own fate. In the second section, I argue that these contrasting views which established and opposed two categories of 'native women' can still be found in the media treatment of two contemporary French 'post-colonial' troubles, that is the issue of Islamic *hijab* for school girls of North African origin, and the excision trials of a number of black African women (mothers and *exciseuses*).[1] In addition, both the colonial and contemporary polemics are to be placed within the context of French historical understandings of cultural difference. Previously unchallenged aspirations to universalism for French identity and civilization have given way to tensions between two different versions of French identity as ethnic (Gallic/Christian) or as adherence to universal principles. Thus, both the colonial and contemporary polemics, and their contexts, articulate shifting contradictions between sameness and difference, visible and invisible, public and private. The third part of the article attempts to unpack the continuities and dissimilarities in the production of these dichotomies.

OTHER WOMEN IN FRENCH COLONIAL SEXUAL POLITICS

To some extent the phrase 'French colonial sexual politics' is a misnomer as it reads a singularity of purpose in, and overemphasizes a supposed homogeneity of, 'colonial sexual politics'. For while the eroticization of 'native women' in colonial discourses is easy to demonstrate, and no new theme for scholarship, whether feminist or not (Fanon, 1952; Martinkus-Zemp, 1973; Kabbani, 1986; Apter, 1992; Jolly, 1994), the value, erotic or otherwise, attributed to these women by their (male) colonizers varied greatly. Arab/Muslim women of North Africa, and particularly from Algeria, were perceived and eroticized, in ways very dissimilar from the eroticization of black African women.

In her study of French colonial literature written between 1919 and 1939, Martinkus-Zemp argues that black African women were functionalized and animalized. 'Naked African females' were perceived as not quite belonging to the human order. At best they were 'pretty animals that obey custom and instinct' (Randeau, 1935: 9, quoted in Martinkus-Zemp, 1973: 63), who could be 'domesticated' but were not to be trusted.[2] Exoticism and eroticism were linked through the white male's appreciation of *naked* black female beauty. Her nakedness and 'animal grace' confirmed her sexual fetishization and her subhuman status which could hardly be improved upon as, clothed, the black woman did not only lose her grace, she became ridiculous (Martinkus-Zemp, 1973: 69). Black women's nakedness was also an indicator of their 'ignorance' and 'naturalness', including in sexual matters. Martinkus-Zemp shows how this naturalness was used in white males' writings to denigrate *all* women. On the one hand, the promise of exotic sensuality was an illusion. Black women were cold and stupid in bed, altogether a disappointment: 'she laid on the mat, docile, indifferent, her gaze fixed on the ceiling' (Megret, 1937, quoted in Martinkus-Zemp, 1973: 77). On the other hand, their ignorance, otherwise a sign of brutality and insensitivity, was perceived, when sexual, as natural, a sign of healthy sexual morals. 'White women, by comparison, appear[ed] perverse' and their companionship a deadening constraint (Martinkus-Zemp, 1973: 78).

The eroticization of Muslim women, especially Algerian women, followed a different course. While the black woman's eroticization essentially rested on perceptions of her offered nakedness, which tended to amalgamate all black women under the same stereotype, Muslim women's desirability depended on the play between their unavailability and their fantasized sexual abilities, in other words on the erotic dynamics of the harem. Such eroticization also recognized some diversity across various types of Muslim women.

Much has been written on the harem as a trope of orientalist discourses (Kabbani, 1986; Alloula, 1986). Apter (1992) in particular characterizes Algerian veiled women as essentialized by French male colonizers as containing the secret of ultimate Otherness. Male colonial desire for veiled Muslim women eroticized a fantasy of colonial mastery and 'aestheticize[d] exotic eroticisms' (Apter, 1992: 208). Arab/Muslim women became both more and less than black African women.

They were more, for though the Arab/Muslim woman's first characteristic was also her submissiveness, unlike black women's, it was one devoid of all connotations of animal passivity. It was a cultivated submissiveness, in the same way as her beauty was a cultivated beauty. Arab/Muslim women were knowing: they knew in fact all sorts of artifices, from the artifices of *la toilette* and *la parure*[3] to the numerous wiles of seduction. Such artifices were seen as the inevitable consequences of the constraints crushing Arab women, just as the harem, the place of confinement, was also the stage of the 'ancient' art of seduction. The seductiveness of Arab/Muslim women was thus inseparable from their status as deserving victims of their own 'barbarous' males as numerous paintings and literary works show (Kabbani, 1986: 67–85).

Knowledge of the ancient arts of seduction, and victimization, 'prepared' Muslim women for white men in many ways, which allowed a certain differentiation between stereotypes. French colonial literature on Algeria demonstrates this: there were the dignified, fatalistic victims (Eberhardt, 1993), the traditional dancers/prostitutes (the famed Oulednail), the passionate lovers (epitomized in Loti's novels) and the femme fatale through whose embrace romantic French heroes transcended industrial mediocrity, though at the cost of their lives: Benoit's Antinea, the North African fatal heroine of *L'Atlantide* (1918) was a formidable success.[4] Thus, unlike black African women, Arab/Muslim ones were granted the humanity of feelings, however improper these might, at times, have been. Indeed it was the feelings they were capable of, which made them superior sexual objects.

Yet, they were also somewhat less than black African women. The latter, even if they were to be bought or considered as a superior kind of pet (Martinkus-Zemp, 1973: 62), at least existed by and in themselves. Certainly, this was achieved by abstracting black African women from any kind of social environment apart from the relationship with the master. Yet, white men related to *them* as a particular type of women. This was not the case for Arab/Muslim women who were seen first and foremost as the product of their men's oppression. They were the way they were, they felt the way they did, because of their men. Their attractiveness was, in other words, largely due, directly and indirectly, to the fact that they were under other men's control. The French heroes of many novels were painted as animated with the best moral intentions, full of pity for the seductive victims. Muslim men were depicted as brutal, unfeeling and barbarous (Kabbani, 1986: 78). And the women whose fates were the apparent concern of the stories became objectified (aside from their sexual fetishization) as the undeclared stakes, or unwitting means, of the contest between white men and Muslim men. By contrast, black African men were, in general, not mentioned in relation to white men/African black women liaisons.

An examination of colonial policies and concerns in North and black Africa shows parallel discrepancies. In Algeria, French colonial administration saw in Algerian women the 'gateway to penetration' and a range of 'medical, hygienic, philanthropic, pedagogic and social' measures were taken to reach, educate and liberate Algerian women (Woodhull,

1991: 117–19). Woodhull also notes the increase of such specific measures towards the enfranchisement of women in the last years of colonial domination. Such measures were seen as the key to a successful Gallicization of Algeria. The colonial educational agenda, for example, insisted on the importance of Algerian female education, for only through the cultural assimilation of Algerian women would the Algerian people be 'regenerated' (Hélie, 1994: 11). This (minus the French emphasis) echoed similar arguments elsewhere in the Muslim world, where Muslim male intellectuals, religious and political leaders made the 'Woman Question' – centred on the civilizing function of women and the importance of their access to a degree of freedom and equal opportunity – their own business (Ghoussoub, 1987; Badran, 1994). Because of French colonial sexual politics, this could not – and did not – happen in Algeria as, for Algerian men, Algerian women became 'both the guarantors of national identity and the supreme threat to that identity' (Woodhull, 1991: 114). For Algerian men, the 'emancipation' of 'their' women became synonymous with their Gallicization. But it is important to realize that Algerian women were thus constituted as the key symbols of Algeria's cultural identity for *both* Algerian and French men. From colonial times onwards, issues of veiling and of female autonomy were the focus of a male (French and Maghrebi) contest which overshadowed Algerian women's own battle for personal autonomy and access to the public sphere. Indeed, Fanon went so far as to assert that Algeria, as a developing nation, needed at some point to reaffirm its authentic culture as demonstrated in the seclusion and veiling of women (Fanon, 1961), thus anticipating similar arguments being nowadays articulated by Islamist movements in various parts of the Muslim world (Hélie-Lucas, 1993).

It is very difficult to document any such touching concerns for the fate of black African women during colonial times. Colonial administration in black Africa was concerned about family law and the general issues of family and health organization, yet the protracted colonial policy debates in the nineteenth and twentieth centuries never mentioned female excision as a relevant problem. Partly this is due to the fact that, in black Africa, the French abandoned assimilation policy relatively early in favour of association policy (Wooten, 1993). Whereas Algeria was considered as part of France and supposedly administered under the same policies and laws,[5] in black Africa, colonial administration was to respect such native institutions and norms as were morally acceptable to the metropolis (Wooten, 1993: 421). Obviously, female excision and infibulation were such respectable customs, as no attempts were made to question them. French administrators and missionaries kept silent on the subject.[6] Medical practitioners might have written a few learned and obscure articles on the pathology subsequent to the practices (Auffret, 1983), but did not denounce it or take it into account in the elaboration and management of the comprehensive [*sic*] public health policy and administration (Snyder, 1974). Some anthropologists, notably Griaule (1965), analysed clitoridectomy as playing important ritual and ideological functions, notably in legitimizing a sexual order founded on extreme sexual dimorphism and on the necessity of the violent subjugation of the potentially subversive feminine. The emphasis in these studies is on the technical discussion of the psychoanalytical aspects of cultural elaboration (Lyons, 1981). No relation is drawn to what it might mean for the real women involved, and certainly not to the possible status of such rituals in terms of human rights. This colonial indifference to the fate of black women contrasts violently with both the colonial 'outrage' and concern about Muslim women, and sits uneasily besides the recent excision trials in France.

NORTH AFRICAN AND BLACK AFRICAN WOMEN IN FRANCE TODAY: THE PROBLEM OF THE 'ISLAMIC SCARVES' AND EXCISION TRIALS

The Excision Trials

The history of the excision[7] trials in France dates back to 1979 when an *exciseuse* was tried (and received a one-year suspended sentence by a magistrate in a police court) after a baby girl died at three months from haemorrhage following excision. Indeed, the next two cases in the following years also involved death or near death of very young infants after severe haemorrhaging. However, 'excision' legally became a crime in August 1983 after a severely disturbed white French woman mutilated her daughter (Winter, 1994: 944). All other cases involved black African migrants, though in one other case (the Corval/Soumare trial June 1990) a white French woman was implicated as her male black African companion organized the excision of their daughter without her consent and, indeed, knowledge. Since 1983, there have been a dozen more trials. In two cases, the excised girls died, one other girl was saved *in extremis* and the other cases were classified as 'excision non-mortelle'.

A number of self-identified feminist associations[8] have been at the forefront of the campaign against genital mutilation, and were instrumental in its criminalization. Since 1983, 'excisions' are tried as 'criminal action against minors, bringing about mutilation, i.e. the ablation of healthy organs' (Article 312 of the Code Penal). There are no specific condemnations of excision per se in the Code Penal. The trials have encountered a number of difficulties, which mostly have to do with the inadequacies of a legal system based on the concept of individual responsibility, when it comes to evaluate matters to do with individual compliance to customs. Whom to charge is one problem as matters of individual responsibility and guilt are far from clear: the *exciseuse* who has done the deed? The mother who organizes the excision? The father whose decision it is to do it? All of the parties involved are far from the ideal 'free agents' of the legal system, considering the social pressure to have one's daughters excised, and the social penalties for those who do not conform. What penalties to impose is another problem, and so is the conducting of the trials as 'courts are there to judge individuals, not to judge customs' in the – ineffectual – words of a judge objecting to the trial taking on, as in many other such cases, 'the allure of a colloque' (Le Monde, 8 March 1991).

These difficulties are reflected in the inconsistencies of the various judgements which range from the acquittal of parents to their condemnation to suspended or actual jail sentences of various lengths. Exciseuses are usually condemned to jail sentences which, however, can vary from one year, suspended, to five years, actual. Nor are sentences given in any increasing order of severity as earlier sentences can be more severe than later ones.

As matters stand, in the course of some 17 trials – though Me Weil-Curiel, the lawyer of SOS Femmes Alternatives has several dozens more briefs (Le Figaro, 3 October 1989) – two have concerned the exciseuse only, in two others the parents were also charged along with the exciseuse, in two trials only fathers were charged. In all of the others, the mothers were charged either by themselves, or with their husbands as accomplices. It is extremely difficult to identify exciseuses due to the private, indeed often clandestine, nature of the operations in France. Thus, in the majority of cases, it is the mothers who are condemned to jail sentences whether actual or suspended, though the feminist associations which stand as partie civile are very aware of the problems this poses. It is, in most cases, easy for the father to pretend ignorance as 'excision is a woman's business' and, of course, they always absent themselves while the act itself is performed. They cannot be charged as perpetrators. On those occasions where fathers were condemned, it was because it could be proved that they actually gave money to the exciseuse or to the mothers, after their daughters had been excised (see Winter, 1994 for a detailed history of the excision trials in France).

Thus, black African women figure predominantly in the media reports on excision, both as past victims[9] and as offenders. The cliché descriptions found in press reports uneasily echo earlier representations. They are presented as exotic women, dressed or 'draped' in colourful boubous of uncertain origin. Here are the descriptions of the same woman in one particular instance: 'dressed in her traditional boubou' (Le Figaro, 4 October 1989), 'draped in her boubou woven with golden threads' (Libération, 5 October 1989), 'dressed in some kind of emerald green gandoura' – a boubou is a specifically black African dress, a gandoura is a North African garment – (Le Monde, 5 October 1989), 'D.F. and her green and embroidered boubous . . . her turban swaying above her huge cheekbones' (Libération, 5 October 1989). This might, on the other hand, be what lends them 'dignity'. Or maybe this dignity is due to to their posture ('straight and proud') or to their muteness. For these are silent women, possibly because they cannot speak French and, sometimes, the official interpreter cannot understand their dialect either (see Libération, 28–29 May 1988), and/or because they cannot understand what the trials represent. 'This strange judicial ritual for A.T., dressed in her traditional *boubou*, facing a judge wearing a curious customary red dress' (*Le Figaro*, 4 October 1989), and/or because they cannot understand what they are accused of: 'they watch the audience with an incredulous look . . . [they show] a calm tempered by fatalist resignation' (*Libération*, 28–29 May 1988). It is unclear what such women – 'directly arrived from the bush' – can understand as, for example, this 'unhappy, underdeveloped [*sic*] and illiterate Malian woman, a victim of the dead weight of her [traditional] society' (*Le Figaro*, 6 October 1989).

In other words, black Africans and black African women, in particular, are presented as dumb, ignorant and silent, although maybe with some native cunning insofar as their ignorance of French language and of the illegal nature of excision is more feigned than real (see Winter, 1994: 948–9). In many cases, doctors and nurses attached to the baby health centres (PMI) come to testify that indeed the mothers had been warned not to excise their daughters. This is used to show that whether their ignorance and silence is feigned or not hardly matters since they are presented as totally submissive to traditions. This submission to traditions they cannot possibly critically evaluate, deprives black Africans of the freedom of action necessary to act on what warnings they understand. This denial of their critical intelligence, individuality and autonomy as subjects is compounded, in the women's case, by their perceived subjection to their husbands' will. Furthermore, not only is 'the degree of autonomy relative to this custom weak or even nil' in the words of Erlich, the expert witness of many such trials (Winter, 1994: 956), but the women themselves are so culturally conditioned that they hardly feel any pain at all. A mother telling about her own excision assures Erlich that it happened 'after a cold bath, painlessly, with a somewhat joyful emotion' (*Le Monde*, 8 March 1991). The parallel with the subhuman brutality described in the colonial literature is inescapable. But before trying to unravel the continuities and discontinuities with colonial discourses, let us turn to that other category of 'Other' woman on metropolitan soil, the Maghrebi (North African) women.

The Problem of the 'Islamist Scarves'

I have elsewhere written about the original 'affair of the Islamic scarves' (Bloul, 1994) which started in October 1989 when three girls of Maghrebi origin refused to remove their headscarves in classrooms. This local incident sparked a national controversy which, at its peak, would figure daily and prominently in all national media until mid-December. The 'affair of the headscarves' as it was called was not resolved then, in spite of it being referred to the Conseil d'Etat, but disappeared very suddenly from the media in mid-December, because of the costs of its political exploitation which momentarily silenced everyone, except the Front National (see *Le*

Monde, 28 October 1989: 9, 14 November 1989: 15, 28 November 1989: 1 and 10, 6 December 1989: 10 for an account of the Front National's political exploitation of the affair).[10] The Conseil d'Etat had issued an ambiguous statement (27 November 1989) which more or less left the decision as to the wearing of the headscarves at school in the hands of each school committee, on the understanding that they were the best placed to judge the local conditions. Some general principles were set down as the relative freedom of any student to express religious convictions provided it was done with due respect to other people's convictions and provided that 'signes d'appartenance' were 'not ostentatious' and did not 'constitute an act of pressure, provocation, proselytism or propaganda'.

In spite of the acrimony of the debates, they were more or less stifled, aside from a few occasional flare-ups. But the issue of headscarves in classrooms came to prominence again with the Bayrou Administrative Directive of September 1994 when the Minister for Education ordered the heads of schools to forbid the wearing of ostentatious 'signes d'appartenance religieuse'. The ostentatious signs in question referred to the 'Islamist headscarves',[11] though the latter were never specifically designated. Debates are ongoing.

In 1989, the debates around the headscarves were remarkable for the breadth and seriousness of the questions debated: the modalities of integration of ethnic and religious minorities, the possible organization of Islam in France and its effects on modernization/secularization of Islam as a religion, the questioning of the meaning of secularity for French society and its expression in the republican ethos, a debate over the school system and its functions, and a deeper questioning of French culture and identity. These debates were also monopolized by men, notwithstanding their apparent concern with the question of women's rights in Islam. French men, Muslim men, male intellectuals and politicians, male personalities gave their opinion ad nauseam over the wearing of the scarves and its sociopolitical and cultural consequences. Women, on the other hand, whether Muslim, Maghrebi or French, were hardly heard.[12] Details were given of the students' families, uniquely represented by the two involved fathers described as 'very pious Muslims' concerned with the religious education and well-being of their daughters. Nonetheless, they insisted that 'the decision to take off the veil is [their daughters'] only'. This was greeted with some scepticism as the girls were in their early teens (12–14 years old), and reporters were prompted to comment that: 'though they are circumscribed in their behaviour, the two young girls are presented as autonomous beings on the subject of their conscience' (*Le Monde,* 7 October 1989: 13).

In general the issue of women's rights blurred the previous parameters of political discourses. The Rightist Opposition in particular delighted in taking an unusual position in favour of women's rights. The Left parties and the usual anti-discrimination associations, as traditional supporters of women's rights (in lieu of the muted feminist organizations), were in an ambiguous situation. This translated into belated attempts to diffuse the question of women's rights as much as possible. The use, and attempted control, of the representation of Maghrebi females by both French and Maghrebi men thus made a striking contrast to both the silencing of women in the media, and the increasing reluctance, of the Left in particular, to discuss women's issues as the debate deepened.

By 1994, the terms of the debate had degenerated. Sophisticated arguments about secularity, universal human rights vs cultural relativism were replaced to a great extent by denunciations of the political manipulations represented by the wearing of the veil. To don the 'Islamist scarf' is now described as a deliberate strategy of Islamist militants who fight for the recognition of a special status for Muslims in France. Moreover, this strategy is seen as part of an international Islamist plot to destabilize the West by any means.

One of the interesting threads running through the debate is the paradoxical media presentation of the young women concerned. They are described as being 'manipulated' (*Le Figaro*, 20 October 1994; *L'Express*, 17 November 1994). Their religious fervour is not denied, but is described as the natural outcome of both normal adolescent rebellion and idealism, and the search for identity of the 'second generation'. Such feelings are explained as being very easily used by militant Islamist associations whose final objectives are political. This 'manipulation' is described as an insidious form of terrorism which uses the very language of human rights and equality to propagate its own unequal and intolerant order (*L'Express*, 17 November 1994: 63) – an order which affirms the preeminence of its version of Islam over the republican ethos, French values and Western stability in general. Moreover, once they give in to the seductive call of the 'Islamist version of religious authenticity', Beurettes (daughters of North African migrants) become regimented, deaf to more reasonable Muslim voices and muzzled. Care is taken to stress that the problem is not Islam per se, but Islamism, i.e. its politically militant and anti-Western faction.[13]

These dangerous victims are also presented as blind victims whose religious fervour is politically manipulated by enemies of the republic for ultimate goals which would work against them as women. They are sincere, if misguided young women, whose future is in France, whose stand for equality of rights is made possible by them being brought up in France, whose freedom of choice in France blinds them to the totalitarian tendencies of the Islamist movement their *hijab* publicizes and supports (see *Nouvel Observateur*'s 'scoop' in staged debate: 'Talisma Nasreen faces veiled schoolgirls', 8–14 December 1994: 40–3). Such freedom of expression as they find in France is opposed to the repressive terror to which Algerian women are today submitted in Algeria by the Front Islamique du Salut (FIS). Finally, they and those described as 'their French supporters of the Left' – a sweeping statement which refuses to consider the extreme division of the Left on this issue (*Le Figaro*, 13 October 1989) – are deluded when they take French opposition to the headscarves in school as a manifestation of racism. In fact, the 'tolerance' of the Left rests on assumptions of essentialized differences which necessarily impose a racist hierarchy. The assimilationist assertion, however, is universalist and ultimately desires equality through intermingling, interestingly characterized by 'our sons as husbands [for your daughters]'.

> Their [the Left's] own tolerance (following the English model) rests, in fact, upon a differentialist turn of mind, that is, on the idea that there are different races and that they must stay separate. On the contrary, French attitude rests on universalist assumptions: if people behave in a way similar to us, then they are welcome. . . . The assimilationist assertion, the refusal of the veil is the opposite of racism . . . [but, unfortunately it] is expressed only in a negative way. . . . The true message would add: 'Because we want you to become French women like the others, to take our sons as husbands'. (Emmanuel Todd, anthropologist, in an interview for L'Express, 17 November 1994: 71–4)

CONTINUITIES AND DISSIMILARITIES IN SEXUAL POLITICS

The idea for this article originated in my appreciation of a discrepancy between the relative degrees of public outrage around the various 'affairs of the headscarves' which at best implicated a maximum of 2000 schoolgirls, and around the excision trials when it was estimated that 36,000 young girls in France were 'at risk'.[14] Though any such comparisons are risky, it is arguable that female genital mutilation is, at the very least, as serious a crime against female integrity and autonomy as 'veiling' could be. It is also more definitive. Thus, it may come as a surprise to realize that the French public has been considerably more concerned by the wearing of the headscarves than by the excision trials. Such dissimilarity echoes the dissimilarity of French colonial sexual politics in North Africa and black Africa respectively, and points to the fact that concern about women (whether Maghrebi or black African) is not the key issue.

Nonetheless, the key terms of both debates are the same, with one exception. The 'veiling' debate centres around universal human rights, cultural relativism, women's rights, individualism vs communitarianism and French secularism as necessitating the modernization of Islam, at least in France.[15] And the key terms around the excision debate are: universal human rights, cultural relativism, women's rights, individualism vs communitarianism and the legal status of customs. Though the black Africans practising female genital mutilation in France are mostly Muslim and believe that excision is a Muslim obligation, all French commentators have been remarkably fair. They always note that Islam does not, in fact, enjoin excision, but rather accommodates itself to a pre-Islamic practice. Such accommodation also characterizes other religions as excision is practised by Christian, Jewish and Animist Africans. Islam has, thus, been dismissed as immaterial to the debate on excision as 'an African custom',[16] while it, or rather its 'modernization' (by which French means its adaptation to a secular culture) is debated at length over the issue of veiling. Certainly, the global prominence of the Islamic resurgence influences French debates over the 'veil', so that the perceived danger of Islam conditions much of the French responses. But why, then, is the Muslim dimension downplayed in the excision debate to the benefit of 'customs'?

One reason is that the public, visible veil, in the republican institutions, is perceived as threatening French secularism, in a way that black African *customs* especially 'private' and 'invisible' ones such as excision do not. Thus a French anthropologist could write in defence of excision that:

> Demanding a penal sentence for *a custom that does not threaten the republican order, and which nothing prevents from being considered as a matter of private choice* . . . would be tantamount to demonstrating an intolerance . . . which manifests a singularly narrow conception of democracy. (Lefeuvre, 1988, quoted in Winter, 1994: 951)[17]

It appears that French reactions relative to the Islamic veil as threatening 'our' identity, and to unthreatening excision as 'their' private custom, have actually little to do with a concern for women, whether they be Arab/Muslims or black Africans. It has more to do with the central role of French secularism in the construction of French identity.

French secularism, as a mediation of the usual Western dichotomy between public and private, attempts to reconcile individual equality with the universality of republican principles. As such, it can recognize only those individuals who agree to respect a neutral space constituted around public institutions, and understood as unmarked by power relations. Against the recognition of any particular status for any ethnic or religious group, Kaltenbach quotes one of the most famous speeches of the French Revolution, that of Clermont-Tonnerre of the 23 December 1789 'Against Discrimination toward Executioners, Actors, Protestants and Jews':

> One must refuse everything to Jews as a nation and give Jews everything as individuals; one must refuse to recognize their judges (as) they must have only ours; one must refuse legal protection to their Jewish corporation; they must constitute in the State neither a political body nor an order, they must be individual citizens. . . . (quoted in Kaltenbach and Kaltenbach, 1991: 149–50)

The veil, then, is an unbearable invasion of ethnic differences in institutional spaces. It threatens the contractual solidarity of individual citizens, based on their respecting the 'neutrality' of republican institutions.[18]

Feminists have long recognized this supposed 'neutrality' as spurious. They have criticized the building of citizenship on the transcendence of these 'personal' differences which have traditionally privatized women and delegitimized them as citizens (Pateman, 1988). Paradoxically, here, this otherwise spurious neutrality seems to be harnessed to a defence of Muslim women's rights as individual citizens (against the excesses of

Muslim misogyny). Or is it rather harnessed to a vindication of Muslim women's duty as French citizens to dissolve the unbearable public mani-festation of Muslim specificity? Indeed, media constructions of veiled Beurettes alternate between presenting them as victims of Muslim patri-archy, or as blind to their public duty to uphold the republican order that offers them individual freedom and autonomy (*Nouvel Observateur*, 8–14 December 1994). The issue is always to convince Muslim women, to plead with them, to seduce them or to intimidate them into forming an alliance with the French and against patriarchal and undemocratic forms of Islam or 'Islamism'. Muslim women are presented as the natural allies of French democracy (in support of a universalist conception of French identity) against Islamism – and Muslim males – though some of these women have not yet realized this. The possibility that veiling might be the free/private choice of individual women is derided. The continuity with colonial sexual politics in Algeria is obvious and so is the persistence of colonial female stereotypes of 'sexy victims' to be 'protected' from their men, and even from themselves, particularly if this upholds French identity and purposes.

The other reason why the Muslim dimension is downplayed in the excision debate is precisely the persistence of colonial stereotypes and imagery which insist upon seeing black Africans as the unwitting captives of 'immutable' customs. The hold of such customs seems to remove black Africans from the realm of historicity and subjecthood. Their historical adoption of Islam is, in the final analysis, immaterial. Thus, the Muslim dimension is abandoned in the excision debate which centres instead around the legal status of customs.

The defenders of excision in the trials point out that excision, as a customary practice of 'a general, continual and obligatory nature' (Article 327 of the Code Penal, quoted in Winter, 1994: 954) is recognized as a suf-ficient legal justification for individual behaviour by French law itself. Here again, in a move reminiscent of French 'association policy' in black African colonies, the universalist dimension of republican principles so constitutive of French identity is pushed aside. Indeed, those French feminist associations which constitute themselves *partie civile* in the trials (in the best tradition of universalist republican principles) are condemned (by the very conservative newspaper *Le Figaro*) for their racism and cul-tural colonialism:[19]

> There is something fundamentally perverse in the ways of certain French intellectual movements which behave arbitrarily through a surfeit of proper feelings. The trial of FDT . . . denounced by feminist associations, is an example in kind.
>
> Of course, these associations have commendable intentions. But . . . they can only propose to further oppress . . . an unhappy, underdeveloped and illiterate Malian woman, a victim of the dead weight of her traditional society. . . .
>
> The more feminine [*sic*] associations have insisted on necessary and

exemplary punishments, the more Africans have hardened, perceiving [such demands] as an infringement in their way of life and cultural colonialism. (*Le Figaro*, 6 October 1989)

Why is there such an affirmation of cultural difference in the debate at the same time that the veil debates reaffirm the universalism of the republican principles and the secularism which sustain French identity? Is it that black Africans are different Others? Or is their difference just different? The construction of excision as 'invisible', unthreatening to the republican order and the 'private choice of individuals' otherwise perceived as 'totally subjected to customs' abounds in ironies and contradictions.

Female genital mutilation, that most enduring, visible, social marking of difference on women's bodies being reinscribed as private, invisible and inconsequential, a matter of personal choice, demonstrates that concern for women is not the driving force behind the debates. So does the simultaneous construction of the *hijab*, a traditional guarantee of women's invisibility in the public sphere, as an untolerable symbol of the difference which makes Muslim women conspicuous in French streets, and, additionally, transforms French men into champions of women's rights.

It is my contention that the contradictions emerge from different stakes in the two debates. The real concerns in the debate over 'veiling' are with French identity and the perception of an overwhelming Muslim threat. Such 'collective' concerns are not involved in the excision debate. Thus, not only has one grounds to think that 'collective' here characterizes cultural communities as 'communities of males' (Appadurai, 1990: 19), it is also apparent that the politics behind the debates follow the same imperialist and androcentric logic that inspired colonial sexual politics.

NOTES

1. Few fathers have ever been accused, as French law, based as it is on an understanding of individual rights and responsibilities, can only deal with actual perpetrators of illegal deeds. Fathers, being absent during the proceedings, can and do usually plead ignorance of 'women's business'. Judges, plaintiffs (feminist associations) and lawyers are well aware of the difficulties. Judges often complain that 'we are not here to judge a custom' and would like to keep to a strict, but inappropriate, legal procedure. The feminist associations acting as plaintiffs, however, aim to enlarge debates as much as possible, though some have also recently resolved to use the punitive potential of the law as the only dissuasive method (Me Linda Weil-Curiel, interview 12 January 1995).

2. Martinkus-Zemp notes the importance and frequency of descriptions of black African women which stress their 'animality', either because of their appearance (nakedness, 'animal grace'), actions ('they move like she-tigers', they 'jump up and down and bark in our direction') or the treatment they receive (they can be bought with the house, but can never reach the status of companions: the *mousso* – black mistress – doesn't even share her master's bed but sleeps on the floor, maybe at the foot of his bed). Martinkus-Zemp quotes R. Marchand (*La Nuit verte*, written in 1928–9): Margot (the *mousso*)

sleeping at the foot of her master's bed is one day frightened by a snake. 'Since that incident, Margot always slept near me [i.e. *in* the bed]. Thus, for some futile motive, one sets aside human respect, conventions, and one becomes entangled in the snare of black life' (Martinkus-Zemp, 1973: 63–4).

3.   Though Orientalist paintings of women in the *hammam* are certainly concerned with revealing the hidden, they also echoed a parallel concern of contemporary painters obsessed with white women at their toilette: to the prurient interest in nakedness is associated a desire to reveal 'female artifices'.

4.   *L'Atlantide* was the first true French best-seller, almost immediately made into an extremely popular cinematographic version which had an international career. It was translated into 18 languages, inspired many plays and popular songs, five movies, an opera and a TV film. At the time of its first publication, its heroine's name endorsed various commercial products (perfume, hats, etc.) (see Bouzar, 1984).

5.   In fact native Algerians were not, for most of the colonial occupation, considered as French citizens, but merely as French subjects with limited political rights.

6.   This was not the case for British colonies as feminists and missionaries opposed the practice (see Pederson, 1991).

7.   French use the term 'excision' as a blanket term to cover clitoridectomy as well as the possible removal of the labia. Though media do report infibulation as a further aggravating possibility, excision is the generic term used for all cases of genital mutilation.

8.   Among them SOS Femmes Alternatives (represented by Me Weil-Curiel), CAMS-F (Commission pour l'Abolition des Mutilations Sexuelles, section Française) and Enfance et Partage decided to associate themselves with the public prosecutor as *partie civile*, i.e. gaining the right to present their arguments in court (Winter, 1994: 945). CAMS-F is an offshoot of GAMS (Groupe des Femmes pour l'Abolition des Mutilations Sexuelles). The latter disagreed with the criminalization of excision, while CAMS-F has adopted the position taken by SOS Femmes Alternatives, which has demanded more severe punishments (i.e. actual jail sentences rather than suspended sentences). SOS Femmes Alternatives argues that symbolic sentences fail as deterrent, and that only actual punishment will have any effect, especially as the illegality of excision is well known and understood among the relevant migrant communities in France after 10 years of information and warnings in baby health centres (PMI) (personal interviews, Paris, December 1994–January 1995). The many differences of opinion and strategies between feminist associations are not reported in the media, who use the term 'feminist' as a blanket term.

9.   Unlike in the past, and maybe unlike what still happens in some parts of Africa, excision in France is performed exclusively on very young babies and infant girls (for them 'not to remember the pain'). Thus many of the traditional legitimations of excision as 'a ritual' do not apply. The babies do *not* learn to control pain and show their courage. It is *not* an initiation into womanhood. Of course, it still functions to mark female bodies and transform them into 'pure', 'clean', 'feminine', 'beautiful' bodies by eliminating the clitoris, seen as a 'dirty' organ, source of pollution, or of sexual difficulties because it is regarded as a competing penis inhibiting male sexuality. The 'unclean', 'impure' woman still in possession of her clitoris is also a source of sexual disorder as she cannot control her sexual appetite (Erlich, 1988). In other words, excision performed on female infants still functions as a mark and a medium of sexual domination, but it is empty of the positive connotations often found in various initiation rituals whose main components include the show of initiates' mastery over bodily pain.

10. The Front National, capitalizing on the affair, was particularly successful in the local elections of 4 December 1989. This victory prompted Mr Le Pen to make various threatening statements which hit the front pages. He variously called for a referendum on immigration and for the dissolution of the parliament (*Le Monde*, 6 December 1989: 10). Two days later, the affair disappeared from the paper, although nothing had been resolved. In fact, one father gave in on the wearing of the headscarves the following January on orders from the King of Morocco, Hassan II.

11. These are not simply 'headscarves' anymore, but 'Islamist headscarves' by reference to militant Islamism, and in opposition to 'Muslim' or 'Islamic'. Other terms now used include: *hijab, veil, chador*.

12. I complained about the male monopolization of the debate among French feminists. It is true that female scholars have since published various analyses of the affair, but in terms of media/public debate, women, in general, were silenced. One interlocutress assures me that many press releases were sent, to *Le Monde* in particular, but were disdained and generally never published.

13. Indeed, official attempts at organizing French Muslims (or even a 'French Islam') are still vigorously pursued by the government. Thus, in January 1995, the Paris Great Mosque made public a 'Charter of French Muslims', immediately disclaimed by a number of Islamist organizations, including AOIF (Association of Islamic Organizations in France, personal interview with AOIF president, January 1995).

14. Of course these 2000 girls, who have apparently now dwindled to 800, represent a small proportion of all girls of Maghrebi origin in France. This is because the headscarf is an issue hotly debated by the girls themselves, as many are opposed to its wearing. However, all 36,000 girls are more seriously and permanently 'at risk', if their parents do not become convinced to abandon excision.

15. Thus, a book was published in 1991, advancing the thesis that France, and the presence of an important Muslim minority in a country like France with strong secular traditions, 'offer' Islam the possibility it needs to modernize (i.e. secularize) (see Kaltenbach and Kaltenbach's *La France, une chance pour l'Islam*).

16. I know of only one short newspaper article mentioning the 'veil' and excision as instances of the same problem. As this article was entitled 'Tchador, excision, cannibales', and indeed amalgamated all three customs as equally undesirable manifestations of otherness not to be tolerated, it may be more useful as an indication of the depth of collective unconscious malaise than as an exemplar of French arguments in multicultural debates (*Le Figaro*, 13 October 1989).

17. One must add that some of the Leftist, liberal anti-racist defences of the veil also stress its character of individual, and thus private, 'free' choice, an argument which, in that case, is derided by its opponents in the name of women's rights (see above).

18. Significantly, opinion polls have shown that 75 percent of French are opposed to the veil in school, while only 31 percent are opposed to it being worn in the streets (*Le Monde*, 30 November 1989: 15).

19. This must not be read as a wholehearted approval of the criminalization of excision. What is of interest are the accusations and counter-accusations of racism. The feminist associations counter by saying that to see Africans as unable to make individual decisions and cultural adjustments is in itself racist (and also does not fit the evidence of cultural adjustments being made by Africans in other areas). Also of interest is *Le Figaro*'s own racism (the 'underdeveloped illiterate Malian') side by side with its denunciation of political opponents' racism.

REFERENCES

Alloula, M. (1986) *The Colonial Harem*. Minneapolis: University of Minnesota Press.
Appadurai, A. (1990) 'Disjuncture and Difference in the Global Cultural Economy', *Public Culture* 2(2): 1–24.
Apter, E. (1992) 'Female Trouble in the Colonial Harem', *Differences* 4(1): 205–24.
Auffret, S. (1983) *Des couteaux contre des femmes*. Paris: Eds des Femmes.
Badran, M. (1994) 'Gender Activism: Feminists and Islamists in Egypt', pp. 202–27 in V. Moghadam (ed.) *Identity, Politics and Women: Cultural Reassertions and Feminisms in Perspective*. Boulder, CO: Westview Press.
Benoit, P. (1918) *L'Atlantide*. Paris: A. Michel.
Bloul, R. (1994) 'Veiled Objects of Post-colonial Desire', *The Australian Journal of Anthropology* 5(1 and 2): 113–27.
Bouzar, W. (1984) *Lectures Maghrébines*. France: OPU Publisud.
Eberhardt, I. (1993) *In the Shadow of Islam*. London: P. Owen.
Erlich, M. (1988) *La Femme blessée: essai sur les mutilations sexuelles féminines*. Paris: L'Harmattan.
Fanon, F. (1952) *Peau noire, masque blanc*. Paris: F. Maspero.
Fanon, F. (1961) *Les Damnés de la terre*. Paris: F. Maspero.
Ghoussoub, M. (1987) 'Feminism – or the Eternal Masculine – in the Arab World', *New Left Review* 161: 3–18.
Griaule, N. (1965) *Conversations with Ogotommelli: An Introduction to Dogon Religious Ideas*. London: Oxford University Press.
Hélie, A. (1994) 'Les Institutrices de l'Algèrie coloniale: agents du pouvoir ou agents de changements?', *Resources for Feminist Research* 33(1/2): 9–13.
Hélie-Lucas, M. A. (1993) 'The Preferential Symbol for Islamic Identity: Women in Muslim Personal Laws', *WLUML Dossier* 11–13: 5–12.
Jolly, M. (ed.) (1994) 'Women's Difference: Sexuality and Maternity in Colonial and Post-Colonial Discourses', special issue *The Australian Journal of Anthropology* 5(1 and 2).
Kabbani, R. (1986) *Europe's Myths of Orient*. London: Pandora Press.
Kaltenbach, J. H. and P. P. Kaltenbach (1991) *La France, une chance pour l'Islam*. Paris: Eds du Felin.
L'Express (1994) 'Foulard: Le Complot. Comment les islamistes nous infiltrent', special file 17 November: 62–80.
Lefeuvre, M. (1988) 'Le Devoir de l'excision', *Bulletin du MAUSS* 1: 65–95.
Le Figaro (1989) 'La Coutume contre la loi', 3 October.
Le Figaro (1989) 'Excision: le choc de deux civilisations', 4 October.
Le Figaro (1989) 'Le Procès de l'excision: chacun sa loi', 6 October.
Le Figaro (1989) 'Tchador, excision, cannibales', 13 October.
Le Figaro (1994) 'Foulard islamique: la manipulation', 20 October.
Le Monde (1989) 'L'excision en cour d'assises', 5 October.
Le Monde (1989) 'Trois foulards contre la sérénité laïque' and 'L'Islam dans l'école de la République', 7 October: 17 and 13.
Le Monde (1989) 'M. Le Pen dénonce "la colonisation de la France"', 28 October.
Le Monde (1989) 'M. Le Pen invite à "la résistance contre l'immigration"', 14 November.
Le Monde (1989) 'Le Regain du Front National', 28 November.
Le Monde (1989) 'Les Français face au voile: un sondage IFOP-Le Monde', 30 November: 14–15.
Le Monde (1989) 'M. Le Pen demande la dissolution de l'Assemblée Nationale et l'organisation d'un referundum sur l'immigration', 6 December.
Le Monde (1991) 'L'Excision, crime coutumier', 8 March.
Libération (1988) 'L'Excision de Mantessa aux assises', 28–29 May.

Libération (1989) 'Excision: trois ans de prison avec sursis', 5 October.

Lyons, H. (1981) 'Anthropologists, Moralities, and Relativisms: The Problem of Genital Mutilations', *Revue Canadienne de Sociologie et d'Anthropologie* 18(4): 499–518.

Marchand, R. (1928) *La Nuit verte*. Paris: L. Fournier, et Cie.

Martinkus-Zemp, A. (1973) 'Européocentrisme et exotisme: l'homme blanc et la femme noire (dans la littérature française de l'entre-deux guerres)', *Cahiers d'Etudes Africaines* 13(1): 60–81.

Megret, C. (1937) *Les Anthropophages*. Paris: A. Fayard et Cie.

Nouvel Observateur (1994) 'Taslima face aux filles voilées', 8–14 December: 40–3.

Pateman, C. (1988) *The Sexual Contract*. Cambridge: Polity Press.

Pedersen, S. (1991) 'National Bodies, Unspeakable Acts: The Sexual Politics of Colonial Policy Making', *Journal of Modern History* 63 (December): 647–80.

Randeau, R. (1935) *Des blancs dans la cité des Noirs*. Paris: A. Michel.

Snyder, F. (1974) 'Health Policy and the Law in Senegal', *Social Sciences and Medicine* 8: 11–28.

Winter, B. (1994) 'Women, the Law and Cultural Relativism in France: The Case of Excision', *Signs* 19(4): 939–76.

Woodhull, W. (1991) 'Unveiling Algeria', *Genders* 10 (Spring): 112–31.

Wooten, S. (1993) 'Colonial Administration and the Ethnography of the Family in French Soudan', *Cahiers d'Etudes Africaines* 33(3): 419–46.

7 Sex as Usual

Body Politics and the Media War in Serbia

Dubravka Zarkov

In summer 1991 the Yugoslav National Army started the war against Slovenia. In autumn 1991 the war began in Croatia, and in spring 1992 in Bosnia. These wars were variously categorized both within former Yugoslavia and internationally. Most often they were taken as one single war and called 'civil war' or 'ethnic war'. By the parties directly involved it was called the 'war of aggression' as often as the 'war of liberation'.[1]

Before the 'civil war' was even possible to imagine, the word *war* was already familiar to people in former Yugoslavia. Since the early 1980s it was a word used often in the media and about the media: the 'media war'. The term was first used by politicians, and later adopted by the public. It refers to the intensive engagement of the media in the nationalist politics of the former Yugoslav republics. The specific feature of the 'media war' was that it engaged in the defence of the leaders and politics of their own nation or republic, while at the same time fiercely attacking other nations' and republics' leaders and politics. And, it was always the other nation's media that was accused of launching the 'media war' against one's own nation and its media.[2] Plotters, conspirators and culprits were seen everywhere, not least among members of one's own nation where the glorification of national heroes and traditions went hand-in-hand with the witchhunt of national traitors.[3]

Thus, the 'media war' was first described by politicians and media of former Yugoslavia as a mode of hostile communication between the quarrelling factions. Aggressive accusations, claims, insults, name-calling and mocking were the characteristics of the journalistic style that maintained the idea that the 'media war' was primarily concerned with attacking others and defending oneself. As former Yugoslavia disintegrated, however, the access to the media and to information from other territories became largely limited, and an almost exclusive media space was created within each republic, and later within newly established states. The closed and exclusive media space became another element of the 'media war', and the censorship and self-censorship exercised by politicians and journalists alike was yet another.[4] All these elements together were both the necessary conditions for, and the results of, the 'media war'.

Nevertheless, attacking the others and censoring information available to one's own recipients, however significant, was not the main purpose of the 'media war'. The hostile media communication with the others makes no sense when these others have no access to the media. Attacking Croats in Serbian papers means nothing to Croats if they cannot read it anyway. But it makes all the sense to readers within Serbia. My argument is that the real target of the 'media war' is, paradoxically, as exclusive as the access to the media: it is the recipient within the closed media space, not outside of it. 'Media war' is thus not so much a mode of hostile communication between the warring parties, as it is a mode of auto-communication. Ivan Colovic (1994) was first to approach 'media war' from that point of view. He defined the concept of 'hate speeches', and characterized the 'media war' as auto-communication. He also pointed to the cohesive and mobilizing functions of the 'media war' (1994: 163). Thus, 'media war' is not only an effect of nationalist processes but their constitutive practice. Just as the gruesome practices of the 'civil war' construct the ethnic Self and the Other, so do the media practices. For, the 'media war' is not only directed towards a specific territory but towards a specifically defined ethnic group. Newspapers in Serbia, while writing about Croatia, do it primarily for the Serbs in Serbia, as much as the Croatian papers write basically for the Croats in Croatia. The pictures and the stories developed in the media are there for the recipients defined as 'one's own' – they are defining the nation for the nationals. Those who are defined as 'enemies' are not the target, they are the message itself, the explanation of who the nationals are, or could be. At the same time, the definition of 'enemy' carries a warning: do not be like them. The hostility with which the 'enemy' is addressed is there for the sake of one's own group: so that 'we' learn well who the enemy is, how to recognize him, how to deal with him, and ultimately what 'our' fate will be if 'we' are like him.

But the enemy in the 'media war' is not only a he. It has been, in fact, increasingly a she. A significant feature of the 'media war' is that women and so-called women's issues, especially issues with regard to female sexuality, have gained prominence within the media rhetoric. This was somewhat surprising given that previously only policy-makers and women-centred and feminist groups had discussed such issues. Moreover, the context of the public discussions had largely been within the frame of the official socialist discourse of women's emancipation. Since the mid-1980s, however, references to child-care, maternity leave, abortion rights, legislation of rape, etc. were discussed in the light of the population questions, traditional values or the so-called historic dreams of a particular nation.

When the 'civil war' began, in 1991, the 'media war' did not stop. On the contrary, the media became even more engaged with reports from the battlefields and stories about the evils of the other side. The tales of the suffering of one's own people joined stories about medieval heroes.

Likewise, the interest of the 'media war' in issues concerning women and female sexuality did not cease. Quite the reverse happened, and women became prominent issues in the 'civil war' as well. In winter 1992 gendered practices of sexual assault, torture and rape were revealed to an astonished world. The systematic way in which these practices were conducted by the military forces of Bosnian Serbs, together with the fact that the other warring sides also used these practices, accounted for both the outrage and the actions of women's groups on an international level, as well as in former Yugoslavia, to put an end to them.

Nevertheless, these practices themselves soon became new elements of the 'media war' while being at the same time the bitter reality of women living in the zones of the 'civil war'. Other issues regarding body politics were simultaneously practised in both wars: for instance, forced pregnancies in the 'civil war' and the pro-natalism and abortion debate in the 'media war'. Different issues became relevant at the given time, in the given territory, but the practices of the 'civil war' and the practices of the 'media war' were, clearly and increasingly, gendered. The female body and female sexuality became an essential site through which nationalism was pursued in both the 'civil war' and the 'media war'.

In Serbia, the two wars have a very specific context. The denial of any responsibility for the war in which former Yugoslavia disintegrated is one of the crucial public discourses in Serbia. Merged with the discourse of 'the whole world is against us' they create the narrative of the Serb victimization which is told in many different ways. Sadly enough, there are many facts that support that narrative and make it difficult to resist. First, on the international level, the Serbs are indiscriminately seen as the only villains, while the suffering of the Serb population in Bosnia and Croatia is noticeably overlooked. In the nationalist discourses in Serbia, every unacknowledged Serb victim is one more argument in support of the narrative of victimization – and one which allows for the denial of the responsibility for the war. Serbs-as-unacknowleged-victims offers the justification to that denial, and the representation of the war as a non-war, as a defence, or as a struggle for survival.

Second, for a large portion of the population in Serbia – which is formally not at war but nevertheless suffers in many different ways the effects of the war – the narrative of Serb victimization and isolation provides the convenient tool for making sense of the everyday humiliations which their lives have become. It is an escape, a refusal to see things differently, or simply a way to conserve energy for better days, if they ever come. Economic deprivation has been overwhelming: industrial production largely reduced, unemployment increased, with hyper-inflation reaching its peak in the winter of 1993–94. An enormous percentage of the population lives below the 'poverty line'.[5] International isolation and the increased activities of oppositional groups within the country have added to the ambiguity of the political situation. As a consequence, denial, depression and resignation rule everyday life. A high increase in crime and violence, especially violence against women, suicide rates and health problems, reflect the decomposition of the society. Enormous energy is necessary just for survival. The strategy is to live a life of here-and-now, and not to think about the future, or the past. For old and young alike there is nowhere to go, even though they may not like the place where they are.

Thus, the narrative of victimization makes sense to people in Serbia for many reasons, even if these reasons seem unlikely to the others. With the 'media war' which has persisted in ex-Yugoslavia with greater or lesser intensity for over a decade now, with isolation, deprivation and resignation in Serbia this narrative has enormous interpretative power: the power of stories that make sense of everyday hardship. The fact that the interpretation simultaneously constructs the nation and normalizes the war may not be obvious to the recipients, and indeed, at first sight it is not. Practices of victimization, normalization or the construction of an ethnic Self are conducted through texts which seem to be about entirely different matters: namely, sexuality. My argument is, first, that precisely because 'media war' operates through body politics these practices remain obscure and second, that through these media practices, sexuality and the female body become constitutive elements of nationalist processes.

ANALYSING THE TEXT: VOICES AND FRAMES OF THE TWO WARS

The wide range of tabloids provide particularly good examples of how sexuality works with nationalism. Their range of topics already included the theme of sexuality: in the life of celebrities, of politicians, or ordinary people. Stories about sex and money, fame, politics, crime or love were already a familiar fare in the tabloids. The war only added an additional topic: sex and war became the order of the day.

In February 1994 such a text appeared in the Serbian tabloid, *Duga* (Rainbow). *Duga* is one of many tabloids in Serbia, but of a special kind. It claims to be 'the forerunner of Serbian democracy'. That claim is not only written on the top of the first inside page of this issue, but is substantiated in many texts where the Serb fighters and the Serb victims tell their side of the war story. A few well known journalists have regular columns in *Duga*. Their stories are not only full of glorification of Serb nationalist myths, but are often told in explicitly sexist language. In their texts, male and female sexuality are often taken as the dividing line in defining the Self and the Other ethnically. The discursive space in ex-Yugoslavia, largely appropriated by the 'media war', gives this type of journalism almost unlimited space in the media. In different contexts different topics are taken up, new interpretations are given to old themes, or completely new themes are introduced. Nevertheless, the issues of sexuality persist in one way or another.

When I read the text in *Duga* for the first time, there was something in it that drew me back, causing me to read it again and again. Something in it was puzzling but I could not immediately see what it was. It appeared to be just another journalistic story about sex and war – at points perhaps moving, but basically in bad taste, sexist and patronizing. But these things in themselves were nothing new. There was something else, however, which somehow did not 'fit'. Only slowly I discovered what that something was.

The title of the text – 'Little Eagles for "Those Things" '[6] – is composed of the nickname for German currency, the Mark, which has an eagle on the coin, and the commonly used expression for sex and sexuality, 'those things'. The story covers four pages in *Duga*: one comprises photographs, the other three text. A big photo – a panorama of Sarajevo – covers one whole page, with two small inserted photos of broken cars. The text consists of three parts: the first two columns form the introduction and the last column the conclusion. The middle part is composed of five columns, which in many respects are different from the rest, being a transcript of a radio programme.

The author of the text claims that this is an authentic transcript of a talk show on a local radio station from Sarajevo, *Radio Zid* (Radio Wall). This is one of several similar radio stations which started up in a Muslim part of Sarajevo during the war. The talk show transcribed in *Duga* has a special theme – 'those things' – and a special guest – a young woman from Sarajevo who was a technical student before the war, but started working as a prostitute when the war broke out in Bosnia. Her pseudonym is Vanja. Besides Vanja and the host of the programme, the listeners take part, too: they are able to call in and ask Vanja various questions about 'those things'.[7] In the conversation the issues of prostitution, money and morality are discussed in relation to fighting, problems of everyday life in Sarajevo, or hopes and worries about the future. One recurrent topic is whether Vanja supports the Bosnian government fighters, either in terms of money or services. Another is whether the listeners might profit from Vanja's profession. They offer themselves as customers, pimps or colleagues. Sometimes, the conversation has a grim atmosphere, but there are moments when participants seem to be having fun. This is particularly so when one of the listeners suggests a quiz in which the winner would get Vanja as a prize. Many listeners decline the opportunity to be anonymous. Most of the names given in the text are clearly Muslim, but some – like Vanja – are of Slavic origin, used both among Serbs and Croats. It is often impossible to distinguish between the latter two, but the Muslim names would be immediately recognized by both the listeners of the talk show and the reader of the text in *Duga*.[8]

In my first reading of the text in *Duga* the transcript of this talk show affected me so strongly that I almost disregarded the introduction and the conclusion. After I read the whole text over and over again a puzzling question came up: what is a transcript of a talk show in Sarajevo doing in a newspaper text in Beograd? I could not know whether the transcript was original, nor whether the talk show ever existed. Nevertheless, the structure and the dynamics of the conversation appeared highly probable and true to life. The more I read it however, the more clearly I saw the source of the puzzle. The photos gave me the first clues: the big photo, the panorama of Sarajevo, covering the page opposite the text was a peacetime photo.

In this text I will try to resolve the puzzle made by the peacetime photo of the city which has since been largely destroyed by war, the text from a tabloid in Serbia and the voices from a talk show in Bosnia. I will approach the talk show and text with the photo in *Duga* as two frames which construct the reality of war for their listeners and readers. The framing in photography has a special meaning. It indicates not only that something is in the photo while something else is left out, but also that there is a special angle of the camera, the close-up or the wide lens, the clear focus or sfumato.[9] I find this concept particularly suitable for the text in *Duga* because many different realities seemed framed together in it: Sarajevo and Beograd; war and peace; sex and survival. At another level, the transcript of the talk show is carefully framed into the text with the photography. Each of the frames will be addressed separately. Besides the concept of frames, I will use the concept of the voices. Listening to the voices of the participants of the talk show, but also that of the author of the text in *Duga*, I will analyse both what is talked about and how, and what is left unspoken.

I will start my analysis with the transcript of the talk show, at its face value, as a frame of its own: voices of Sarajevo. Then I will bring the transcript back into *Duga* where it was published with the encircling introduction and the conclusion, and I will analyse the whole text together with the photographs as a second frame: voices of Serbia. In each of these frames I will analyse the role of body politics – metaphors of female body and definitions of sexual morals. The specific context of the two wars – 'civil war' and 'media war' – in Serbia, and their gendered practices, already elaborated above, form a basis against which I analyse the frames. I will pursue the argument that the media engage in practices of normalization of war and in the construction of the Serbs as the ultimate victims of the war through body politics. My objective is to show how this occurs, using the text in *Duga* as a case in point.

THE FIRST FRAME: THE TALK SHOW

According to the transcript,[10] the theme of the talk show seems to be the life of a young woman – Vanja (non-Muslim name) – who started working as a prostitute in Sarajevo 1994. Vanja justifies her choice of job by referring to the war situation and the necessity of survival: 'We simply needed money . . .' she says of herself and the female friend with whom she works. This justification displays her concern about the morality of her job and her desire to keep the job secret from her family and friends. One of the ways to make her job more acceptable to herself was to be selective:

> We [she and her friend] thought that it is not so terrible if it is done under certain conditions, with certain customers. We try to keep it that way, to work only with selected men.

Her job is her main reason for thinking of leaving Sarajevo. Although she admits that she went into the job consciously, she is afraid that the truth will be revealed:

> Something tells me that I should go away from here, that I will feel much safer morally. . . . What I do has not been disclosed up to now, but it will be to-morrow. This is a small city. And how can I face people then?

During the conversation it becomes clear that Vanja feels highly uncom-fortable with her profession and that she insists on making a sharp differ-ence between what she does and who she is. Throughout the programme she is struggling to control and defend her own definition of herself, against the listeners and the host. It is very striking, however, that throughout the conversation both listeners and the host consistently dis-regard her attempts to distance herself from her profession. They do it in different ways: asking her about the types of services she provides, the prices and the forms of payment, about how she looks and whether she is clean and healthy. Many callers obviously enjoy making rude jokes about her.[11] There are two particularly striking examples in which she is drawn back into 'being a prostitute'. The first happens in the conversation with the host. At one point Vanja explains that she will try to leave Sarajevo before the end of the war in order to finish her studies and find a job. She says:

> I want to use the knowledge I have gained so far, except, of course, for what I am doing now. That is never, ever to be considered again.

The host's immediate response to her words is: 'Is there any work these days?' Thus, although she struggles to explain that she is a student and that prostitution is only an episode in her life, to be forgotten and dis-regarded as soon as possible, he re-positions her as a prostitute. Just after the above-mentioned exchange, one of the male listeners calls in and the following dialogue occurs:

> C: Milan [non-Muslim male name] calling, Vanja knows me. I respect what she is doing and I wish to ask her would she accept my offer to be her pimp when she leaves the city?
> V: No, not yours nor anybody's, because, as I said already, I do not intend to do this once I am out, nor ever again.
> C: Do you really think that this – what you are doing now – is your life?
> V: No, I do not think that this is my life. Far from it.

Unlike Vanja who maintains persistently that prostitution is morally bad, whatever the circumstances, the callers take a different approach. Many of them express the opinion that prostitution is a normal job, a job like any other. Or they insist that they personally have nothing against it. Others perceive the morality of prostitution from the perspective of the war. This is apparent in the following conversation.

> C: Good evening, Munib [Muslim male name] speaking. I am a butcher from Hrasnica. I would like to ask Vanja what she thinks of the colleagues in her profession who left us in these difficult times and went over to the side of the aggressor?
> V: Nothing.
> C: Aren't they really disgusting? Should they be allowed to came back here at all after the war?
> V: Why not? It's all the same.
> C: Let me ask you, I could come through the tunnel [under the Sarajevo airport] if we can agree. I see that you are the right person for me.
> V: How do you see it?
> C: Simple, I have been dealing with your kind before and I see that for you it is really only a job that comes out of need, and that you are a woman of character. But those others who went over to aggressor's side, well . . .
> V: All right, if you think so . . .
> C: What? Imagine, she slept with Ljuban [non-Muslim male name], and then to come here, and I have not had electricity for two years. No way!

Obviously, the caller has a particular woman in mind, and a particular non-Muslim man with whom the woman slept. So, although he excludes Vanja from the questionable morality of the others 'of her kind', he sets the framework of discussion. According to him, it is not prostitution *per se* that is morally bad, but the prostitute. Her morality is questionable, depending on her attitude towards the warring sides. Thus, it is not Vanja's profession but her relation towards the parties involved in the war that becomes crucial in defining her sexual morality. Other callers take this framework a step further. They question Vanja directly about her own attitudes and, unlike Munib, give a negative moral judgement of her as a person:

> C: I would like to ask whether there is any reduction in price for members of the Bosnian Army? (everybody laughs in the studio).
> H: You are appealing to her patriotism.
> V: No, no, there isn't really any reduction.
> C: But there should be, even if just a little bit, for people who defend this city, this country.
> V: And why do you think I am doing this?
> C: I know why you do it, but still you should find some time to give it with a reduction.[12]

While this caller only asked for reduction in price, others requested a financial contribution:

C1: I would like to ask the lady if she is paying a contribution to the Bosnian armed forces (Vanja is laughing)

V: No, this lady is not paying anything.

C1: How come you don't? When I see how much you charge, well, this is the value of one gun, of a 'zolja' [a nick-name for a type of gun] for me. You should help a bit. Considering how much you work, we could all be getting good ammunition. So not everything is against us, poor Muslims. It would even things out.

C2: Think of paying some financial contribution to the armed forces.

The advice is not always as polite, and aggression is sometimes expressed openly, as in the following dialogue.

C: I have some advice for our Vanja. I think that she shouldn't give a hen[13] to UNPROFOR[14] men, let their balls dry, they should fuck their mother. Give it to our poor men, for coupons, too.

V: It is not possible for coupons.

C: There are no German Marks now, fuck it. Give a bit to the fighters, and they'll be sharper, too.

The dissatisfaction and aggression towards Vanja's way of practising her profession is clear: she asks for foreign currency (German Marks), she does not give reductions and she does not accept any other forms of payment but cash. But the real source of frustration is that she does not help 'the cause'. She does not even acknowledge the difference between 'us' and 'them'. Instead, she says, 'it's all the same'. And this is exactly what makes her, and not her profession, morally bad in the eyes of callers. One woman caller states this explicitly:

C: Due to the force of circumstances, I have also started doing this job, now in war. But I help the fighters, and everybody, and I will be able to look everybody in the eye tomorrow with a clear conscience.

The host reacts: 'Oh, you are colleagues!' This total disregard of Vanja's self-definition by both the host and callers continues throughout the conversation. It is enforced by the moral claim: Vanja is not only a prostitute, she is a morally bad prostitute because she does not help the fighters. Nevertheless, she is there, in the studio, and many callers seem to hope to get some profit out of the fact. Milan was one among those who made attempts to profit from Vanja as a pimp. Others also called in offering to be pimps, or customers, or to ask Vanja to consider financial or other contributions to the armed forces. The only caller who does not ask anything from Vanja is another woman caller. She talks with Vanja about the prospects of a job in the West and chats with the host about her own life. At one point the host asks her whether she is happy:

C: I am, as much as one can be in Sarajevo.

H: Vanja told me, before this official part, that she is very unhappy in love, that she has had a lot of disappointments and doesn't believe she could fall in love again.

C: Listen, I do not believe that this could have been a reason to start doing this job. After her job, if it is disclosed, I do not believe she will ever be happy in love, at least not in Sarajevo, or Bosnia.

H: Well, she doesn't see her perspective here, anyway . . .

C: This pessimism is really not what we need tonight in this city.

There is a group of callers who also do not want pessimism. One man calls in with the following question:

C: Good evening. May I ask if there is going to be a quiz, so that one who wins can . . .

The implication is clear: Vanja will be the prize. The host explains that Vanja would not allow such a quiz, but adds that it would cost money and, anyway, he would win because he would know the answer to the quiz question. Throughout the transcript the issue of a quiz is repeated by callers, each time with a bit more enthusiasm. Callers offer to collect money or look for a sponsor. The gradual change of the tone – from a question of whether there will be a quiz to the assertion that there is one – makes everything else seem irrelevant: who Vanja is or what she does, her attitude towards the fighters or prostitutes, maybe even her looks. For men who want a prize – both the host and the callers – the only thing which is relevant seems to be sex and fun. Unlike the other callers who insist on connecting sex, war, morals and money, the connection now is between sex and fun and not war or morals.

Voices of Sarajevo

The talk show speaks, in the transcript, through a few different voices. Vanja's voice is strong and consistent. Its source is a moral claim: prostitution is morally bad, under all circumstances, at all times, in all places. Her strategy is to distance herself from her job, by refusing to define herself as a prostitute. By that same move, Vanja also refuses to acknowledge the war. She never uses the word 'war', but rather 'circumstances'. She thinks nothing of 'her colleagues' who went to the 'aggressor's side'. Her customers are those who can pay, regardless of ethnicity. She does not want to contribute to the armed forces. She has problems with water and electricity like everybody else, but she still 'has her bath regularly', as she states at one point. Thus, nothing connected with the ethnic war seems to affect her, despite the undeniable fact that the war made her choose prostitution.

Her attempts to disconnect what she does from who she is makes physical distance a necessity. She will have to leave the city in which she was born and start somewhere else. The new start provides a continuity with her pre-war life. What she learned in war – prostitution – is knowledge never to be used again. What she lives in war – prostitution – is not her life: 'far from it'. Her true self is a 24-year-old student of engineering. That is the public persona she defends in the talk show. For Vanja, both war and prostitution belong to the same hidden, private experience which will be erased, once 'circumstances' change. The only connection she makes between war and prostitution is a moral rejection of both. Her definition of sexual morality has not changed because of war. It still belongs to peace-time: when it was normal to have a bath regularly, when 'those things' were not talked about in public, and when a student was a student and a prostitute a prostitute.

The male callers speak with a different voice. Their moral claims are an inversion of Vanja's. They say they respect her job and that it is a normal job which is not morally bad *per se*. What is morally questionable for them, however, is Vanja's attitude towards her job. For these callers, sexual morality is defined through the prism of ethnic war. War has moral pri-ority: in defence of the people, of the city, everybody should help, prosti-tutes included. This is the only morality possible. Only if she does not help the cause of the just ethnic war, a prostitute is rejected as morally bad. As one of the women callers puts it, she can 'look everybody in the eye . . . with a clear conscience', even as a prostitute, because she takes responsi-bility for the war effort. For these callers, both the ethnic war and sexual morality are public affairs, and as such both need public intervention and even control.

In the talk show control is exercised by setting a special framework within which the themes of war and prostitution can be addressed. While prostitution, morality, profit, sex and fun are explicitly mentioned in the conversation, the theme of war tends to disappear. The word war is never used. There is talk about fighters and aggressors or problems with water, energy and food. However, the talk show as a whole generates a lot of laughter in the studio, often among all the participants – Vanja, the host and the callers. War seems to be pushed aside and sex, money and fun are in the forefront. The most explicit statement with regard to the apparent denial of war is voiced by the second woman caller: 'This pessimism is really not what we need tonight in this city'. The men who call for the quiz could not agree more. Their own denial of war was total: all they wanted to talk about was the female body for sex and fun.

Paradoxically, while sexual morality in the talk-show is controlled through the ethnic definition of the war, war seems to be controlled through the denial of conflict.

THE SECOND FRAME: THE NEWSPAPER TEXT

The text to which I refer here is made up of two columns that appear in *Duga* before the transcript, and one concluding column. Together with the photos, they frame the talk show in Sarajevo for the readers in Serbia. Unlike in the transcript, where the word war never appears, the first sen-tence of the text already uses the word:

Zlaja [non-Muslim male nickname] is one of my pre-war friends. . . . A lucky thing for Zlaja is that he was, and remained even in the war – a non-smoker. 'I always have cigarettes, I get them in my regular supplies', he said. 'Otherwise, it is difficult to get them. Only for a hell of a lot of [German] Marks. And there are so many girls who are smokers. The supplies are gone, the Marks are gone. So we meet in a tavern, just like ordinary neighbours, with no apparent reason. I take a few boxes of cigarettes with me and 'those things' are quickly done. . . . Until the next supply.

The war which is talked about in the text in *Duga* is a war that brings unexpected sexual advantages to some men as well as loose sexual attitudes among the inhabitants of Sarajevo. Sarajevo is a 'new empire of sex'. International media reports and officials from Sarajevo are quoted saying that 'sex became almost the only pleasure in a grim, war ridden, everyday life'. They explain that 'in war conditions [sex is] even more loose than in normal circumstances'. After that, the text introduces the radio talk show, quoting its host saying that 'in male–female relations in Sarajevo there are, on average, 23 (!) members of the fairer sex to every man'. The text continues:

One lad quickly calls in: 'So where are my 23? I haven't been able to even get one during the whole war.'
'There are those who can, nevertheless' the host answers him, and after a curse that comes as a reply from the caller the line is cut off.
Despite that almost unreal quantitative ratio between the fairer sex and the stronger sex in Sarajevo, not even officials hide the fact that prostitution is flourishing in the city, especially among secondary school girls and unemployed women who took on the oldest profession while their husbands are on the front, says [Mr] Smajo Karacic, the head of the Criminal Prevention Office in [Mr] Izetbegovic's Internal Affairs Department.

At that point, a new sub-title is introduced in the text and the transcript of the contact programme follows. The discontinuity of the two parts of the text – the introductory columns and the transcript – is striking: from a story of 23 women to every man, the text shifts into a story of many men for one woman, i.e. a woman who is a prostitute. The 'empire of loose sex' turns into an empire of 'little eagles'.

There is an element of continuity, however, between the introduction and the transcript. It is provided by merging two empires together. And it is not Vanja in whom the two meet – for she showed no interest in 'loose sex', only in money. It is a Muslim man:

C: Greetings from Tanovic Ergin [Muslim male name]. . . . This oldest profession is not very prosperous here in Bosnia, you know how it is viewed. I am interested in Vanja's opinion if I, as a male, could do the kind of job that she is doing?
V: You could. . . .
C: Then let me suggest an arrangement. You are interested in powerful men, I've got them. I am interested in powerful women, but I do not mind men either. Could we, say, make a deal? I will, here, publicly leave my phone

number: 440-741. So, there it is – Tanovic Ergin at your service. You know
what it is about, it's winter, food supplies are needed, heating, etc. . . .

H: That's good, that's good.

V: That's it!

In the short concluding column, which together with the introduction
frames the transcript, a moving empathy is shown for Vanja:

> After night fell, heavy as lead, Vanja was at her work place, probably until the
> next day, drowned in Sarajevo's stream of destinies. Or maybe, on one of those
> days, she had already met her piece of shrapnel or the bullet of death.

This empathy connects the concluding part of the text with the transcript.
For, the question is whether empathy would have been displayed if the
woman had a Muslim name, and, indeed, whether there would have been
any text at all. Readers in Serbia do not even have to ask themselves these
questions. The names of the actors in the text create images which are
taken for granted. It is a fact that there are Serbs living in Sarajevo and the
readers in Serbia know that life there must be hard. In the text in *Duga* it
is a non-Muslim woman whose life is hard. She lives in a Muslim-held area
of Sarajevo. She has a non-Muslim name: Vanja. She is a victim of double
Muslim aggression, on one hand war, on the other, sexual exploitation. In
the transcript, all men but one have Muslim names. They all ask something from Vanja: contribution to the armed forces of Bosnian government,
her services, or her money. A few wanted to be her pimps. But Tanovic
Ergin only wants information for he is willing to go into prostitution
himself. More than that, he does not even mind homosexual relationships,
stating explicitly that it does not matter for him whether his customers are
women or men. Thus, even if he does not exploit Vanja the fact that she
would share her living space with him might be seen as reason enough for
empathy.

Voices of Serbia

The loudest voice in this text is the voice that names. Through this naming
sexual morality is defined ethnically. Muslim men are represented as
morally bad. For not only do they fight a war against Serbs, and exploit
Serb woman sexually, but they are moral perverts: male prostitutes and
homosexuals. The taboos of male prostitution and male homosexuality
have been very strong in ex-Yugoslavia. Only in Slovenia and parts of
Croatia has homosexuality been a part of an alternative public scene, and
even then it has seldom been part of mainstream public debates. Male
prostitution is never even acknowledged, and simply does not exist in
public discourse. Thus, in the figure of Tanovic Ergin, the text in *Duga*
simultaneously breaks the taboos about male homosexuality and sexu-
ality-for-sale. And it does it in a very specific manner: it attributes them to
one specific group, to Muslim men.

Here also, as in the transcript, it is sexual morality that reflects the dynamics of ethnic identities. In the transcript, the callers defined the sexual morality of Vanja not through her profession but through her attitude towards the war. At the same time the ethnic names of the participants in the talk show assert the existence of two different moralities through two different ethnicities: Muslim men accepting prostitution as morally unproblematic, Serb woman rejecting it. In the text, Muslim men are defined as morally questionable, while the Serb woman is beyond reproach. In that respect the text in Serbia speaks with the same voice as the callers from Sarajevo: in both cases sexual morality is defined through the prism of ethnicity.

The naming in the text has yet another effect. If Muslim men make Sarajevo an 'empire of sex' by having so much sex and fun, this has direct bearing on the perception of war. Sex and fun do not sound like war at all. The problems concerning water, food and electricity are not specific to war. In Serbia the vast majority of people have the same problems. They, of course, know that there is a war going on 'there', but while reading the text, they may wonder whether it really exists, after all. The war that the text talks about appears tragic only from the perspective of one actor: Vanja. Because there are no signs of war-as-destruction or war-as-collective tragedy, but only the general problems facing the citizens of Sarajevo and Serbia alike, the story in *Duga* obscures the war from its readers.

The war is obscured in yet another way by the photo that covers the whole page opposite to the text in *Duga*. As already stated, it shows Sarajevo in peacetime: white buildings, red roofs, green trees. Two small photos inserted at the bottom of the big one both show broken cars on the street, with people in the background. They look like any other broken cars one could see in any other city in the world. By looking at these pictures we cannot possibly conclude that there is a war in this city.

According to John Taylor (1991) the role of photography in the press is to present proof of authenticity. Sewn into the web of rhetoric of the text it accompanies, the photo is its pictorial analogue. Even more, Taylor states, photography has a power to present itself as a simple equivalent to reality. Thus the photographic representation is a part and parcel of textual representation in media. 'Below the horizon of the reportable war' (Taylor, 1991: 8), there is the never-reported-news that clashes with the presented picture, hidden by censorship and self-censorship. Thus, photography and text in the media cannot be seen as 'innocent, transparent or true; they do not simply "reflect" reality. They help constitute it' (Taylor, 1993: 36). They are not harmless pictures reflecting reality, nor are they secondary to the reality (Meijer, 1993). In the context of the two wars these photos and texts construct the identities of Self and the Other, and they say that these identities are worth dying and killing for. But even more, they provide the reality in which dying and killing will be done. Thus, they are constitutive of the power and processes that construct reality.

What the text and the photos from *Duga* tell to the readers in Serbia is simple: there is no war. If there is no war, there cannot be any responsibility for the war either. One individual non-Muslim woman's 'destiny' does not call for a responsibility about the war. It only calls for human empathy for one of the 'drowned', maybe even a re-calling of all the other 'drowned' non-Muslims. Thus, it mourns Serb victims, while rejecting any Serbian responsibility for the war.

A TWICE TOLD STORY OF WAR AND BODY POLITICS

The story about the war-which-is-not-the-war in the text in *Duga* is told twice: once through the conversation in the alleged talk show, where it is a story about sex, money, morals and fun, and yet also in the journalist's introductory and concluding arguments where it is a story about easily available sex, prostitution and empathy for one woman whose moral purity rises above her actions. However different these versions seem to be, they make the same connections and create the same impression: the war is somewhere else.

For readers in Serbia a story about the war, but without the war, may feel familiar. A story about a woman who finds herself in a place where she would rather not be, may be close to their own experience. And a story of moral purity untainted by an immoral job may reflect their convictions about their own situation. In the context of the two wars – where the 'civil war' is not on the territory of Serbia but its effects are, while the 'media war' is there but not necessarily obviously so – this story has manifold effects.

It normalizes war. Different elements of the text have this effect by constructing one particular war zone as the 'empire of sex' coupled with the use of the peacetime photo of the city or by constructing the people living in the war zone as being basically concerned about sex and fun. If people do not suffer, the effects of war can be denied. Thus the war is not really a war, but something else, something that can be lived with. The adherence to the 'pre-war' realities in the definition of moral values is used to re-establish continuity and normality in the daily life of readers in Serbia exactly on that ground: that this war does not really disturb the normality of everyday life.

But the normalizing use of the 'pre-war' sexual morals in the text is also selective. On the one hand, through Vanja's voice it maintains that female prostitution, as well as male homosexual prostitution, is morally bad. On the other hand, the disregard for sexual taboos expressed by one Muslim man and other Muslim men's attempts to profit from Vanja, make them almost inhuman. Vanja is their victim. The effect is that while the Muslims are defined through the sexual morals of Muslim men, the Serbs are defined through the suffering of a Serb woman. Vanja is a metaphor of the

Serb suffering, a symbol of their victimization. For her life is constructed as reflection of the daily life in Serbia: opportunistic but resigned, pessimistic but enduring, humiliating but pure. She tells the Serbs that they are the only ones who really suffer the consequences of this non-war.

Normalization and victimization in the text in *Duga* construct ethnicity, for they name both the sufferer and the cause of the suffering ethnically. Vanja's morality is upheld beyond her profession on an entirely different basis: she is a victim, and thus beyond moral judgement. The Muslim men and their sexual morals are the real culprits. In the classical orientalist fashion, gender and sexuality are used to define the two groups: Muslim men do not have a counterpart in Serb men and they do not need to have one. In the text the Muslim men and Serb woman represent the Muslims and the Serbs, in general.

In the context of the 'media war' in Serbia, thus constructed ethnicities have yet another significant effect: they cast the doubt on the reality of sexual violence as war strategy. The text in *Duga* was published in February 1994, while the accusations about sexual atrocities against Muslim women committed by Serb soldiers in Bosnia have been growing in the international media since winter 1992. In Serbian media, a story about ethnic war in which a Serb woman is a victim of the Muslim sexual exploitation, precludes all the other stories about ethnicity and sexual assault.

The practices of constructing groups ethnically, of normalizing war and of victimizing Serbs, are interwoven in the body politics of this text – in the explicit use of sexual morality in defining ethnicity and in the metaphoric use of the female body. The very topic through which this war story is told – prostitution – makes the female sexual body the site through which these practices operate. The story about the war is told through the story about prostitution. The oldest profession of women is used to tell a story about the oldest profession of men. The sequence about the quiz is particularly significant for the metaphoric use of the female body in this text. It has a double effect. On one hand, it is an ultimate denial of the war. It is sex and fun that concerns the callers, and Vanja's body. She is not a person with a name any longer, she is just a body through which the war is denied for those who live in it and normalized for those who read about it. On the other hand, however, Vanja always has a name, and ethnicity; her body is not only female, but it is also an ethnic body. It is the body of the Serb woman.

Only as such – female and ethnic at the same time – a body of a woman is a site of nationalist processes, be it normalizing and victimizing practices in the 'media war' or the rape in the 'civil war'. Both highly symbolic and utterly physical, these practices rely on the representational capacity of the female body – the capacity to integrate individual experience with social and cultural meanings. In nationalist discourse it is the experience and the meaning of ethnicity. And the body of one woman becomes the body of all Serbs.

NOTES

I am indebted to Lena Inowlocki for opening the world of textual interpretation before me, for stimulating suggestions about the text in *Duga* and for inspiration for the title. I am grateful to Willy Jansen for insightful comments, and to Kathy Davis for patient editing and steady encouragement.

This text is a part of my PhD thesis, 'From "Media War" to "Civil War" – Female Body and Nationalist Processes in Former Yugoslavia'. It has been funded by the Dutch Organization for Scientific Research, NWO.

1. These different names have different political platforms behind them, and different interpretations of reality. I resent calling the war through which Yugoslavia disintegrated an 'ethnic war' for several reasons, and I think the situation is a bit more complicated than 'aggression' versus 'liberation'. To go into the debate here, however, is beyond the scope of this paper. Some of the problems associated with the characterization 'ethnic war' have been explored elsewhere (Zarkov 1995). I stay with the name 'civil war', but not without cynicism, for I see civilians as much the victims of this war as its proponents. For that reason I keep it in inverted commas.

2. Political and analytical language in former Yugoslavia did not use the term ethnicity, but rather nation or peoples. Thus the people living in former Yugoslavia belonged to one of six nations (*narodi*): Croats, Macedonians, Montenegrians, Muslims, Serbs and Slovenians (Muslims were granted the status of 'nation' in the late 1960s and in the census of 1971 for the first time appeared as a separate category), or to minorities (*narodnosti* or *nacionalne manjine*): Albanians, Bulgarians, Czechs, Hungarians, Italians, Rumanians, Ruthenians, Slovaks, Turks and Ukrainians, among the most numerous. Each republic had within its population people from almost all nations, and many minorities.

    National minorities were enjoying substantial rights to their own language, education and broadcasting, as well as to the promotion of their cultural interests (cf. Ramet, 1992). In the territories with an especially heterogeneous population, more than one language was in official use. In Kosovo, Albanian and Serbo-Croatian; in Vojvodina five languages, Hungarian, Slovak, Serbo-Croatian, Romanian and Ruthenian; in some parts of Croatia, Italian and Croatian. Since the beginning of the 1980s the situation has worsened considerably in Kosovo, and since 1989 it has deteriorated in all former Yugoslav territories.

3. This is not to say, however, that all the media always had the same attitude to either nationalist projects and practices or to the issues regarding women and sexuality. There has been, throughout the last decade, democratic opposition with many, if small, political organisations, parties and groups engaged in anti-war and anti-nationalist activities, women's groups being the most prominent. Many of them have had their own newspapers, or TV programmes, some even had whole TV stations. An organization called Press Now, based in Amsterdam, supports the independent media from the former Yugoslavia. Also, the International Organization of Journalists acknowledges the role of independent media in disrupting the media blockade and the censorship imposed by the governments of the newly established states in ex-Yugoslav territories (cf. L'OIJ, 1992). Nevertheless, many newspapers and TV programmes took it upon themselves to support and advance the nationalist projects of their governments or nationalistic political parties.

4. See Thompson (1994) and L'OIJ (1992).

5. It is necessary to note that not everybody lives through either economic hardship or disillusionment. There are those who have made high material and political gains from the war. On the economic level especially some have

profited enormously, and the social strata of the newly rich is very visible on the streets of many cities in Serbia. Their connections to crime are privately condemned but seldom publicly pursued.

Furthermore, as the economy broke down, the 'grey economy' (already a familiar and necessary source of income in ex-Yugoslavia) expanded to include many activities that used to be considered petty crime (like for instance tobacco smuggling and dealing). Hence, the ideas about crime have changed, as more and more people engaged in some form of it, and profited from it.

6. Maljukan, G. (1994) 'Little Eagles for Those Things', *Duga*, No. 520, pp. 44–7.
7. In the transcript I will mark the participants of the talk show as follows: V, for Vanja; H, for the host; and C for the callers. When more than one caller is quoted in the same excerpt they will be marked subsequently as: C1, C2, etc.
8. Because the naming plays a particular role in this text, I will indicate the origin of the name for the reader.
9. The same concept is used by scholars analysing both literary and visual representation of the female body precisely because of its capacity to mark the boundaries: in and out, Self and Other. Cf. Lynda Nead (1992) and Maaike Meijer (1993).
10. The square brackets in the text are used for my own explanations, the round brackets appear in the original text.
11. At several points in the transcript there are brackets with the words: (the laughter in the studio), making it clear for the readers of *Duga* that participants in the talk show are having fun.
12. 'To give' is a slang expression, usually used by men, referring to woman's attitude to sexual relations, for example 'she gives easily', 'she does not give'.
13. A slang for female genitals, but the same word is also used for a woman, especially 'old hen'.
14. United Nations Protection Force that was stationed in Bosnia with the mission to aid humanitarian efforts and enforce peace.

REFERENCES

Colovic, I. (1994) *Brothel of the Warriors*. Beograd: Kultura.

L'OIJ (1992) *Reporters and Media in ex-Yugoslavia*. Paris: Les Cahiers de l'Organisation Internationale des Journalistes, No. 2.

Meijer, M. (1993) 'Countering Textual Violence, On the Critique of Representation and the Importance of Teaching its Methods', *Women's Studies International Forum* 16(4): 367–78.

Nead, L. (1992) 'Framing and Freeing: Utopias of the Female Body', *Radical Philosophy* 60: 12–15.

Ramet, S. (1992) *Nationalism and Federalism in Yugoslavia, 1962–1991*. Bloomington and Indianapolis: Indiana University Press.

Taylor, D. (1993) 'Spectacular Bodies: Gender, Terror and Argentina's "Dirty War"', pp. 20–40 in M. Cooke and A. Woollacott (eds) *Gendering War Talk*. Princeton, NJ: Princeton University Press.

Taylor, J. (1991) *War Photography, Realism in the British Press*. London and New York: Routledge/A. Comedia Book.

Thompson, M. (1994) *Forging War – The Media in Serbia, Croatia and Bosnia-Hercegovina*. London: Article 19.

Zarkov, D. (1995) 'Gender, Orientalism and the History of Ethnic Hatred in the Former Yugoslavia', pp. 105–20 in H. Lutz, A. Phoenix and N. Yuval-Davis (eds) *Crossfires, Nationalism, Racism and Gender in Europe*. London and East Haven: Pluto Press.

Feminist Interventions
in Body / Politics

8 Erotic Bodies

Images of the Disabled

Gon Buurman

Passion in Plenitude: Handicap, Body Image and the Erotic (Ploegsma/De Brink, 1991), from which these photographs are taken, was commissioned by the Council for the Disabled in the Netherlands. It is a candid and refreshing exploration of the embodied experiences of the disabled that displays their struggles, but also their pleasures and seductiveness. The perspective is an unusual one: it does not view the disabled stealthily, with shame or as objects of pity. It shows that a handicap does not mean that the body has become nothing more than a burden; it may function differently, but it does function – and sexually, too. This prize-winning book gives a central place to the individual rather than her disability.

9 Women's Public Toilets

A Serious Issue for the Body Politic

Julia Edwards and Linda McKie

Our research on the topic of the provision of public toilets for women began with the question 'Why is it that women invariably have to queue for the toilet in public places, whereas men do not?' The answer we initi-ally received from many women, as well as most men, is that women spend longer attending to their dress, hair and make-up and, as a conse-quence, queues form. However, from personal knowledge we recognized that queues do not build up outside women's toilets because there is a crush of bodies in front of the mirrors, but because the toilet cubicles them-selves are occupied. Nevertheless, it is indicative of the fixity of cultural 'norms' that despite substantive changes to women's socioeconomic and political status, the idea of women as preoccupied with appearance should so persist in many people's perceptions. Such myths are, of course, useful excuses for doing nothing about the problem of queues and blaming women rather than asking more relevant questions of the providers of the service. Questions like, for example, are there more toilets for men than for women? Or, if there are equal numbers of toilets for women and men, do women require more toilets than men? If so, why? And why aren't providers responding to this greater demand from women?

Our investigations into such questions form the basis of this article in which we describe our analyses of some of the cultural and political struc-tures which not only sustain the myth of vanity, but also diffuse attempts to get this issue taken seriously by public policy-makers. While our research is presently limited to the UK, we know from reports from an international symposium on public toilets held in Hong Kong,[1] that the problem is common enough worldwide, although in countries like France, Japan and Australia, the willingness to address it appears to be greater. All three of these countries have national Toilet Associations dedicated to the promotion of more and better facilities; the Japanese Toilet Association, for example, is currently campaigning for three times the number of toilets for women as for men. Yet in most European countries the inadequate pro-vision of public toilets for women is trivialized by most policy-makers and accepted by many women.

In the first part of this article we address the question of women's need for more public toilets in terms of women's different biology and the historical and social factors in the social construction of toilet provision and the etiquette of using public toilets in the UK. Second, we examine women's own responses to the problem and the obstacles they encounter from male-dominated professional and political institutions, when they campaign for more and better public toilets. In the conclusions we discuss the interactions between the two previous sections and draw out the implications for women as unequal citizens. The lack of public toilets, we conclude, is much more than an inconvenience for women. It is a denial of women's different public policy needs; an abuse of their time and therefore a denial of opportunities to engage with, and transform, the patriarchal power relations which continue to structure and regulate society.

DO WOMEN NEED MORE PUBLIC TOILETS?

This question needs to be addressed in two interrelated ways. First, the biological differences between women and men; and second, the social construction of toilet provision, dress and toilet etiquette.

Biological Differences

As social scientists we are concerned that the study and application of biology can emphasize anatomical differences between men and women which may appear to support the reductionism or essentialism of biology. It may also detract from the exploration of the role of culture in defining and determining resultant social differences in toilet etiquette. However, with these provisos we do need to recognize the complex biological differences between the female (internalized) and the male (externalized) genitourinary systems. In addition, about a quarter of all adult women are menstruating at any one time, adding to the length of time that a woman may spend in the toilet, and adding to the number of occasions a woman needs to visit a toilet compared to men. Moreover, while urination and defecation are bodily functions which are subject to conscious control (at least to an extent), menstruation is not. Thus, while men can tolerate a reasonable time lag in seeking a toilet to relieve their excretory functions, women cannot always do so.

Increased visits to the toilet for women are also occasioned by other biological differences from men such as pregnancy, when pressure on the bladder is greater. Furthermore, a wide range of specifically female conditions, including childbirth, may also result in continence problems for women (see, for example, Shapiro, 1989), lengthening still further the list of biological reasons as to why women need more public toilets than men if they are to have equality of access to the service.

Of course, many men suffer from incontinence due to medical conditions such as a prolapse of the prostate gland, loss of muscle tone and

stress-related causes. Comparative information for the lay reader is difficult to come by, since the issue is rarely discussed openly. However, the
Continence Foundation in Britain (a voluntary agency for incontinence
sufferers) claims that one in every 12 women compared to only one in 60
men experience incontinence. In contrast, Shapiro comments that 'many
doctors believe that nearly 50% of young, normal women have some
degree of urinary-control problem' (Shapiro, 1989: 377). This seems to
imply that strong control over the bladder may not be natural for women
due to the combination of a different genitourinary system and hormonal
differences. The woolliness of our comments here is not due to our laity
alone, for as Shapiro (1989: 379) points out:

> As shocking as it is, even experts know little about the basic anatomy and
> physiology of the female genitourinary system. The classic text, *Gray's
> Anatomy*, devotes several pages to the male genitals and urinary tract but only
> one sketch of the female urinary system. Most doctors see the female urinary
> system as an inadequate or defective system, rather than as a complex system
> in its own right.

As a result of medical education many doctors (and nurses) consider the
female genitourinary system as less effective and prone to problems,
rather than studying this system in its own right. Nevertheless, inconsistencies (in the statistics of incontinence, and what constitutes
normal/abnormal behaviour) do not detract from the fact that due to biological differences alone, women need greater access to public toilets than
men.

Social Differences

The catalogue of socially constructed differences in the way that women
and men urinate includes factors like sitting down as opposed to standing up, adjusting dress, having to enter an enclosed cubicle as opposed to
walking directly to an unenclosed urinal and the use of toilet paper. All of
these factors may increase the length of time it takes for women to urinate
compared to men.

Research conducted in various parts of the world between 1957 and
1991 and collated by Kira (1994) shows that women, on average, take twice
as long to urinate as men. These studies record the time taken, measured
in seconds, from entering to exiting a toilet. There are eight studies on
men's urination times showing averages of between 32 and 47 seconds
and six studies on women showing averages of between 80 and 97
seconds. These figures illustrate the total time needed by both sexes to
perform their urination in the context of current Western culture, and primarily reflect differences in clothing management and the nature and
number of toilets available.

Further research is required to ascertain how far the longer urination
times for women cited in Kira's data are accounted for by differences in

time needed to adjust dress before and after actual urination. But of the six studies on women's urination times, the first was carried out in Japan in 1960 (97 seconds) and the last also in Japan in 1991 (93 seconds). We think it fair to say that in those 31 intervening years, women's dress has become more convenient to manage, perhaps accounting for the four-second difference, but the men's figures for these same studies were 32 and 33 seconds respectively, suggesting that dress can only account in part for the differences in urination times.

Women's need to sit down to empty the bladder may be inhibited by fears of contaminated toilet seats. The hovering position over the toilet can slow the flow and result in the bladder not being fully emptied which in turn tends to cause infections like cystitis with its attendant symptom of urge incontinence – the feeling of wanting to visit the toilet very frequently (Moore et al., 1991). Further, although there have existed women's urinals in the past in Britain, this would be regarded as socially unacceptable in modern times. Likewise, the practice of urinating in public, although illegal in many countries and socially frowned upon, tends to be accepted when men do it (for example, late at night or in a motorway lay-by), when young children, especially boys, need to urinate at short notice when visit-ing public spaces, but would be unacceptable if women did it. Yet in previous centuries it was accepted that women working in fields wearing long skirts would squat and urinate beneath the folds of the skirt.

Today the social pressures on women to wait in line for an enclosed toilet cubicle, can be contrasted with the wider range of options available to men where, within the male toilet-room[2] there are choices between urinals and cubicles. As Kira (1994) points out 'men's facilities are vastly overfitted with WCs'. In contrast, women's toilets are underprovided with facilities as evidenced by research cited by Jones (1993): '. . . 75% of coun-cils fall short of a reasonable level of toilet provision for women and 54% did not even reach half the desired standard of provision for women'. Queuing may also cause women to hurry the process of urination and again not fully empty the bladder leading to infections and, in turn, further increased demand for toilets.

One of the main differences between women and men using the toilet is that women still tend to carry the main responsibility for the care of chil-dren in families, and may have to visit the toilet for a child's needs rather than their own. Similarly, it is still predominantly women who have the care of elderly relatives for whom incontinence may be a problem as it is for the very young. While attitudes to the gendered division of domestic labour and childcare are changing, the evidence from recent research (Kiernan, 1992) is that men's practice of taking a greater share of house-hold tasks and childcare still lags far behind their stated egalitarian beliefs. Moreover, men have been slow to demand the necessary facilities, such as unisex baby-changing rooms, which would enable them to take a greater share in parenting work. For nursing mothers, the taboo against breast-feeding in restaurants or other public spaces often forces them to, inappropriately, feed their babies in toilets thus adding to the pressure of use.

Finally, there is a historical legacy of underprovision of public toilets for women rooted in Victorian middle-class attitudes towards their place in society. Although, as Hollis (1987) tells us, it was women who were the main campaigners for public sanitation in nineteenth-century Britain, then (as now) it was predominantly men who decided where and how many public toilets would be built. This is most noticeable in bars and public houses where the ratio of provision is 75 : 25 in favour of men (Greed, 1995).

Thus, in answering the question as to why women need more public toilets, we have argued that women's bodies function differently from men's, at times causing them to spend longer in the toilet at each visit and to visit the toilet more frequently. Within the culture of Western medicine the female urinary system is defined within a particular sociohistorical context as inferior and thus prone to medical problems. It would therefore not be unreasonable to presume that greater provision of toilets for women would follow, but it is interesting to note that there are fewer toilets for women than men.

CAMPAIGNING FOR MORE AND BETTER PUBLIC TOILETS

Campaigning for more and better public toilets in Britain can be broadly described in three categories, namely:

1. highly localized lobbying of local authorities, which in more recent times has been focused on preventing closures of public toilets as councils cut back on what is a discretionary service;
2. part of the agenda of national organizations representing the interests of specific groups such as elderly and disabled people and pregnant women, e.g. Age Concern, InconTact, National Childbirth Trust; and
3. a specific campaign addressing the issue of women's equality of access to public toilets.

The campaign which we have researched, All Mod Cons (AMC), originated as a women's campaign and has placed the issue of equality of access as central to its activities. We first briefly describe how the campaign started and what it has achieved in the 10 years of its existence, and then draw out the relevant issues through our analysis of the obstacles which the campaigners have encountered.

All Mod Cons

The campaign began in Cardiff in the early 1980s by one woman (Mrs Susan Cunningham) initiating a letter-writing campaign in the local press to complain about the impact of underprovision of public toilets on

women with small children. More support for the campaign was soon
attracted when the local county council announced plans for a new public
library in the city centre which was deliberately designed without toilets
for library users. In the council's view, toilets in other libraries had been
forced to close because of 'unsavoury use' by vandals, drug abusers and
shoplifters, making maintenance and supervision costs too high. Moreover, since 'a large modern toilet facility had recently been opened
immediately to the rear of the central library . . . the decision was taken
not to provide generally available public toilets' (letter from South Glamorgan county librarian dated 11 July 1995).

The revised BS 6465 incorporates substantive improvements in the construction and location of public toilets for women. What it does not do,
however, is to make the provision of public toilets a mandatory duty of
local authorities, nor does it require there to be twice the number of
women's toilets as men's. Such regulations are the province of parliament.
AMC has been successful in persuading a local MP to raise the issue in the
House of Commons. A private member's Bill by Jon Owen Jones (MP for
Cardiff Central) did attract cross-party support and was published as the
Public Conveniences Bill on its second reading in 1994. Had the Bill
become law, local authorities would have had a statutory duty to provide
one toilet per 550 female and one per 1100 male members of their local
populations. But, since such a duty would have required the Treasury to
provide the necessary resources, the government was unwilling to

  Although AMC failed to persuade the council to change its mind, the
public debate which the campaign generated attracted attention nation-
wide from the media, from voluntary organizations, from parliamentari-
ans, from commercial organizations, academics and individuals, such that
the main activity of AMC shifted from being a local campaign to that of a
national organization for the coordination and dissemination of information. One of the academics taking an interest in the campaign was Professor Alexander Kira at Cornell University, New York State, whose
research on urination times is discussed above. It was from this body of
evidence, and contact with Toilet Associations in other parts of the world,
that AMC's objective of campaigning for twice the number of toilets for
women as for men, came about.

  Moreover, as part of the process of marshalling their arguments against
the council's decision, AMC found that the British Standards Institute
(BSI), which regulates the design and construction of toilets in public
buildings, was in process of revising that particular standard (BS 6465). By
bombarding the BSI with questions arising from women's perceptions
about where and how public toilets should be built, which the BSI found
difficult to answer, representatives from AMC were eventually invited on
to the committee revising BS 6465. This, in 1991, was the first time that a
woman had sat on that particular committee, indicating how deep rooted
is the assumption by male policy-makers that women have no needs,
values or priorities different from their own.

support the Bill and accordingly it ran out of time at the end of the parliamentary session in November 1994.

Nevertheless, because of the amount of support which the Bill received in the House of Commons, encouraged by effective lobbying by AMC, the government did make one minor concession in asking the Audit Commission (which measures the performance of local authorities) to collect data on existing levels of public toilet provision. Although the unit of measure which the Audit Commission has requested from local authorities is inadequate (number of sites of public toilets, not number of individual facilities) the campaigners hope to use this information, eventually, as a springboard for putting further pressure on the government and to resurrect the Public Conveniences Bill in the future.

This is the barest of outlines on the origins and development of AMC to set the scene for our following analysis of the obstacles which have beset the campaign. While we have indicated some of the campaign's achievements – not least in exposing it to wider public debate in Britain – the question must be addressed as to why more progress has not been made. To examine the underlying causes for this, we have analysed the obstacles to progress in terms of (1) cultural attitudes to women and bodies, (2) access for women to resources, and (3) structures of political and professional control. All three are, of course, interrelated and as such form, in our view, a web of gendered power relations which not only account for lack of progress in this particular case, but also the continuing lack of progress for women's social, economic and political equality.

CULTURAL ATTITUDES TO WOMEN AND THE BODY

In this section we identify three interrelated aspects of cultural attitudes to women and to excretory functions generally. They are:

1. An undercurrent of traditional assumptions about women as objects of desire; as carers of men, children and other dependent relatives; as dependent homemakers rather than economically independent breadwinners. Women's magazines, newspaper articles, popular music and advertising all continue to promote these traditional attitudes, albeit often side by side with more egalitarian views of women.
2. Embarrassment (by both sexes) and reluctance to speak about excretory functions. An apparent association of these functions with weakness and/or vulnerability in contrast to popular images of the body which exemplify beauty, strength, fitness and perfection.
3. Sexualization, mainly by men, of the excretory functions – their own as well as women's. Although most men urinate at unenclosed urinals, they have an etiquette which includes not using a urinal immediately next to one that is occupied, and avoiding eye contact and conversation with strangers during urination (Kira, 1995). While homophobia may

be an aspect of this etiquette, it also appears to be bound up with fears of heterosexual judgement.

Men's sexualization of women's bodily functions can best be illustrated by the following two quotations: Clara Greed (1995), an expert in town planning, has observed that men have a:

> predilection to 'sexualise' the toilets issue . . . by a school-boyish smutty mentality, and much sexual innuendo, when the topic of toilets is raised, but also in genuine embarrassment and ignorance when discussing women's excretory requirements. Unfortunately these attitudes mean that women's needs are unlikely to be taken seriously.

Sophie Laws (1990: 91), in her study of men's attitudes to menstruation, observes:

> Many of the men who told me about jokes about menstruation emphasised that menstruation was not a central topic of such joking. What is central is 'sex' – meaning the sexual degradation of women. If the male culture regards menstruation as purely discrediting, entirely disgusting, then it is only to be expected that well-intentioned men will tend to avoid talk with women about it. . . . The silences and the obscenities are intimately connected.

These three interrelated aspects of cultural attitudes towards women and bodily functions create formidable obstacles for campaigners seeking to promote public debate about the need for more and better toilets. In an interview with Mrs Cunningham (21 June 1994) she told us of one campaigner, an expert nutritionist, who when he was invited to speak on BBC radio a few years ago was told:

> no, you can't talk about that on the radio; don't you dare say that people should eat more roughage and they should go to the toilet more often.

The Cardiff MP, Jon Owen Jones (interview, 28 September 1994), who led the campaign in parliament, also observed:

> I've come to the conclusion that unless women's organisations and women councillors in particular take a leading role, it [better provision of public toilets] won't happen. It seems to be one of those issues which men don't seem to see as their business for some reason . . . [it's] embarrassment.

The implication here is that it is mainly men who are embarrassed, more so than women.

In spite of these obstacles, and as we indicated above, AMC has been successful in opening up the debate. There have now been several articles in national newspapers and two networked television programmes on the subject as well as news items on local television. However, there is still a tendency for the media to treat the issue at arm's length – as a problem for specified groups such as elderly and disabled sufferers of incontinence, or as an anxiety for parents of small children. The issue of lack of toilets as discrimination against women is rarely highlighted.

WOMEN'S LACK OF RESOURCES

From the early 1980s until 1993 when the Continence Foundation (CF) stepped in with administrative support, AMC operated on a financial shoestring. The following quotation encapsulates the catch 22 which entraps many women's campaigns, including AMC, namely that subordinate socioeconomic positions in society deny many women the time, energy and money resources to fight for political change:

> But I'm a housewife, I've never received any money for this. I do get some help now from the Continence Foundation, but I've put in tremendous amounts of time and money . . . but when I started totting it all up, it was costing me about £20 per week and you know we're [her family] not in that league . . . but it actually takes time and money to set up as a charity. . . . (interview with Susan Cunningham, 21 June 1994)

CF is an umbrella organization set up with grant aid from the Department of Health and a group of private companies whose products relate to incontinence. CF is funded (initially for three years) to collect and disseminate information on incontinence reflecting the concern which policy-makers are beginning to show towards the needs of an increasingly elderly population. The first Director of CF, Christine Norton, formed a close working alliance with AMC to relieve Mrs Cunningham from some of the burdens in time, money and energy which have been spent in developing AMC into a nation-wide organization.

The support for AMC from CF was timely, since, as she indicates in the quotation above, Mrs Cunningham and her small band of local supporters were getting close to the limits of their personal resources to sustain the ever-growing campaign. However, there is an acknowledged danger that the women's rights aspect of the campaign will become subsumed to the primary objective of CF, namely, campaigning on behalf of those disabled by incontinence.

Getting financial support from independent sources is, as Mrs Cunningham said, a time-consuming and expensive process. Most grant-giving organizations are obliged to have a set of bureaucratic processes through which they scrutinize the disbursement of their funds. The problem for campaigns like AMC, where the work is being done virtually single-handedly by one woman, is that the time, money and effort required to meet the bureaucratic regulations in order to apply for grant aid are simply unavailable. Given that women have, on average, three hours less leisure time per day than men (Kelly, 1992); that the majority live highly fragmented lives, splitting their time between paid and unpaid labour in a variety of settings in and outside of the home and have to rely on public transport more than men (Graham, 1993); that they earn, on average, significantly lower wages than men (MacEwen Scott, 1994); it is a wonder that women's campaigns are established and survive at all.

WOMEN AND THE STRUCTURES OF GOVERNMENT

In this final set of obstacles, we use the term 'government' in its broadest sense to incorporate the professions as well as the politicians involved in public policy-making. In combination, they can present a formidable array of obstacles to all but the most well-resourced pressure groups, and particularly so, if the issue concerned is not socially condoned. The three main obstacles which AMC encountered in dealing with the structures of government were:

1. male-dominated professions and their influence on public policy-making;
2. the lack of feminist representation in local and central government (meaning women who promote positive actions to redress gender inequalities);
3. unequal distributions of power in parliament and between local and central government in Britain.

These obstacles may be illustrated in one example, namely the design of the new public library in Cardiff. This building was designed without public toilets through a process which involved professional architects, planners, lawyers, accountants, librarians as well as the politicians. The most senior of these professionals can have a very strong influence on policy, even if their official stance is impartiality. Being overwhelmingly male (on average less than 5 percent of senior British local government advisers are women) they rarely have experience of intimate care tasks or the fragmented lives of women. Thus, although influential in public decision-making, they tend not to have first-hand experience of using public services in the way that most women do. In addition, their professional training is male dominated too, which, as Clara Greed (1995) explains (in relation to town planning) gives them a distorted view of the world:

> male town planners have tended to look at the city from above, peering down on layouts on the drawing board. . . .

This 'view from above' was true in the Cardiff case, as evidenced by the county librarian's statement (above) that the decision against public toilets in the new library was partly because 'a large, modern public toilet facility had recently been opened immediately to the rear of the Central Library'. The toilets in question are only 'immediately to the rear' on the plans; in reality they are one floor down (the library is built on the first floor of the building); outside into the shopping precinct; and some 500 yards up the road and round the corner from the front door of the library. An elderly person with restricted mobility, or a mother with toddlers and pushchair, would take a minimum of ten minutes to reach the toilet from the library checkout desk.

The problem for women of living with professional men's view of the world is ubiquitous. Before AMC was coopted on to the BSI committee dealing with standards in toilet provision, it was only men who decided how much space was needed within cubicles. Since, as Kira (1995) points out, men rarely use the cubicles available to them in public toilets, opting for the more accessible urinal instead, they have little concept of the problems which their inadequate standards cause women. Undersized cubicles, into which sanitary towel bins are awkwardly placed, make manoeuvring within the cubicle difficult for many women, particularly if they are accompanying small children or frail elderly relatives.

These literally different perspectives (between service planners and service users) make dialogue with male professionals extremely difficult for campaigners. So much has to be explained to them to present a women's perspective which is time/energy/money consuming. Elected politicians (at both local and national government levels) are meant to represent the views and claims of the people; but since these, too, are overwhelmingly male, a similar problem occurs. Mrs Cunningham told us of the hours she had spent both at the BSI and with local councillors explaining the problems for women with the lack of public toilets, but, as Jon Owen Jones's comment (above) shows, 'men just don't seem to see it as their business'.

The lack of women's representation in political forums is problematic. The national average of women councillors is 23 percent; at the parliamentary level in Britain, women MPs form approximately 10 percent of the House of Commons. Gross underrepresentation is, however, only part of the problem. As the research on feminist action in local government shows (see, for example, Edwards, 1995; Cockburn, 1991) competitive party politics often results in women's perspectives on policy being subsumed to male-dominated party priorities in the processes of helping the party to gain or hold on to power. Moreover, in our experience, very few of the women who have achieved status and power as councillors, senior officials or MPs, would identify themselves as feminists. This is unsurprising since neither party structures (Lovenduski and Norris, 1993) nor professional training (e.g. Greed, 1994) are conducive to feminism. Consequently, there is a lack of receptive milieux for women's campaigns for better public services within the majority of governmental institutions.

This is compounded at the local level by the subordinate nature of local to central government in Britain. Unlike many of our European partner countries, local government in Britain has no power of general competence. Such a power would enable local authorities to do anything other than that forbidden by parliament. Instead, and simplifying the matter somewhat, local government in Britain does what parliament tells it to do.

Campaigning for more and better public toilets in the current restrictive economic climate is therefore increasingly difficult. Those councils sympathetic to the cause may be powerless to respond effectively to the campaign, particularly if their financial advisers (who now have special powers over spending decisions) are against them. However, according to MP Jon Owen Jones (interview, 28 September 1994) who was formerly a councillor in Cardiff:

> Personally, I don't believe that the financial burden [of more toilets] is anything that local authorities couldn't afford. I think it comes down to how many councillors would want to see their names on plaques outside a local toilet which has been provided rather than say a local swimming pool.

Thus, in this analysis of obstacles for the campaigners, we come full circle. According to Mr Jones, the male-dominated culture which accounts for the embarrassment about toilets, inhibits male-dominated councils from prioritizing spending on toilet provision over other public amenities. As we have shown in this analysis, the issue is much more complex than the simple causality implied. A web of gendered power relations exists which inhibits open debate about public toilets, trivializing it with embarrassed laughter or silencing it with sexual innuendo – and sustains the myth of women's vanity. We now bring together the issues raised in the foregoing two sections in order to address this question in our final discussion within a framework of citizenship theory.

CONCLUSIONS: CITIZENSHIP AND THE BODY

After centuries of struggle and the achievement of basic political rights, why is it that women are still wasting their time in queues, suffering discomfort, even accumulating extra domestic work if a toilet is not found in time for themselves or their children/elderly relatives? While many women are tolerating the situation in silence, yet more are vigorously protesting against it. But as we have shown, these campaigners (notwithstanding their achievements within the BSI) have been unable to change what is clearly a case of institutionalized discrimination against women in the provision of a public service.

David Held (1994: 49–50) refers to this situation as 'nautonomic':

> Nautonomy refers to the asymmetrical production and distribution of life-chances which limits and erodes the possibilities of political participation. . . . The attempt to control, if not monopolise, any range of resources according to particular social criteria, such as class, race, ethnicity or gender, can be denoted a form of social exclusion or 'social closure' (see Parkin, 1979). Any system of power in which particular life-chances and opportunities are subject to closure can create nautonomic outcomes and thereby, undermine or erode the principle of autonomy. Thus, those who do not have access to, for instance an adequate income, educational opportunities or the organised media are unlikely, in societies like our own, to be able to exercise their potential as active citizens.

The primary cause of 'closure' is the gendered division of labour; nevertheless, on all the countless occasions when women are absent because they are seeking out/queuing for a toilet – be that at political gatherings, conferences or theatre intervals – not only are they denied participation, but myths of their vanity and their lesser worth as autonomous beings, are reinforced. How then, are women to become equal citizens? As Elizabeth Meehan (1994: 73) notes:

> To ensure equal citizenship there must be a polity that respects the outlooks of marginalised people sufficiently strongly to create opportunities for them to put across their views.

How far can it be argued that women are 'marginalised people'? One of the many problems for the equality debate has been the difficulty of defining women as a group in order to claim that women's citizenship is different and/or inferior to men's citizenship. Group identity debates have usually floundered in attempting to reconcile the many differences between women – class, ethnicity, able-bodiedness, religious affiliation and the dreaded et cetera – as much as in distinguishing the differences from men. In focusing on the excretory functions of women's bodies we claim that women's biological difference from men constitutes a criterion for their groupness. We do not suggest that women are therefore defined by their excretory functions, just as women are not defined by their capacity to gestate, nor that one of us who is hearing impaired is defined by her deafness. These specific functions or characteristics do not constitute the whole individual, but they do provide a reason for affinity with others with the same characteristics and to be empowered by group membership.

In making this argument we follow Iris Marion Young (1990: 48) who emphasizes the value of a plurality of groups for democratic citizenship. Social groups, she argues:

> are not themselves homogeneous, but mirror in their own differentiations many of the other groups in the wider society. In American society today, for example, Blacks are not a simple, unified group with a common life. Like other racial and ethnic groups they are differentiated by age, gender, class, sexuality, region [sic] and nationality, any one of which in a given context may become a salient group identity.

If women, as individuals with comparable bodily functions that are different from those of men, are forced to queue in order to relieve those bodily functions because men (as decision-makers) refuse to acknowledge women's different needs, then, we contend, women are a marginalized group in that particular context. The notion that we all identify with a variety of groups at any one time better expresses, we think, the embodiedness of human individuality and sociability.

Almost all 'new democracy' models are problematic, not least, we think, because they overemphasize structure, forgetting that any system of government is only as good as the people and processes for practising it.

In this regard, we would suggest that a model already exists for developing the necessary practices, this being local government women's committees (see Edwards, 1995). Although few in number, these examples of feminist action in British local government have successfully developed democratic ways of expanding women's representation and participation in public policy-making. At the heart of their praxis is empowerment – the application of power in positive ways – to facilitate reciprocity between, and achievement by, others rather than to govern or control. As such, we think them worthy of much more attention from 'new democrats' than they have received so far. The group in Birmingham, for example, has already been instrumental in improving attitudes to and provision of public toilets for women (BPWG, 1993).

In this article we have explored some of the problems for women in getting policy-makers to take their demands seriously. The network of obstacles we have described is an embodiment of male power within cultural and political institutions, and sustained by male (mis)interpretations of democratic principles which are exclusive of women. But as we have also shown, women's tenacity and commitment to each other can result in achievements, albeit at disproportionate costs in time and energy. It is, we suggest, only through such solidarity in organized group politics that they will achieve an equal citizenship.

NOTES

1. International Symposium on Public Toilets, hosted by the Hong Kong Urban Council and held 25–27 May 1995.
2. The language of toilets is complex and confusing. In the USA for example the room for excretory functions is the bathroom; in Britain the word toilet is used both for the room and the lavatory. Lavatory in other countries is a place to wash hands rather than excrete. Since toilet is used internationally, we have kept to that term.

REFERENCES

BPWG (Birmingham for People Women's Group) (1993) *Caught Short in Brum: Toilets for Women in Birmingham City Centre*, report. Birmingham: Birmingham for People.
Cockburn, C. (1991) *In the Way of Women*. Basingstoke: Macmillan.
Edwards, J. (1995) *Local Government Women's Committees*. Aldershot: Avebury.
Graham, H. (1993) *Hardship and Health in Women's Lives*. Hemel Hempstead: Harvester/Wheatsheaf.
Greed, C. (1994) *Women and Planning: Creating Gendered Realities*. London: Routledge.
Greed, C. (1995) 'Planning For Convenience', paper delivered at 'Street Ahead' conference, University of the West of England.
Held, D. (1994) 'Inequalities of Power, Problems of Democracy', pp. 47–59 in D. Miliband (ed.) *Reinventing the Left*. Cambridge: Polity Press.

Hollis, P. (1987) *Ladies Elect: Women in English Local Government 1865–1914*. Oxford: Clarendon Press.

Jones, J. Owen (1993) 'Not At Your Convenience: A Survey of Local Authority Public Convenience Provision', pamphlet, House of Commons, London.

Kelly, E. (1992) 'The Future of Women in Scottish Local Government', *Scottish Affairs* 1 (Autumn).

Kiernan, K. (1992) 'Men and Women at Work and Home', pp. 90–111 in R. Jowel, L. Brook, G. Prior and B. Taylor (eds) *British Social Attitudes Ninth Report*. Aldershot: Dartmouth Press.

Kira, A. (1994) 'Urination Measurements', personal communication to All Mod Cons, April.

Kira, A. (1995) 'Culture and Behaviour of Public Toilet Users', paper delivered to International Symposium on Public Toilets, Hong Kong.

Laws, S. (1990) *Issues of Blood: The Politics of Menstruation*. Basingstoke: Macmillan.

Lovenduski, J. and P. Norris (1993) *Gender in Politics*. Cambridge: Polity Press.

MacEwen Scott, A. (1994) *Gender Segregation and Social Change*. Oxford: Oxford University Press.

Meehan, E. (1994) 'Equality, Difference and Democracy', pp. 67–79 in D. Miliband (ed.) *Reinventing the Left*. Cambridge: Polity Press.

Moore, K. et al. (1991) 'Crouching over the Toilet Seat: Prevalence among British Gynaecological Outpatients and its Effect Upon Micturition', *British Journal of Obstetrics and Gynaecology* 98: 569–72.

Parkin, F. (1979) *Marxism and Class Theory*. London: Tavistock.

Shapiro, J. (1989) 'Urinary Incontinence', pp. 376–400 in *The Boston Women's Health Book Collective, Ourselves Growing Older*, British edn. London: Fontana.

Young, I. M. (1990) *Justice and the Politics of Difference*. Princeton, NJ: Princeton University Press.

10 Chic Outrage and Body Politics

Joanne Finkelstein

CHIC OUTRAGE

On 27 January 1995, on the fiftieth anniversary of the liberation of the Nazi concentration camp at Auschwitz in Poland, the Parisian fashion house, Comme des Garçons, launched its menswear collection in the Place Vendôme. The theme of the fashion show was sleep; but when two tall, emaciated young men with closely shaved heads appeared on the catwalk, wearing dressing gowns and striped pyjamas bearing numbers, the striking resemblance to the uniforms of the concentration camps was decried by the world press. The fashion show had opened on the same day that those who had perished in the Holocaust were being commemorated in ceremonies throughout Europe and the rest of the world. In the same week, another designer (from the fashion house Jean-Louis Scherrer) had also been castigated for employing Second World War iconography, especially Nazi insignia, in a couture collection which had featured Gestapo-like caps adorned with the iron cross. These apparently deliberate gestures toward images of neo-Nazi tailoring were described in the international press as inexcusably tasteless. The designer of the Comme des Garçons pyjamas, Rei Kawakubo, was reported as being dismayed at the furore her collection had created. She claimed her show was unfortunate in its timing, but not intended to give offence. This incident was reminiscent of the fiasco created last season by Chanel's Karl Lagerfeld, when his tight, low-cut dress bodices, which featured Koranic verses embroidered in grey pearls, offended many in the Muslim community. Following press reports of this reaction, the garments were not permitted to go on sale and, like Lagerfeld, Kawakubo has withdrawn her garments from sale in the wake of media interest (Yanowich, 1995a).

The international press picked up these incidents, as it has other fashion campaigns such as those of Benetton, and used them to engender an atmosphere of moral outrage. It is an easy position to assume, but ironically it protects the fashion industries by locating criticism at a banal juncture. The press's criticisms disparage members of the fashion industries for doing what is expected of them, namely, producing popular and stylish goods which resonate with the interests and values of the consumer classes and which aestheticize the tempo of the *Zeitgeist*. To criticize fashion (or any art form) for being pertinent, even if in doing so it promulgates dubious imagery, implies that aesthetic products should always be servile to material interests. In this case, the international press singled out haute couture for being more provocative than politically sensitive. This is a conceit the press have often expressed. When Rei Kawakubo launched the Comme des Garçons label in Paris in the early 1980s with a collection inscribed as post-Hiroshima, the bruised make-up and powder scattered on the clothes were declared by the press to be distasteful. When Zandra Rhodes was invited by the Indian government in 1982 to use and promote local fabrics, she reworked the traditional sari, ripping it and giving it shredded edges. The mutilated sari was seen as an insult. Last year, Comme des Garçons' winter collection featured models wrapped in what appeared to be army blankets and fatigue jackets, torn and worn as if from sleeping rough. In his catwalk parades, Versace has frequently played Phil Collins' popular song, 'Paradise' about a destitute girl living on the streets, to accompany models clad in clothes worth tens of thousands of dollars. Recently, the Italian fashion house, Dolce e Gabbana, dressed its models in slick, natty, sharp suits reminiscent of American gangsters of the 1930s at a time when the Italian community was absorbing the murders of judges and police investigators working to bring the Mafia to justice. These allusions to fascism, poverty, dislocation and violence in a Europe not only concerned about its undeclared wars but also about its expanding underclass have been regarded by the international media as wantonly callous (Hume, 1995; Yanowich, 1995b).

But is this the best criticism to direct at haute couture? There is no easy correspondence to be drawn between fashion styles and commemorative gestures which attempt to mark historic occasions.[1] Indeed, the instances described above, in which the international press assume a position of moral outrage over fashion's well-publicized imbroglios, rest on the tacit expectation that haute couture can and should be politically correct. It is a position which has the consequence of naturalizing the high visibility of haute couture while simultaneously deflecting attention from what fashion does routinely, which is to reinstate ideologically conservative values found in the conventions of the everyday world.

In addition to the moral certainty expressed by the mass media, there are the frequent portrayals of fashion designers being out of touch with the putative real world and inhabiting remote and rarefied environments. Yves Saint Laurent is described as living in a cocoon, shunning any contact with newspapers, radio and television. This isolation, which is now associated with the haute couture industries, creates the expectation that every season some designer somewhere will generate a sensation by stumbling into politically sensitive areas. Although haute couture has a reputation for often being sensational and shocking, displays of political insensitivity as evidenced by Lagerfeld and Kawakubo have been reported as attaining new heights. Yet the shock tactics of fashion have been a trademark of the industry for some time. During the 1960s and 1970s, Vivienne Westwood's and Malcolm MacLaren's shop on the Kings Road – sequentially called Sex, Seditionaries and World's End – provoked chic outrage with their torn clothes, jewellery made of razor blades, safety pins, chains and S&M paraphernalia. This kind of sensationalism was breathtaking in its day but it begins to look quaint in contrast to the post-Hiroshima, neo-Nazi militarization of the current catwalks – or, at least, this is the position taken by fashion commentators such as Marion Hume in the *Independent* newspaper, and the legendary Suzy Menkes in the *International Herald Tribune*.

Fashion as a Contested Cultural Site

The mass media demonstrate a persistent interest in the world of fashion. So much so that the coverage of haute couture verges on surveillance. The reportage rightly figures fashion as a contested cultural site, although the precise interpretative complexities of that assessment are not developed or enunciated in the media reports. That fashion in the twentieth century is such big business may protect it from theoretically informed analysis. The production, marketing and consumption of fashionable items encompasses a vast economic colossus employing millions of people and generating billions of dollars in revenue; it is a golden egg which few want to threaten in these harsh economic times. Additionally, there has been a strong intellectual tendency to condemn fashion as a frivolity because it bestows too great an emphasis on the trivial, and this has also worked to protect fashion from the attention of those who deem it an unimportant cultural field. Even though the polysemic expressions of fashion are evidence of a multifarious and contradictory nature, nonetheless a generalized understanding of fashion as such seems to have been effectively curtailed. Its cooption by other conservative institutions has aided in this: for instance, when fashion found a protective mantle in that bastion of culture, the museum, its cultural status was elevated but its eruptive capacities were simultaneously diminished.

Take the example of the Victoria and Albert Museum's exhibition 'Streetstyle, From Sidewalk to Catwalk, 1940 to Tomorrow', curated by the popular media anthropologist, Ted Polhemus, in 1994–5. This exhibition classified youth culture and style tribes through clothes dating from post-Second World War. Beginning with 1940s zoot suits from New York's Harlem, and extending to the eclecticism of the 1990s (including the New Age traveller, rocker, rasta, punk, biker, surfer, rockabilly, goth and hipster), the exhibition was a successful holiday attraction bringing the spending public into the financially straitened museum. The dominant assumption in the 'Streetstyle' exhibition was deeply conservative. It portrayed clothing styles as unproblematically 'thick' with anthropologically significant meanings which could reveal the political and social positions of those who adopt them. To choose a particular garment, hairstyle or make-up is simultaneously to express a particular subcultural worldview. Polhemus went further and posited that clothes could represent complex ideas, attitudes and values, and that direct connections were discernible between the visibility of one's appearance and the invisibility of one's political and aesthetic values (Polhemus, 1994: 15). The position endorses the simplistic equation that social values, individual character and political beliefs are immanent in appearance. It is ironically the same assumption employed by those criticizing the recent creations of Kawakubo and Lagerfeld. Polhemus unknowingly takes the side of the popular fashion critics by saying dress literalizes various interests, that is, it can signal a concern for environmental issues as expressed through hippie wear or political nihilism and anarchy as embodied in punk wear: 'the Punks' black leather, fetishistic garments, studs and Crazy Colour hairstyles indicate a nihilism, an aggressive stance and a delight in artifice and deliberate perversity' (Polhemus, 1994: 15). Polhemus does not go so far as to identify neo-military garb as signalling nazification, but the logic of the idea is there.

In 'Streetstyle', dress is represented as a literal representation of abstract qualities; as if it were capable of signifying any position along a political spectrum. To see such a close alliance between physical appearances and moral expressions is to invoke a range of pseudo-theories such as that of physiognomy which have been rightly condemned in academic circles but which persist as working assumptions in contemporary life, including the world of the international press (Finkelstein, 1991). If fashion were more rigorously critiqued, it would be required to delineate the arguments undergirding the conclusion that clothing styles can represent subtle and not so subtle political positions. A happy consequence of that might be the emergence of a public discourse that could educate us to see the intertextualizing of aesthetics and politics, and which would in turn make it appropriate to expect the consumer industries to be more self-consciously politically correct. But there is no public discourse which explains the particular obligations of haute couture (or, for that matter, other fashion styles such as retro and diffusion). There is no articulation which ethically obliges haute couture to be properly commemorative of history. Indeed, the dubious ideas undergirding this position – namely, the literalization of abstractions embodied in obvious, material expressions – are a taken-for-granted aspect of social life. This makes the position assumed by the international press, that haute couture should be politically correct, seem ill conceived because it implies that political sensitivity is easy.

The confluence of interests in fashion from museums, department stores and advertising agencies has firmly established it as a spectacle to be analysed like any other aesthetic formation. But in order to do this, fashion must be rescued from the sensationalist criticisms of the mass media, and from the protection of advertisers, bankers and museum curators. To elicit from fashion the critical assessments which would yield more insight into the political and social significance of the consumer industries, we must take fashion more seriously and see it as a technique, an apparatus, which diligently reinstates the conventionalized, thereby making it seem natural, domestic and invisible. As fashion reinforces much that is obvious – such as gender distinctions – it is not a radicalizing phenomenon. But this is not an inescapable and inevitable failure of fashion. Its polysemic and contradictory expressions make it, theoretically, capable of radicalization, and the intentions of this article are to identify ways in which fashion can function on both sides of the divide – as both naturalizing and socially eruptive. By demonstrating its capacity to express anomaly, the significance of fashion can be seen in the use made of styles of appearance as public claims for inclusion within categories (albeit most commonly those representing quotidian positions), and in the formation of cultural values including the embodiment of human subjectivity. A more critically informed intervention in the functions of fashion is often inhibited by fashion's social prominence and its representation in the media with headline-grabbing, sensationalizing commentaries as we have seen above. Indeed, these latter tactics are better seen as deflections which take critical attention away from recognizing the conservatism of many fashion gestures.

BODY POLITICS

The Functions of Fashion

Fashion is swathed in anomalies. On the one hand it is often regarded as a distraction, a form of playfulness and humour; on the other, it is understood to generate the economic potential to rehabilitate failing businesses and restore commercial respect. Fashion can be used to indicate social change and progress, for example, by its weakening of the prescriptions around gender-appropriate dress. But at the same time fashion is a conservative influence, dedicated to the maintenance of the status quo – as the longevity of the business suit could be taken to indicate. The anomalies embodied in fashion make it an important adjunct to commentaries on the cultural formations which effect and shape modern life.

When Fredric Jameson (1990) characterizes the modern sensibility as archetypically schizoid because of its powers to compress and make sense of contradictory images and distorted temporal frames, he could be describing the contemporary fashion lover. The contradictions expressed through fashion parallel the disturbances, disjunctions and conflicts encountered every day. Jameson's modern individual harbours an anarchic, fragmented and protean self, which makes fashionability seem a reasonable and satisfying pursuit. It is a position employed by the fashion marketeers who regard the ideal consumer as 'not the rational sovereign subject of Descartes' but a 'Deleuze and Guattari's "body without organs" – the absolute decentred subject, the irresponsible, unanchored subject' (Hebdige, 1993: 82–3). With every change of style and appearance, fashion demonstrates its power to influence human subjectivity and assert what is described as a postmodern subject position. This is well illustrated with the representation of gender.

Ideas about masculinity and femininity have changed as quickly as the garments. But the enduring message, for theorists and the fashion conscious alike, is that both social identity and gender identity are figments of the imagination. As Caroline Evans and Minna Thornton remark, 'the body can be made, through dress, to play any part it desires, as gender coding is displaced from the body on to dress' (Evans and Thornton, 1989: 62). In their book on women and fashion, Evans and Thornton show how being chic is a flirtation with being overloaded by the different expressions and styles of an incoherent feminine ideal. Such diversities can be read as a failure of that ideal. But instead of paralysing women with a deluge of contradictions, Evans and Thornton rightly suggest that such category confusions are liberating. What they refer to as 'the alienation that is a structural condition of being female' can also enable women to manipulate better their social position. Thus, 'if fashion is one of the many costumes of the masquerade of femininity, then those costumes can be worn on the street as semiotic battledress' (Evans and Thornton, 1989: 14). Fashion need not be either an entrapment, or a mechanism for further disabling and wounding the subordinate. Fashion, because of its inherent anomalies, can be experimental, playful, creative as well as oppressive.

Fashion magazines, with their increasing popularity and seductive appeal, instruct in the creation of image and self-representation. As well as reporting on the availability of goods, they link fantasy with self-production in ways that satisfy desires such as those for control and novelty. As Lipovetsky remarks, 'the psychologising of appearance is accompanied by the narcissistic pleasure of transforming oneself in one's own eyes and those of others, of "changing one's skin", feeling like – and becoming – someone else, by changing the way one dresses' (Lipovetsky, 1994: 79).

These habits can be seen as empowering, especially for the structurally disadvantaged, as women are often depicted. The historian Leslie Rabine explains how the daily act of donning clothing and cosmetics is deeply implicated in the 'process of enacting the fantasies of fashion magazines upon the body'. One of the pleasures of these everyday gestures is that they are 'erotically charged', and at a symbolic level, they ritualize a mastery of biology – they make the body seem tractable. By changing the unclothed, unmade up body into 'a self-produced coherent subject', it becomes apparent that 'the pleasures of fashion include the symbolic replay of this profoundly productive moment when subjectivity emerges' (Rabine, 1994: 64).

Such pleasures are frequently undercut as liberatory by the claim that the ideal female body is always an impossibility, an unmatchable ideal. Even though there are the personal pleasures that fashion provides, as when a well-groomed style gives one a sense of being attractive, it is also the case that we are frequently made aware of having failed to replicate the ideal. But, it is important to reinstall the antinomies of fashion so that its powers of regimentation are not inflated. Rabine (1994) supports this by indicating how the failure to meet the ideals of fashion is not always oppressive. Even though the 'look' is always beyond and out of reach, nonetheless it remains alluring. From a psychoanalytic perspective, this is because fashion is used as a promise to annul the fragmented condition of modernity with the imposition of a coherent subjectivity. In this way, the contemporary woman interested in fashion is encouraged to become a self-reflecting subject. She is enticed to think about and to know how she is being looked at, as well as how her status as an object to be pleasurably gazed upon has been formulated. Yet there is an inherent contradiction in all of this; at the very moment when women are depicted as self-producing, what they are often constructing is the constrained and subjugated image of the heterosexually desirable female.

> The more she is portrayed as independent, the more she is portrayed as an object of the male look. The woman of fashion is invited to assume custodianship of that look, and to find her own empowerment through managing the power that inevitably reduces her to the second sex. (Rabine, 1994: 65)

Rabine provides a muted optimism deduced from her analysis of fashion magazines between the 1960s and 1980s. She argues that women, during this time, were offered a persistent dualism in classifications of femininity. On the one hand, women were given images of themselves as confident, free and sexually powerful individuals who can display these qualities through their skilful use of clothing and cosmetics. On the other hand, during these two decades, the same fashion magazines published reports of women's submission and vulnerability, with articles on domestic violence, increasing rape rates, salary inequalities, sexual harassment in the workplace, and other events and practices which demonstrated that women were merely objects in a man's world (Rabine, 1994: 66). Fashion magazines peddle a bifurcated subjectivity for women, which combines the contrary illusion of an exuberant and self-possessed femininity with the expectation of being vulnerable to the power exercised in male-dominated economic and political spheres. Rabine's important point is not that these images are contradictory and confusing, but that they succeed in shaping female subjectivity in a way that naturalizes the ambivalent social position of contemporary women, whose situation is thus even more dire than being simply seduced by the fashion system. Rabine shows that when women internalize both their power and lack of it, they oscillate between perfect femininity as sexual power, and perfect femininity as object of male pleasure. Nonetheless, at this juncture, it is possible to theorize and imagine situations in which women can escape this trap. The diversity of fashionable guises available to women, and their inherent instability in the fashionable image, equip the fashion *habitué* (who is most commonly female) with an imaginative agility to take greater control of her position in a variety of social contexts.

Styles of clothing shape what we see when looking at the 'natural' body. The public, visible body is always mediated through vestimentary codes.

As the surface of the body is imagined through styles in dress, then clothing and fashionability become constitutive features of subjectivity. Again, from a psychoanalytic interpretation of fashion, Silverman (1986) makes the point that gender differences have become more visible during the last century and are represented in gender-specific dress styles. Men's wear, in particular, has solidified into uniform sobriety and rectitude, whereas by contrast, women's styles have fluctuated rapidly, thus creating the impression of female flightiness. The few attempts at bridging these differences, such as women wearing neckties and business suits, do not challenge Silverman's argument, but merely demonstrate again both the instability and eclecticism of the feminine in matters of dress: 'clothing not only draws the body so that it can be seen, but also maps out the shape of the ego, [such that] every transformation within a society's vestimentary code implies some kind of shift within its ways of articulating subjectivity' (Silverman, 1986: 149). Even though male and female styles in clothing have merged in recent decades, gender differences have not been submerged. Lipovetsky (1994: 109) describes how such differentiation is now much more subtle, and requires a correspondingly closer reading of 'little nothings' – the woman's necktie made of different material from a man's, her shirt tailored with 'feminine' buttons, and the belt buckle gendered into male and female versions.

As women have become more active in the public domain, they have partially abandoned their position as emissaries for men, and begun to use fashion and appearance for their own self-expression. In this reappropriation of an already existing system of social classification, new configurations in meaning have come into play. These have not sparked the kind of category crisis that cross-dressing brings about, yet they do signal a permeability at the boundaries as well as the possibility of disruptions provoked by the designation of the category itself (see Garber, 1992). Styles of appearance are public claims for inclusion within a category, and whenever these styles are toyed with, then fashion is reiterating its ability to influence human subjectivity. Fashion is here in service to the ethic of individualism. How individuals choose to look, how they want others to see them, designates the fashioned body as a site for acting out a variety of social claims. Fashioning the body becomes a practice through which subject positions are also fashioned.

Women have often been intimately linked with fashion as if the latter's frivolousness were enough to explain women's obsession. According to Cathy Griggers (1990), the institutions of fashion, the mass media and advertising, are all deeply implicated in the discursive formation of women's identities. These industries have appropriated the Freudian question, 'what do women want?' and answered it in self-serving terms: 'she wants everything' (Griggers, 1990: 96). Thus, women are ubiquitously portrayed in various and often contradictory poses as 'the "new" woman, the working woman, the sports woman, the family woman, the sexually liberated and educated woman' (Griggers, 1990: 96). This chameleon is capable of looking attractive in 'high-impact shades, reptile gloves, evening gowns by Ungaro, spiked heels, and a divided skirt' (Griggers, 1990: 77). Griggers interrogates this position in order to indicate that the mechanisms of desire which operate in the fashion system draw into their orbit not just women but every consumer, irrespective of gender or age. But having said this, it should not be underestimated that, in contemporary consumer societies, women's identities have been fractured, divided, redivided and newly created in order to multiply the opportunities and niche markets for fashion-driven products. The fashion industries have thrived on the instability of women's identity, and have continued to burden women with the putative need to reinvent themselves.

Griggers' view coincides with Jameson's and Baudrillard's theories of the self in its schizophrenic and ephemeral state. Yet, in a subtle reworking of the idea of the postmodern self, Griggers points out that modern women have long experienced the instability of the feminine. 'The loss of the cultural referent anchoring a normalized feminine subject . . . *is* her history' (Griggers, 1990: 86). No modern woman expects to discover a stable identity in the images found in fashion journalism:

> the average reader of Vogue participates in a discursive game which trembles between fantasy and its failure, but not only in relation to the fashion garments . . . but in relation to the cultural construction of feminine subjectivity, and its splittings, which the fashion discourse articulates. (Griggers, 1990: 87)

In this sophisticated stance towards the fashioned feminine ideal, there is an element of resistance. The pleasure for women in looking at their multifarious images is the recognition that their feminine identity has always been elusive and somewhere else. Men, too, are recognizing that their own dream of a self-empowered subjectivity is better conceived of as merely an ideological ruse. The stability of a social identity, whether masculine or feminine, is now more widely recognized as a myth. And disrupting social mythology has its rewards. The constant display of desirables, which the consumer society daily creates, provides the objects with which both men and women can extract satisfaction (however temporary and fleeting) for their unrestrained and fluid desires. To be knowledgeable about what sustains us on a daily basis is an important source of renewable pleasure, which often gives a sense of autonomy. The significance then of fashion rests not on whether we need haute couture or street style clothing in order to consolidate a sense of identity, or whether these needs are manufactured to serve the interests of capitalist enterprise, rather the point has much more to do with how we resist a coercive conventionality and use fashion to sustain ourselves to become more reflexive in our everyday social activities. Fashion, as a mode of social exchange, functions like other social discourses to maintain cultural continuity. However it is not always so straightforward. The sociation around fashion is commonly ambiguous, thereby making it difficult to assert that fashions necessarily exploit or demean us. The lack of stability and closure is a benefit of the fashion system which we can utilize as a discourse of signs and codes through which desires and subjectivities can be enunciated.

For example, when Hélène Cixous (1994) describes her favourite evening jacket, a black, soft woollen garment designed by the illustrious Sonia Rykiel, she vividly illustrates how fashion, as a technology, can materialize some of the most intimate sensations. Cixous's elaborate meditation on this elegant, expensive and shimmering garment depicts fashion as more than an object; it is a sensibility which pervades and constitutes one's aesthetic inclinations. Whenever Cixous puts on her jacket, she becomes the starry night, the East, the foreign. Fashion transforms her, and she is infatuated with its capacity to do so. Fashion is not just a vestimentary overlay, a disguise of fabric and style which covers and thus rewrites and reshapes the body. Instead, it is a new way of speaking the body, and freeing it from silence. For Cixous, the garment is continuous with her body, it becomes a form of cultural expression, much like writing, which renders the interior exterior. The fashion garment makes the 'inside' the 'right side': 'there is continuity between world, body, hand, garment' (Cixous, 1994: 95).

Cixous regards Rykiel's fashion garments as forms of self-expression. Although she recognizes that clothes can be barriers, these are not the clothes she favours. Cixous's clothes must become part of her; and by expressing her 'self', they will even come to resemble her. In this way, a woman's identity fuses with her appearance to become greater than the parts. Cixous denaturalizes the body by making it synonymous with history and culture, and naturalizes fashion by making the garment part of individual consciousness, memory and sensation.

Yet despite the flashiness and apparent inconstancy of fashion, it is a durable, like the very body it clads. Rykiel, like Cixous, fuses the outer with the inner when she claims that the body and the dress are 'mirrored images of each other, each the consecration of the other' (Rykiel, 1994: 103). Rykiel counters the view that fashion is frivolous, irrational and destructive because it exhibits destabilization and constant change. Like Roland Barthes, she argues that fashion effects the stopping of time, because the designer compresses past, present and future in every garment, every style (Rykiel, 1994: 107). As Barthes (1985: 273) had remarked, fashion is a means of keeping vigilance over the present moment: it is a way of erasing history at the very moment of participating in its making. In the light of the outrage surrounding Comme des Garçons and the commemoration of history outlined at the beginning of this article, Barthes's remarks reinforce the ambiguity of fashion. It is a position Sonia Rykiel already understands as she describes fashion as functioning more like a philosophy or aesthetic which provides both the elements of meaning and the tools for its analysis. Such a viewpoint reinforces the liberatory capacity of fashion to denaturalize the body and reconstitute it as a look, a feel, an imagined aesthetic.

Dressing for Success

The ability of fashion to intercede between individuals and the material world in ways that reflect an appropriated aesthetic or politics has many expressions. It has, for instance, been the assumption supporting the literal reading of an individual's beliefs and morality from the way she or he looks – as Polhemus demonstrated in the museum exhibition, 'Streetstyle'. Such an idea has also circulated through the history of women's social and economic struggles. The wearing of trousers and bloomers, for instance, was regarded as a blatant signal of female sexual abandon and rebelliousness. Even when women wore these items for practical or health reasons, they were frequently accused of violating their feminine roles and advocating a range of unorthodox, even criminal, practices (Luck, 1992). Yet, a more theoretical critique of the physiognomic perspective clearly indicates that to interpret sexual abandon from the wearing of bloomers is as convincing as Polhemus's directive that a spiky hairstyle indicates political nihilism.

In most cultures, styles of dress and body adornment attempt to produce a different body, that is, to reshape it into an aesthetic ideal, whether through scarification, nose- and neck-rings, hair dyeing or fashionable garments. The effect of clothing on the constitution of subjectivity, and the use of dress as a cultural metaphor for the body, bring theories of identity formation directly into contact with the regulation of the body. In *Discipline and Punish* (1977), Foucault charted those structural mechanisms which produced the docile body, one of which was how the body was clothed. Both the increased use of uniforms in the nineteenth century for military and professional purposes, and the general regulation of clothing for specific occasions such as weddings, funerals, civic ceremonies, suggested to Foucault how regimes of discipline were being implemented.

Elizabeth Wilson adds the contemporary example of women's prison dress. Some penal institutions now permit women to wear their own clothes while incarcerated – not as a reward, but as a means of increasing surveillance. The logic is that when female prisoners wear their own clothes rather than a uniform, they reveal a great deal more of their characters or personalities, thereby giving the authorities useful information about how best to police such women (Wilson and Ash, 1992: 11). In the late twentieth century, when some dress styles are self-consciously infused with the wearer's aesthetic taste, when, say, garments have become self-referentially fetishized, sexualized and politicized, the point of fashion is to articulate the individual's worldview. As Wilson has argued,

> clothing . . . has the unique characteristic of being able to express ideas about sex and the body while simultaneously it actually adorns the body. . . . These insights move us away from the simple, moralistic rejection of fashion. . . . We can still acknowledge that dress is a powerful weapon of control and dominance, while widening our view to encompass an understanding of its simultaneously subversive qualities. (Wilson and Ash, 1992: 12, 14)

Wilson is drawn to the conclusion that fashion need not be about regimentation and restriction. It is not always a gesture which undermines the individual while at the same time enhancing an already engorged capitalist system. She argues that the economic exploitation inherent in a consumer-dominated culture will not be reduced simply by putting an end to fashion. Instead, she supports the reverse position, namely that when fashion is understood in aesthetic terms (as a manner of ordering, categorizing and enchanting the lived milieu) then simultaneously it assumes a more radical potential. It is a position also advocated by the notorious fashion designer, Vivienne Westwood, who has suggested that *couture création*, the extension, proliferation and multiplication of fashion, constitutes the more radical act because it is the plurality of fashion which elevates its value to the individual and prevents more fashion simply translating into more profits for multinational corporations. The aesthetic pleasures afforded by fashionability cannot be trivialized since without such pleasures everyday life can become a grinding monotony.

Elizabeth Wilson (Wilson and Ash, 1992) regards fashion as a device which pulls together the fragmented aspects of modern identity, and provides the individual with a means of negotiating the often incoherent aspects of the everyday. Fashion can function ideologically by formally resolving, at the imaginary level, the social contradictions produced by modern, urban living. At the same time, it interpellates the moral location of an individual by questioning how repudiations of or reconciliations with convention are being made. Individuals can thus dress in order to criticize the dominant culture and transcend its homogenizing influences while simultaneously aligning themselves with the conventions of marginalized or dissenting groups. In these ways, fashion provides a symbolic sense of location even for those individuals whose social critique distances them from the mainstream.

Yet all fashions remain ambivalent because the question of whether they are meant to be confrontational or affirmational is indeterminate. When the haute couture gown is paraded in drag, its original value is hard to discern; a point well made by Jennie Livingston in her documentary film, *Paris is Burning* (1990) which records the drag balls attended by African-American and Latino men in New York City and Harlem. Fashion styles selected mainly from the straight 'white' world are here performed and judged in categories of costumes which include Ivy League, executive, the military look, high drag feminine and butch queen. Judith Butler has enquired of these performances: do they subvert the norm or reidealize it, and how does an onlooker know when the appearance coincides with what it means (Butler, 1993: 129)? When other styles are imitated, it is questionable whether the resultant faux-fashion is to be understood as fakery or as failure. Does faux-fashion undercut or concretize the fashion hierarchy?

IN PURSUIT OF CHIC

This is the dilemma faced by Kawakubo and Lagerfeld in their 'politically incorrect' new season styles. It is very easy to misread fashion: the shaved head may allude to a military-style puritanism, parody the institutionalized look, or (as in the Comme des Garçons example) gesture ambivalently towards the victims of war. Body-piercing and tattooing can be seen to recuperate the practices of 'primitive' peoples, but they can also evoke a technoculture in which semi-criminalized individuals are identified by numbers and body-brandings (Ross, 1994: 295–6). Fashion can indicate social crisis, but the capacity for fashion to absorb any stylistic forms makes it unreliable; it is a hungry Moloch which can eventually digest all attempts at oppositional dress. Polhemus naturalizes the position by claiming that the constant renovations in fashion can be expressions of subcultural variations, even expressions of tribal pedigrees. This is particularly apparent in urban settings, where the assertion of identity is felt to be urgent.

> It is no coincidence that the decline of traditional social groupings, which has intensified so markedly since the Second World War precisely parallels the rise of a new type of social group, the *styletribe*. Hipsters, Teddy Boys, Mods, Rockers and so forth arose to satisfy that need for a sense of community and common purpose which is so lacking in modern life. (Polhemus, 1994: 14)

Fashion is a disciplinary power in Foucault's sense in that it coerces the body to shape and rearrange itself in accordance with ever-shifting social expectations. The skills required to diet, apply facial cosmetics, arrange clothes and wear ornamentation are in the service of aesthetic innovations which continually reinvent identity. Foucault's notion of the docile body shows how elements of a fashionable lifestyle – which includes the urban habits of reading fashion magazines, engaging in body-sculpting practices such as dieting, gym workouts, cosmetic surgery and periodic internments at health and fat farms – are techniques for transforming the body into a commodity. The body becomes a site of aesthetic innovation, much like the family car, and, in much the same manner, is subject to periodic upgrading. To redesign the look of a commodity is to give it a new lease of life, specifically by submerging its use-value into its appearance-value. 'Looking good' adds value: those who cannot achieve the fashionable 'look' fail the appearance test, and their social status declines. Urban life, which constantly exposes everybody to the scrutiny of strangers, emphasizes the need to monitor and update one's self-performance.

A point that Una Troubridge seemed to understand well. When she sat for her portrait by the painter Romaine Brooks, she selected masculine dress. In her everyday life she was more likely to wear conventional feminine dress, in contrast to the more masculine attire of her partner,

Radclyffe Hall. In the portrait, however, she would be figured alone, without her partner, and so to communicate her sexuality she dressed in masculine clothes. Violet Trefusis and Vita Sackville-West did much the same when they escaped together for a short-lived honeymoon in Paris. Violet wore feminine dress and Vita masculine clothes in order to live out their relationship in the public domain. This gender masquerade allowed the couple to experience in public some of the privileges of the hetero-sexual, as well as signalling to those in the know who they really were. On their return home to England, both reverted to conventional feminine dress (Rolley, 1992: 37; Leaska and Phillips, 1989: 115).

In the early decades of the twentieth century, when the existence of les-bians was rigorously effaced, clothing could be used as a way of identify-ing its wearers, and in many instances, such dress codes worked to bind individuals into a self-conscious subculture. Katrina Rolley (1990) points out that early twentieth century lesbians dressed in styles that both signi-fied their sexual orientation and suppressed any knowledge of it. By adopting similar modes of dress, women could appear to be sisters and therefore part of a conventional familial grouping, thus concealing their sexual relationship from unsuspecting onlookers. Alternatively, by wearing stylized masculine and feminine garments they could demon-strate the opposite, and enable more discerning others to acknowledge what was before their eyes.

The use of clothing in this fashion, to designate gender appropriateness and exploit the opportunities this creates for masquerade, underlies an important element in the deployment of fashion, namely, that clothing speaks (albeit ambiguously) to both strangers and observers. Styles in appearance simultaneously attract and deflect attention. When clothes are misappropriated, as in gender bending, they fracture conventions; when they are parodied, they satirize those same conventions for allocating clothing in accordance with strict divisions between the feminine and masculine. Particular kinds of clothes allow the wearer to pass as a member of the other sex to the eyes of uninitiated observers; but to know-ledgeable spectators, the cross-dressed communicate pleasure and play. An example of the pleasures of coded dress styles is Vivienne Westwood's 'Half-dressed City Gent' outfit, an ensemble which has women wearing men's shirts (with a dishevelled collar and necktie askew) and tight panty-hose with either a fig leaf appliqued to the crotch or, in the same position, a 'graffiti'd' penis (Ash, 1992: 184).

Given the scepticism provoked by interpretations of fashion and style, it is ironic that a desire to read the obvious should endure as if it were self-revealing – as has been the case with Rei Kawakubo's striped pyjamas, Zandra Rhodes's ripped sari, Westwood's penis-embossed lingerie. This literalization of 'the look' is exemplified in the persistent use of fashion hierarchies to reflect class, status and conventionality, even when the mutual cannibalization of fashion from every position on the political spectrum continues as part of the sartorial cycle. For instance, when street stylists have lost the ability to shock, and the most audacious styles have become elements in mainstream costuming (such as the absorption of S&M fetish wear into haute couture, and the prevalence of cross-dressing on international fashion house catwalks), a belief still endures in the authenticity of appearances, and in the ability of the costumed body to speak and act contrarily as both a manifesto of rebellion and a mirror to convention.

To discern character or politics in appearances is not new. As modern societies eliminated sumptuary laws and rigid codes of dress, opportunities arose for individuals to construct or fashion themselves as they pleased. Such flexibility of self-representation, which has been a driving force in the rapid development of the fashion industries, is also a defining feature of modernity. The modern era is marked by constant innovation and the pursuit of novelty in technical, political, social and aesthetic arenas. By emphasizing the seductiveness of the new and deriding the past, fashion has become synonymous with the urban and the modern. Fashion is a means of acquiring multiple lives. It works best in a social climate saturated with commodities, each of which is infused with promises of new sensations and new opportunities. To subject fashion to instances of chic outrage, then, as the mass media is wont to do, is to limit its scope and overlook much of its political and social significance.

The Benetton fashion company fully understands the new consumer mood of politicized fashion in which individuals seek personal pleasure, psychological gratification and aesthetic rewards from their purchases. Benetton has introduced the idea that fashion spending can be part of a new political platform which is sympathetic to the ambitions of various eco-movements, as well as to liberal causes such as anti-racism, antisexism and those forms of local politics which advocate national pride and tribalism. Benetton has associated political correctness with consumer commodities by successfully blurring the boundaries between images of real social events and representations of a restructured and utopian world where Benetton's 'united colors' suggest a strengthened globalism (Giroux, 1993–4).

Fashion in the West has long been implicated in the formation of subjectivity and cultural values. It is often considered one of those social forces which keeps us ever attentive to the present in one of the worst possible ways; that is, as a source of novelty, distraction and self-absorption. Fashion seems to be about individuality, about standing out from the crowd. It seems to be about change, the constant unravelling of the new and the display of the inventive. But often its effect is the reverse: it can maintain the status quo and encourage conformity and uniformity. On closer examination, fashion is about turbulence and creating a sense of movement without pointing in any direction. As Renato Poggioli has stated,

the chief characteristic of fashion is to impose and suddenly to accept as a new
rule or norm what was, until a minute before, an exception or whim, then to
abandon it again after it has become a commonplace, everybody's 'thing'.
(Poggioli, 1968: 79)

Fashion has the effect of making an idea or commodity or aesthetic perspective into a seemingly inclusive category. Suddenly, everyone knows
and understands that this is the cutting edge, this is where the action is,
this is valuable. The apparent instantaneousness of fashion lends it an
attractive volatility. Fashion is regarded as the site where we come into
immediate contact with human creativity, for it signifies the intervention
of a dominating human mind. When fashion is dislodged from its material
foundations and recast as an aesthetic formation it can become a source of
self-administered individual satisfaction. At the same time, fashion has a
subaltern function which is so submerged and implicit that it comes as a
shock. As Poggioli astutely remarked – fashion is really about maintaining the eternal sameness, preserving the status quo; it is a quixotic gesture,
a con trick, a sleight of hand, which makes us think change is happening
when the opposite is closer to the truth. Poggioli's allusion to the rapid
turnover of the fashionable alerts us to this. Fashions are not about putting
into circulation the really new, because the genuine novelty cannot be
absorbed quickly into the cultural formations of everyday life. Fashion –
in its various guises as a practice, an industry and a social force – provides
no such opportunity for a full engagement with the new. Fashions are continuously being recycled, and new marketing strategies are constantly
being tried out to maintain the recycling impetus. The constancy of circulation, whether in ideas or material goods, indicates that the actual function of fashion may well have more to do with the appearance of change
and novelty without actually precipitating any ruptures to the status quo.
When these considerations are articulated simultaneously with popular
critiques of fashion events, then the full impact of being chic will be better
understood.

NOTES

I would like to acknowledge the generous support of the Arts Faculty, University
of Auckland, New Zealand, for providing a fellowship enabling this research.

1.   The example of commemoration is particularly poignant given that in any
      era it is a difficult gesture to make and especially so in the West in the late
      twentieth century, when many characterize the culture as anti-historical,
      even anti-memorial. Formal institutional responses from agencies with great
      investments in such gestures frequently struggle and fail to be effective in
      this endeavour. Perhaps we should ask if this is why organizations such as
      the entertainment industries get delivered the task.

REFERENCES

Ash, Juliet (1992) 'Philosophy on the Catwalk: The Making and Wearing of Vivienne Westwood's Clothes', pp. 167–85 in Elizabeth Wilson and Juliet Ash (eds) *Chic Thrills*. Berkeley: University of California Press.

Barthes, Roland (1985) *The Fashion System*. New York: Jonathan Cape (originally published 1967).

Butler, Judith (1993) *Bodies that Matter: On the Discursive Limits of 'Sex'*. New York: Routledge.

Cixous, Hélène (1994) 'Sonia Rykiel in Translation', pp. 95–9 in Shari Benstock and Suzanne Ferriss (eds) *On Fashion*. New Brunswick, NJ: Rutgers University Press.

Evans, Caroline and Minna Thornton (1989) *Women and Fashion*. London: Quartet.

Finkelstein, Joanne (1991) *The Fashioned Self*. Oxford: Polity Press.

Foucault, Michel (1977) *Discipline and Punish*. London: Allen Lane.

Garber, Marjorie (1992) *Vested Interests: Cross-Dressing and Cultural Anxiety*. New York: Routledge, Chapman and Hall.

Giroux, Henry (1993–4) 'Consuming Social Change: The "United Colors of Benetton"', *Cultural Critique* Winter: 5–32.

Griggers, Cathy (1990) 'A Certain Tension in the Visual/Cultural Field: Helmut Newton, Deborah Turbeville and the *Vogue* Fashion Layout', *differences* 2(2): 76–104.

Hebdige, Dick (1993) 'A Report from the Western Front: Postmodernism and the "Politics" of Style', pp. 69–103 in Chris Jenks (ed.) *Cultural Reproduction*. New York: Routledge.

Hume, Marion (1995) 'Fashion: A History of Controversy on the Catwalk', *The Independent* 10 February.

Jameson, Fredric (1990) *Postmodernism, or The Cultural Logic of Late Capitalism*. Durham, NC: Duke University Press.

Leaska, Mitchell and John Phillips (1989) *Violet to Vita: The Letters of Violet Trefusis to Vita Sackville-West 1910–21*. London: Methuen.

Lipovetsky, Gilles (1994) *The Empire of Fashion: Dressing Modern Democracy*, translated by Catherine Porter. Princeton, NJ: Princeton University Press (originally published in 1987).

Livingston, Jennie (1990) *Paris is Burning*. New York: Premium Films.

Luck, Kate (1992) 'Trouble in Eden, Trouble with Eve', pp. 200–12 in Elizabeth Wilson and Juliet Ash (eds) *Chic Thrills*. Berkeley: University of California Press.

Poggioli, Renato (1968) *The Theory of the Avant-Garde*. Cambridge, MA: Belknap (originally published in 1962).

Polhemus, Ted (1994) *Streetstyle: From Sidewalk to Catwalk*. London: Thames and Hudson.

Rabine, Leslie (1994) 'A Woman's Two Bodies: Fashion Magazines, Consumerism, and Feminism', pp. 59–75 in Shari Benstock and Suzanne Ferriss (eds) *On Fashion*. New Brunswick, NJ: Rutgers University Press.

Rolley, Katrina (1990) 'Cutting a Dash: The Dress of Radclyffe Hall and Una Troubridge', *Feminist Review* 35: 54–66.

Rolley, Katrina (1992) 'Love, Desire and the Pursuit of the Whole: Dress and the Lesbian Couple', pp. 30–9 in Elizabeth Wilson and Juliet Ash (eds) *Chic Thrills*. Berkeley: University of California Press.

Ross, Andrew (1994) 'Tribalism in Effect' pp. 284–99 in Shari Benstock and Suzanne Ferriss (eds) *On Fashion*. New Brunswick, NJ: Rutgers University Press.

Rykiel, Sonia (1994) 'From *Celebration*', pp. 100–8 in Shari Benstock and Suzanne Ferriss (eds) *On Fashion*. New Brunswick, NJ: Rutgers University Press.

Silverman, Kaja (1986) 'Fragments of a Fashionable Discourse', pp. 139–52 in Tania

Modleski (ed.) *Studies in Entertainment: Critical Approaches to Mass Culture.* Bloomington: University of Indiana Press.

Wilson, Elizabeth and Juliet Ash (eds) (1992) *Chic Thrills*. Berkeley: University of California Press.

Yanowich, Lee (1995a) 'Designer Withdraws Pyjamas after Jews Protest', *Reuter News Service* 7 February.

Yanowich, Lee (1995b) 'Pyjama Gaffe Shakes Fashion World into Reality', *Reuter News Service* 20 February.

11   'My Body is My Art'

Cosmetic Surgery as Feminist Utopia?

Kathy Davis

In August 1995, the French performance artist Orlan was invited to give a lecture at a multimedia festival in Amsterdam.[1] Orlan has caused considerable furore in the international art world in recent years for her radical body art in which she has her face surgically refashioned before the camera. On this particular occasion, the artist read a statement about her art while images of one of her operations flashed on the screen behind her. The audience watched as the surgeon inserted needles into her face, sliced open her lips, and, most gruesomely of all, severed her ear from the rest of her face with his scalpel. While Orlan appeared to be unmoved by these images, the audience was clearly shocked. Agitated whispers could be heard and several people left the room. Obviously irritated, Orlan interrupted her lecture and asked whether it was 'absolutely necessary to talk about the pictures *now*' or whether she could proceed with her talk. Finally one young woman stood up and exclaimed: 'You act as though it were not *you*, up there on the screen'.[2]

This may seem like a somewhat naive reaction. Good art is, after all, about shifting our perceptions and opening up new vistas. That this causes the audience some unease goes without saying. Moreover, the young woman's reaction is not directed at Orlan the artist who is explaining her art, but rather at Orlan the woman who has had painful surgery. Here is a woman whose face has been mutilated and yet discusses it intellectually and dispassionately. The audience is squirming and Orlan is acting as though she were not directly involved.

I became interested in Orlan (and the reactions she evokes) as a result of my own research on women's involvement in cosmetic surgery (Davis, 1995). Like many feminists, I was deeply troubled by the fact that so many women willingly and enthusiastically have their bodies altered surgically despite considerable hardship and risk to themselves. While I shared the commonly held feminist view that cosmetic surgery represented one of the more pernicious horrors inflicted by the medical system upon women's bodies, I disliked the concomitant tendency among feminists to treat the recipients as nothing more than misguided or deluded victims. In an attempt to provide a critical analysis of cosmetic surgery which did not undermine the women who saw it as their best option under the circumstances, I conducted in-depth interviews with with women who had had or were planning to have some form of cosmetic surgery. They had undergone everything from a relatively simple ear correction or a breast augmentation to – in the most extreme case – having the entire face reconstructed. Since the research was conducted in the Netherlands where cosmetic surgery was included in the national health care package, my informants came from diverse socioeconomic backgrounds. Some were professional women or academics, others were cashiers or home-helps and some were full-time housewives and mothers. Some were married, some single, some heterosexual, some lesbian. They ranged in age from a 17-year-old school girl whose mother took her in for a breast augmentation, to a successful, middle-aged business woman seeking a face lift in order to 'fit into the corporate culture'.

These women told me about their history of suffering because of their appearance, how they decided to have their bodies altered surgically, their experiences with the operation itself and their assessments of the outcome of the surgery. While their stories involved highly varied experiences of embodiment as well as different routes towards deciding to have their bodies altered surgically, they invariably made cosmetic surgery viewable as an understandable and even unavoidable course of action in light of their particular biographical circumstances. I learned of their despair, not because their bodies were not beautiful, but because they were not ordi-nary – 'just like everyone else'. I listened to their accounts of how they struggled with the decision to have cosmetic surgery, weighing their anxieties about risks against the anticipated benefits of the surgery. I dis-covered that they were often highly ambivalent about cosmetic surgery and wrestled with the same dilemmas which have made cosmetic surgery problematic for many feminists. My research gave a central role to women's agency, underlining their active and lived relationship with their bodies and showing how they could knowledgeably choose to have cos-metic surgery. While I remained critical of the practice of cosmetic surgery and the discourse of feminine inferiority which it sustains, I did not reject it as an absolute evil, to be avoided at any cost. Instead I argued for viewing cosmetic surgery as a complex dilemma: problem and solution, symptom of oppression and act of empowerment, all in one.

Given my research on cosmetic surgery, I was obviously intrigued by Orlan's surgical experiments. While I was fascinated by her willingness to put her body under the knife, however, I did not immediately see what her project had to offer for understanding why 'ordinary' women have cosmetic surgery. On the contrary, I placed Orlan alongside other con-temporary women artists who use their bodies to make radical state-ments about a male-dominated social world: Cindy Sherman's inflatable porno dolls with their gaping orifices, Bettina Rheim's naked women in their exaggerated sexual posings, or Matuschka's self-portraits of her body after her breast has been amputated. It came as a surprise, therefore, when my research was continually being linked to Orlan's project.

Friends and colleagues sent me clippings about Orlan. At lectures about my work, I was invariably asked what I thought about Orlan. Journalists juxtaposed interviews with me and Orlan for their radio programmes or discussed us in the same breath in their newspaper pieces. Our projects were cited as similar in their celebration of women's agency and our insistence that cosmetic surgery was about more than beauty.[3] We were both described as feminists who had gone against the feminist mainstream and dared to be politically incorrect. By exploring the empowering possibilities of cosmetic surgery, we were viewed as representatives of a more nuanced and – some would say – refreshing perspective on cosmetic surgery.

These reactions have increasingly led me to reconsider my initial belief that Orlan's surgical experiments have nothing to do with the experiences of women who have cosmetic surgery. In particular, two questions have begun to occupy my attention. The first is to what extent Orlan's aims coincide with my own; that is, to provide a feminist critique of the technologies and practices of the feminine beauty system while taking women who have cosmetic surgery seriously. The second is whether Orlan's project can provide insight into the motives of the run-of-the-mill cosmetic surgery recipient.

In this article, I am going to begin with this second question. After looking at Orlan's performances as well as how she justifies them, I consider the possible similarities between her surgical experiences and the surgical experiences of the women I spoke with. I then return to the first question and consider the status of Orlan's art as feminist critique of cosmetic surgery – that is, as a utopian revisioning of a future where women reappropriate cosmetic surgery for their own ends. In conclusion, I argue that – when all is said and done – surgical utopias may be better left to art than to feminist critique.

ORLAN'S BODY ART

Orlan came of age in the 1960s – the era of the student uprisings in Paris, the 'sexual revolution' and the emergence of populist street theatre. As visual artist, she has always used her own body in unconventional ways to challenge gender stereotypes, defy religion and, more generally, to shock her audience (Lovelace, 1995). For example, in the 1960s, she displayed the sheets of her bridal trousseau stained with semen to document her various sexual encounters, thereby poking fun at the demands for virgin brides in France. In the 1970s, she went to the Louvre with a small audience and pasted a triangle of her own pubic hair to the voluptuously reclining nude depicted in the *Rape of Antiope* – a hairless body devoid of subjecthood, a mere object for consumption. In the 1980s, Orlan shocked Parisian audiences by displaying her magnified genitals, held open by means of pincers, with the pubic hair painted yellow, blue and red (the red was menstrual blood). A video camera was installed to record the faces of her viewers who were then given a text by Freud on castration anxiety.

Her present project in which she uses surgery as a performance is, by far, her most radical and outrageous. She devised a computer-synthesized ideal self-portrait based on features taken from women in famous works of art: the forehead of Da Vinci's *Mona Lisa*, the chin of Botticelli's *Venus*, the nose of Fountainebleau's *Diana*, the eyes of Gérard's *Psyche* and the mouth of Boucher's *Europa*. She did not choose her models for their beauty, but rather for the stories which are associated with them. Mona Lisa represents transsexuality for beneath the woman is – as we now know – the hidden self-portrait of the artist Leonardo Da Vinci; Diana is the aggressive adventuress; Europa gazes with anticipation at an uncertain future on another continent; Psyche incorporates love and spiritual hunger; and Venus represents fertility and creativity.

Orlan's 'self-portraits' are not created at the easel, but on the operating table. The first took place on 30 May 1987 – the artist's 40th birthday and eight more have taken place since then. Each operation is a 'happening'. The operating theatre is decorated with colourful props and larger-than-life representations of the artist and her muses. Male striptease dancers perform to music. The surgeons and nurses wear costumes by top designers and Orlan herself appears in net stockings and party hat with one breast exposed. She kisses the surgeon ostentatiously on the mouth before lying down on the operating table. Each performance has a theme (like 'Carnal Art', 'This is My Body, This is My Software', 'I Have Given My Body to Art', 'Identity Alterity'). Orlan reads philosophical, literary or psychoanalytic texts while being operated on under local anaesthesia. Her mood is playful and she talks animatedly even while her face is being jabbed with needles or cut ('producing', as she puts it, 'the image of a cadaver under autopsy which just keeps speaking').[4]

All of the operations have been filmed. The seventh operation-performance in 1993 was transmitted live by satellite to galleries around the world (the theme was omnipresence) where specialists were able to watch the operation and ask questions which Orlan then answered 'live' during the performance. In between operations, Orlan speaks about her work at conferences and festivals throughout the world where she also shows photographs and video clips of her operations. Under the motto 'my body is my art', she has collected souvenirs from her operations and stored them in circular, plexi-glass receptacles which are on display in her studio in Ivry, France. These 'reliquaries' include pieces of her flesh preserved in liquid, sections of her scalp with hair still attached, fat cells which have been suctioned out of her face, or crumpled bits of surgical gauze drenched in her blood. She sells them for as much as 10,000 francs, intending to continue until she has 'no more flesh to sell'.

Orlan's performances require a strong stomach and her audiences have been known to walk out midway through the video. The confrontation of watching the artist direct the cutting up of her own body is just too much

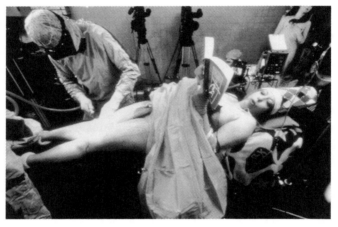

FIGURE 1
'Before'

for many people to bear. Reactions range from irritation to – in Vienna –
a viewer fainting.[5] While Orlan begins her performances by apologizing
to her audience for causing them pain, this is precisely her intention. As
she puts it, art has to be transgressive, disruptive and unpleasant in order
to have a social function. ('Art is not for decorating apartments, for we
already have plenty of that with aquariums, plants, carpets, curtains,
furniture. . .').[6] Both artist and audience need to feel uncomfortable so that
'we will be forced to ask questions'.

For Orlan, the most important question concerns 'the status of the body
in our society and its future . . . in terms of the new technologies'.[7] The
body has traditionally been associated with the innate, the immutable, the
god given or the fated-ness of human life. Within modernist science, the
body has been treated as the biological bedrock of theories on self and
society – the 'only constant in a rapidly changing world' (Frank, 1990: 133).
In recent years, this view has become increasingly untenable. The body –

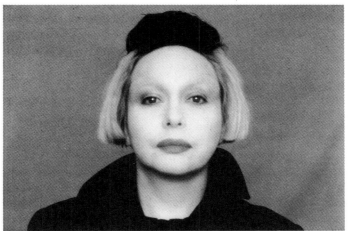

Figure 2
'After'

as well as our beliefs about it – is subject to enormous variation, both within and between cultures. Postmodern thinkers have rejected the notion of a biological body in favour of viewing bodies as social constructions. Orlan's project takes the postmodern deconstruction of the material body a step further. In her view, modern technologies have made any notion of a natural body obsolete. Test-tube babies, genetic manipulation and cosmetic surgery enable us to intervene in nature and develop our capacities in accordance with our needs and desires. In the future, bodies will become increasingly insignificant – nothing more than a 'costume', a 'vehicle', something to be changed in our search 'to become who we are'.[8]

The body of which Orlan speaks is a female body. Whereas her earlier work explored gender stereotypes in historical representations of the female body, her present project examines the social pressures which are exercised upon women through their bodies – in particular, the cultural beauty norms. At first glance, this may seem contradictory, since the goal of her art is to achieve an 'ideal' face. Although she draws upon mythical beauties for inspiration, she does not want to resemble them. Nor is she particularly concerned with being beautiful. Her operations have left her considerably less beautiful than she was before. For example, in operation seven she had silicone implants inserted in her temples (the forehead of Mona Lisa), giving her a slightly extraterrestrial appearance. For her next and last operation, she has planned 'the biggest nose physically possible' – a nose which will begin midway up her forehead. Thus, while Orlan's face is an ideal one, it deviates radically from the masculinist ideal of feminine perfection. Her ideal is radically non-conformist. It does not make us aware of what we lack. When we look at Orlan, we are reminded that we can use our imagination to become the persons we want to be.

Orlan's project explores the problem of identity. Who she is, is in constant flux or, as she puts it, 'by wanting to become another, I become myself'. 'I am a bulldozer: dominant and aggressive . . . but if that becomes fixed it is a handicap . . . I, therefore, renew myself by becoming timid and tender. . .'.[9] Her identity project is radical precisely because she is willing to alter her body surgically in order to experiment with different identities. What happens to the notion of 'race', she wonders, if I shed my white skin for a black one?[10] Similarly, she rejects gender as a fixed category when she claims: 'I am a woman-to-woman transsexual act'. However, Orlan's surgical transformations – unlike a sex-change operation – are far from permanent. In this sense, Orlan's art can be viewed as a contribution to postmodern feminist theory on identity.[11] Her face resembles Haraway's (1991) cyborg – half-human, half-machine – which implodes the notion of the natural body. Her project represents the postmodern celebration of identity as fragmented, multiple and – above all – fluctuating and her performances resonate with the radical social constructionism of Butler (1990, 1993) and her celebration of the transgressive potential of such performativity.

For Orlan, plastic surgery is a path towards self-determination – a way for women to regain control over their bodies. Plastic surgery is one of the primary arenas where 'man's power can be most powerfully asserted on women's bodies', 'where the dictates of the dominant ideology . . . become . . . more deeply embedded in female . . . flesh'.[12] Instead of having her body rejuvenated or beautified, she turns the tables and uses surgery as a medium for a different project. For example, when Orlan's male plastic surgeons balked at having to make her too ugly ('they wanted to keep me cute'), she turned to a female feminist plastic surgeon who was prepared to carry out her wishes. The surgical performances themselves are set up to dispel the notion of a sick body, 'just an inert piece of meat, lying on the table'.[13] Orlan designs her body, orchestrates the operations and makes the final decision about when to stop and when to go on. Throughout the surgery, she talks, gesticulates and laughs. This is her party and the only constraint is that she remain in charge. Thus, while bone breaking might be desirable (she originally wanted to have longer legs), it had to be rejected because it would have required full anaesthesia and, therefore, have defeated the whole purpose of the project. Orlan has to be the creator, not just the creation; the one who decides and not the passive object of another's decisions.

ART AND LIFE

I now want to return to the issue which I raised at the outset of this article: namely, the puzzling fact that my research is continually being associated with Orlan's art. As one journalist noted after reading my book: the only difference between Orlan and the majority of women who have cosmetic surgery is one of degree. Orlan is just an extreme example of what is basically the same phenomenon: women who have cosmetic surgery want to be 'their own Pygmalions'.[14]

At first glance, there are, indeed, similarities between Orlan's statements about her art and how the women I interviewed described their reasons for having cosmetic surgery. For example, both Orlan and these women insisted that they did not have cosmetic surgery to become more beautiful. They had cosmetic surgery because they did not feel at home in their bodies; their bodies did not fit their sense of who they were. Cosmetic surgery was an intervention in identity. It enabled them to reduce the distance between the internal and external so that others could see them as they saw themselves.[15] Another similarity is that both Orlan and the women I spoke with viewed themselves as agents who, by remaking their bodies, remade their lives as well. They all rejected the notion that by having cosmetic surgery, they had allowed themselves to be coerced, normalized or ideologically manipulated. On the contrary, cosmetic surgery was a way for them to take control over circumstances over which they previously had had no control. Like Orlan, these women even regarded their decision to have cosmetic surgery as an oppositional act: something they did for themselves, often at great risk and in the face of considerable resistance from others.

However, this is where the similarities end. Orlan's project is not about a real-life problem; it is about art. She does not use cosmetic surgery to alleviate suffering with her body, but rather to make a public and highly abstract statement about beauty, identity and agency. Her body is little more than a vehicle for her art and her personal feelings are entirely irrelevant. When asked about the pain she must be experiencing, she merely shrugs and says: 'Art is a dirty job, but someone has to do it.'[16] Orlan is a woman with a mission: she wants to shock, disrupt convention and provoke people into discussing taboo issues. 'Art can and must change the world, for that is its only justification.'[17]

This is very different from the reasons the women I spoke with gave for having cosmetic surgery. Their project is a very private and personal one. They want to eliminate suffering which has gone beyond what they feel they should have to endure. They are anxious about the pain of surgery and worried about the outcome. They prefer secrecy to publicity and have no desire to confront others with their decisions. While their explanations touch on issues like beauty, identity and agency (although not necessarily using those words), they are always linked to their experiences and their particular life histories. Their justification for having cosmetic surgery is necessity. It is the lesser of two evils, their only option under the circumstances. They do not care at all about changing the world; they simply want to change themselves.

Thus, cosmetic surgery as art and cosmetic surgery in life appear to be very different phenomena. I, therefore, might conclude that there is little resemblance between Orlan's surgical experiences and those of most women who have cosmetic surgery, after all. Orlan's celebration of surgical technologies seems to have little in common with a project like my own, which aims to provide a feminist critique of cosmetic surgery. Consequently, comparisons between my research and Orlan's project can only be regarded as superficial or premature.

But perhaps this conclusion is overhasty. After all, it was never Orlan's intention to understand the surgical experiences of 'ordinary' women. Nor is it her intention to provide a feminist polemic against the unimaginable lengths to which women will go to achieve an ideal of beauty as defined by men. Hers is not a sociological analysis which explicitly attacks the evils of cosmetic surgery and its pernicious effects on women (Lovelace, 1995). Nevertheless, her project is an implicit critique of the dominant norms of beauty and the way cosmetic surgery is practised today. It belongs to the tradition of feminist critique which imaginatively explores the possibilities of modern technology for the empowerment of women. As such, Orlan's project might be viewed as an example of a feminist utopia.

COSMETIC SURGERY AS FEMINIST UTOPIA

Feminists have often envisioned a future where technology has been seized by women for their own ends. Take, for example, Shulamith Firestone's *Dialectic of Sex* (1970) in which she fantasizes a world in which reproductive technology frees women from the chores and constraints of biological motherhood. In a similar vein, the novelist Marge Piercy depicts a feminist utopia in *Woman on the Edge of Time* (1976) where genetic engineering has erased sexual and 'racial' differences, thereby abolishing sexism and racism.[18]

More recently, the feminist philosopher Kathryn Morgan (1991) applies the notion of utopia to cosmetic surgery. She claims that refusal may not be the only feminist response to the troubling problem of women's determination to put themselves under the knife for the sake of beauty. There may, in fact, be a more radical way for feminists to tackle the 'technological beauty imperative'.

She puts forth what she calls 'a utopian response to cosmetic surgery': that is, an imaginary model which represents a desirable ideal that because of its radicality is unlikely to occur on a wide scale (Morgan, 1991: 47). Drawing upon feminist street theatre, on the one hand, and postmodern feminist theory – most notably Judith Butler's (1990) notion of gender as performance – on the other, Morgan provides some imaginative, if somewhat ghoulish, examples of cosmetic surgery as feminist utopia.

For example, she envisions alternative 'Miss . . .' pageants where the contestants compete for the title 'Ms Ugly'. They bleach their hair white, apply wrinkle-*inducing* creams or have wrinkles *carved into* their faces, have their breasts pulled *down* and *darken* their skin. (Morgan, 1991: 46). Or, she imagines 'beautiful body boutiques' where 'freeze-dried fat cells', 'skin velcro', magnetically attachable breasts complete with nipple pumps, and do-it-yourself sewing kits with pain-killers and needles are sold to interested customers.

These 'performances' can be characterized as a feminist critique of cosmetic surgery for several reasons.

First, they unmask both 'beauty' and 'ugliness' as cultural artefacts rather than natural properties of the female body. They valorize what is normally perceived as ugly, thereby upsetting the cultural constraints upon women to comply with the norms of beauty. By actually undergoing mutations of the flesh, the entire notion of a natural body – that linchpin of gender ideology – is destabilized.

Second, these surgical performances constitute women as subjects who use their feminine body as a site for action and protest rather than as an object of discipline and normalization. These parodies mock or mimic what is ordinarily a source of shame, guilt or alienation for women. Unlike the 'typical' feminine disorders (anorexia, agoraphobia or hysteria) which are forms of protest where women are victims, Morgan's actions require '*healthy*' (*sic*) women who already 'have a feminist understanding of cosmetic surgery' (Morgan, 1991: 45).

Third, by providing a travesty of surgical technologies and procedures, these performances magnify the role that technology plays in constructing femininity through women's bodies. At the same time, they usurp men's control over these technologies and undermine the power dynamic which makes women dependent on male expertise (Morgan, 1991: 47). Performances show how technology might be reappropriated for feminist ends.

Morgan acknowledges that her surgical utopias may make her readers a bit queasy or even cause offence. However, this is as it should be. It only shows that we are still in the thrall of the cultural dictates of beauty and cannot bear to imagine women's bodies as ugly. Anyone who feels that such visions go 'too far' must remind herself that she has merely become anaesthetized to the mutilations which are routinely performed on women by surgeons every day (Morgan 1991: 46–7). Where the 'surgical fix' is concerned, 'shock therapy' is the only solution.

DOES COSMETIC SURGERY CALL FOR A UTOPIAN RESPONSE?

The attractions of a utopian approach to cosmetic surgery are considerable. It enables feminists to take a stand against the cultural constraints upon women to be beautiful and dramatically exposes the excesses of the technological fix. It destabilizes many of our preconceived notions about beauty, identity and the female body and it provides a glimpse of how women might engage with their bodies in empowering ways. However, most important of all – and I believe this is why such approaches appeal to the feminist imagination – it promises the best of both worlds: a chance to be critical of the victimization of women without having to be victims ourselves.

While I am entertained and intrigued by the visions put forth by Morgan and enacted by Orlan, I must admit that they also make me feel profoundly uneasy. This unease has everything to do with my own research on cosmetic surgery. On the basis of what women have told me, I would argue that a utopian response to cosmetic surgery does not just open up radical avenues for feminist critique; it also limits and may even prevent this same critique. It is my contention that there are, at least, four drawbacks.

First, a utopian response discounts the suffering which accompanies any cosmetic surgery operation. One of the most shocking aspects of Orlan's performances is that she undergoes surgery which is clearly painful and yet shrugs off the pain ('Of course, there are several injections and several grimaces . . . but I just take painkillers like everyone else')[19] or explains that the audience feels more pain looking at the surgery than she does in undergoing it. ('Sorry to have made you suffer, but know that I do not suffer, unlike you . . .').[20] This nonchalance is belied by the postoperative faces of the artist – proceeding from swollen and discoloured to, several months later, pale and scarred. Whether a woman has her wrinkles smoothed out surgically or carved in has little effect on the pain she feels during the surgery. Such models, therefore, presuppose a non-sentient female body – a body which feels no pain.[21]

Second, a utopian response discounts the risks of cosmetic surgery. Technologies are presented as neutral instruments which can be deployed to feminist ends. Both Orlan and Morgan describe surgery as conceived, controlled and orchestrated by the autonomous feminine subject. She has the reins in her hand. However, even Orlan has had a 'failed' operation: one of her silicone implants wandered and had to be reinserted – this time, not in front of the video camera. Such models overstate the possibilities of modern technology and diminish its limitations.

Third, a utopian response ignores women's suffering with their appearance. The visions presented by both Orlan and Morgan involve women who are clearly unaffected by the crippling constraints of femininity. They are not dissatisfied with their appearance as most women are; nor, indeed, do they seem to care what happens to their bodies at all. For women who have spent years hating their excess flesh or disciplining their bodies with drastic diets, killing fitness programmes or cosmetic surgery, the image of 'injecting fat cells' or having the breasts 'pulled down' is insulting. The choice of 'darkened skin' for a feminist spectacle which aims to 'valorize the ugly' is unlikely to go down well with women of colour. At best, such models negate their pain. At worst, they treat women who care about their appearance as the unenlightened prisoners of the beauty system who are more 'culturally scripted' than their artistic sisters.

Fourth, a utopian response discounts the everyday acts of compliance and resistance which are part of ordinary women's involvement in cosmetic surgery. The surgical experiments put forth by Orlan and Morgan have the pretension of being revolutionary. In engaging in acts which are extraordinary and shocking, they not only entertain and disturb, but also distance us from the more mundane forms of protest.[22] It is difficult to imagine that cosmetic surgery might entail *both* compliance *and* resistance. The act of having cosmetic surgery involves going along with the dictates of the beauty system, but also refusal – refusal to suffer beyond a certain point. Utopian models privilege the flamboyant, public spectacle as feminist intervention and deprivilege the interventions which are part of living in a gendered social order.

In conclusion, I would like to return to the young woman I mentioned at the beginning of this chapter. At first glance, her reaction might be attributed to her failure to appreciate the radicality of Orlan's project. She is apparently unable to go beyond her initial, 'gut level' response of horror at the pictures and consider what Orlan's performances have to say in general about the status of the female body in a technological age. She is just not sophisticated enough to benefit from this particular form of feminist 'shock therapy'.

However, having explored the 'ins' and 'outs' of surgical utopias, I am not convinced that this is how we should interpret her reaction. Her refusal to take up Orlan's invitation may also be attributed to concern. She may feel concern for the pale woman before her whose face still bears the painful marks of her previous operations. Or she may be concerned that anyone can talk so abstractly and without emotion about something which is so visibly personal and painful. Or she may simply be concerned that in order to appreciate art, she is being required to dismiss her own feelings.

Her concern reminds us of what Orlan and, indeed, any utopian approach to cosmetic surgery leaves out: the sentient and embodied female subject, the one who feels concern about herself and about others. As feminists in search of a radical response to women's involvement in cosmetic surgery, we would do well to be concerned about this omission as well.

NOTES

1. This festival was organized by Triple X which puts on an annual exhibition including theatre, performance, music, dance and visual art. I would like to thank Peter van der Hoop for supplying me with information about Orlan. I am indebted to Willem de Haan, Suzanne Phibbs and the participants of the postgraduate seminar 'Gender, Body, Love', held at the Centre for Women's Research in Oslo, Norway in May 1996 for their constructive and insightful comments.
2. *De Groene Amsterdammer* (23 August 1995).
3. See, for example, a recent article by Xandra Schutte in *De Groene Amsterdammer* (13 December 1995) or 'Passages and Passanten' (VPRO Radio 5, 17 November 1995).
4. Quoted in Reitmaier (1995: 8).
5. *Falter* (1995, No. 49: 28).
6. Quoted in Reitmaier (1995: 7).
7. See Reitmaier (1995: 8).
8. Quoted in Tilroe (1996: 17).
9. *Actuel* (January 1991: 78).
10. Obviously, Orlan has not read John Howard Griffin's (1961) *Black Like Me* in which a white man chronicles his experiences of darkening his skin in order to gain access to African-American life in the mid-1950s. For him, becoming the racial Other was a way to understand the material and bodily effects of racism – an experiment which was anything but playful and ultimately resulted in the author's untimely death from skin cancer. See Awkward (1995) for an excellent discussion of such experiments from a postmodern ethnographic perspective.
11. While Orlan has been cited as a model for postmodern feminist critiques of identity, her project is, in some ways, antithetical to this critique. She celebrates a notion of the sovereign, autonomous subject in search of self which is much more in line with Sartre's existentialism than poststructuralist theory à la Butler. See, for example, the debate between Butler and others in Benhabib et al. (1995).
12. Quoted in Reitmaier (1995: 9).
13. *De Volkskrant* (5 June 1993).
14. *De Groene Amsterdammer* (13 December 1995: 29).
15. Quoted in Reitmaier (1995: 8).
16. Quoted in Reitmaier (1995: 10).
17. Quoted in Reitmaier (1995: 7).
18. See José van Dyck (1995) for an excellent analysis of feminist utopias (and dystopias) in debates on the new reproductive technologies.
19. Quoted in Reitmaier (1995: 10).
20. Statement given at performance in Amsterdam.
21. This harks back to the notion that women – particularly working-class women and women of colour – do not experience pain to the same degree that affluent, white women and men do. This notion justified considerable surgical experimentation on women in the last century. See, for example, Dally (1991).

22. It could be argued that in the context of the art business where success depends upon being extraordinary, Orlan is simply complying with convention. This would make her no more, but also no less, revolutionary than any other woman who embarks upon cosmetic surgery.

REFERENCES

Awkward, Michael (1995) *Negotiating Difference. Race, Gender, and the Politics of Positionality*. Chicago and London: The University of Chicago Press.
Benhabib, Seyla, Judith Butler, Drucilla Cornell and Nancy Fraser (1995) *Feminist Contentions. A Philosophical Exchange*. New York and London: Routledge.
Butler, Judith (1990) *Gender Trouble: Feminism and the Subversion of Identity*. New York: Routledge.
Butler, Judith (1993) *Bodies that Matter. On the Discursive Limits of 'Sex'*. New York: Routledge.
Dally, Ann (1991) *Women Under the Knife*. London: Hutchinson Radius.
Davis, Kathy (1995) *Reshaping the Female Body. The Dilemma of Cosmetic Surgery*. New York: Routledge.
Firestone, Shulamith (1970) *The Dialectic of Sex. The Case for Feminist Revolution*. New York: Bantam.
Frank, Arthur (1990) 'Bringing Bodies Back In: A Decade Review', *Theory, Culture and Society* 7: 131–62.
Griffin, John Howard (1961) *Black Like Me*. New York: Signet.
Haraway, Donna J. (1991) *Simians, Cyborgs, and Women. The Reinvention of Nature*. London: Free Association Books.
Lovelace, Cary (1995) 'Orlan: Offensive Acts', *Performing Arts Journal* 49: 13–25.
Morgan, Kathryn Pauly (1991) 'Women and the Knife: Cosmetic Surgery and the Colonization of Women's Bodies', *Hypatia* 6(3): 25–53.
Piercy, Marge (1976) *Woman on the Edge of Time*. New York: Fawcett Crest.
Reitmaier, Heidi (1995) ' "I Do Not Want to Look Like . . ." Orlan on becoming-Orlan', *Women's Art* 5 June: 5–10.
Tilroe, Anna (1996) *De huid van de kameleon. Over hedendaagse beeldende kunst*. Amsterdam: Querido.
Van Dyck, José (1995) *Manufacturing Babies and Public Consent*. London: Macmillan.

12　The Researching Body

The Epistemophilic Project

Monica Rudberg

The critical attack on positivism from the 1960s onwards also laid the foundation for a deconstruction of the abstract – unsituated and disembodied – rationality which characterized the scientific ethos of the times (see Merton, 1949, cited in Mitroff, 1974). To point to the fact that it is impossible *not* to interact with your data – that the researcher is always a participant – does in fact imply a situated body: *who* is speaking here and from which *standpoint* do you speak? However, it was in many ways a rebellion *within* a disembodied philosophical discourse – where the body was still lingering in the prediscursive 'wings of social order' (Morgan and Scott, 1993: 2). And even though the body seems to be the topic of the day, the embodied experience of the researcher has not often been in focus. The self-reflexive strand of postpositivist methodology, where researchers are told to take their 'selves' into account not only as bias but even more as resource of empirical research, has not resulted in a particularly great interest in the bodily anchorage of all those free-floating selves.[1]

In this article I connect the desire for knowledge to the body, a connection that in my view often makes the research process into both such a passionate and frustrating affair – a sort of epistemophilic project. It is this passion that the scientific ethos, stressing emotional neutrality and disinterestedness, tries to keep in check. 'Epistemophilia' is originally a Freudian term, where the human urge to gain knowledge (*Wisstrieb*) is associated with the child's sexual curiosity (Freud, 1923). The American scholar Peter Brooks (1993) makes use of this term in his illuminating analysis of the body as object of desire in modern narrative. As he points out, the body is the obvious point of departure for any processes of knowing. The fundamental prerequisite for symbolization is found in the earliest experiences of the infant: its experience of its body in relation to the body of the mother; its experience of spacial orientation; its first efforts to gain bodily equilibrium. This is of course not only a cognitive accomplishment, but a process full of infantile desire. However, although this symbolization is driven *by* the body, it also alienates us *from* the body. The sign is not identical with the signified, the body is always absent even when it is incessantly talked about. This alienation will make us even more obsessed with explicating and making sense of the body, putting it into discourse. Thus, knowing is connected with the body in two ways: the body is the departing point for all our knowledge, as well as the great secret to be discovered; the epistemophilic project is propelled by bodily desire with the ultimate aim to know the body itself.

Traditionally the epistemophilic project has been associated with masculine subjectivity. The gendered character of science has for a long time been the target of important feminist critique (see Keller, 1986; Harding, 1986), but the body has to my knowledge not very often been the focus of these discussions. My intention here is therefore to analyse the researching process in light of a gender-specific *bodily* history, which in my view is important in order to understand both the passions implicated and the disciplining of these passions. The analysis is divided into three main parts: in the first part of the article, the epistemophilic project will be illustrated with an impressionistic analysis of three pictures of 'textbook bodies'. Although the choice of these pictures might seem a bit arbitrary to the reader, they are in fact important reasons for my writing this article, as those pictures, contrary to textbooks in general, had a great emotional impact on me in my student days. Second, the 'male' version of the epistemophilic project is explored through the reading of Mary Shelley's *Frankenstein*, a fictional character that illuminates the gendered passions involved in an exemplary manner. Through this story we can follow the research process step by step, from the first stirring urges of knowledge all the way to the horrid revenge of the monstrous research product – a process which seems especially significant today, as the fiftieth anniversary of Hiroshima coincides with French nuclear bombs in the colonies. However, today the academic world has lost the sexual homogeneity that made this male story into a sort of self-evident prerequisite for research. Maybe this implies that the epistemophilic project itself will change as women, who once were the more or less monstrous objects of this project, suddenly become active researching bodies in their own right. In the final part of the article I make a few suggestions as to how such a 'female' version of the epistemophilic project might be understood as both the same as and different from the one that led to Frankenstein's destruction.

TEXTBOOK BODIES

The feeling of boredom was often acute during my years as a student in psychology, as I waded through the pages of the introductory textbooks. The fact that others (men) seemed to be passionately involved in this kind of fragmented, cool, disembodied research never ceased to puzzle me. Nevertheless, there were some parts of the textbooks that really made an impression, namely exactly three pictures portraying bodies in different contexts. These were concrete pictures of material people, telling moving stories about the difficult conditions of the subject in search of knowledge, and I could definitely relate to that.

In the textbook of social psychology, *Individual in Society* (Krech et al., 1962: 510–11) we are presented with the picture of a deceived college student in the conformity experiments of Salomon Asch, where all the other participants are in cahoots with the investigator (the task is to match lines – and the majority are instructed to give evidently wrong answers). One of the deceived young men describes his 'inner conflict' in this way: 'I felt disturbed, puzzled, separated, like an outcast from the rest. Every time I disagreed I was beginning to wonder if I wasn't beginning to look funny' (Krech et al., 1962: 508). And, believe me, he *does*: the sequence of photos shows a gang of young men in dark suits, white shirts and ties (the well-groomed college student of the 1950s) who sit back in their chairs in carefree positions. Only one person, who even in the first picture seems to stand out, being the only one in a short-sleeved shirt (which gives him a sort of vulnerable look), leans forward with his forearms on the table. In the following pictures his bodily position becomes more and more tense, and his frown deeper and deeper. In the last picture he shrugs his shoulders in a resigned gesture and looks apologetically towards the camera. The subtext of the picture tells us that he says, 'He has to call them as he sees them' (Krech et al., 1962: 511). This experiment has been interpreted in light of the human need to conform, but it evidently also tells us about the need to hold on to what one 'knows' despite the uninformed opinion of the majority. This is a young man who with regard to bodily demeanour as well as competence is definitely part of the group from which he is artificially excluded. He illustrates the epistemophilic project, in which sticking to what one thinks is the truth can be experienced as an almost bodily necessity. Looking at his picture one can sympathize with his temporary predicament, but then we all know, of course, that everything will turn out right in the end. Just like in candid camera.

The next picture is from a book on developmental psychology (Smedslund, 1967), and depicts a little boy in braces and striped T-shirt, smiling awkwardly at the camera while he fumbles with his fingers. The small insecure child is here in sharp contrast to the bombastic scientism of the title of the thesis from which the picture is reproduced. The subtext goes: ' "Smile after having failed" (Heckhausen, H. und Wagner, I.: Anfänge und Entwicklung der Leistungsmotivation: (II) in der Zielsetzung des Kleinkindes. Zur Genese des Anspruchsniveaus. Psychologische Forschung. Bd. 28, s 179–245. Berlin–Heidelberg–New York: Springer, 1965).' In the text there is a meticulous description of all the bodily symptoms shown by the children of his age group, when they cannot solve a weight-lifting problem: 'One observes blushing, shameful lowering of the eyes, lowering of the head, especially changes around the mouth, pressing the lips together, sucking in the lower lip, opening the mouth, stretching out the tongue, sighing, rapid breathing – all signs that the child is hurt and upset' (Heckhausen and Wagner, 1965, cited in Smedslund, 1967: 144, my translation). In this case we are not confronted with the competent student who in a Copernican manner sticks to his conviction. This is an image of a child who has been narcissistically wounded, and it tells us about the intense emotional investment that our efforts to understand and handle the world entail. The only comfort is that he eventually will tackle it as he grows older.

Finally, there is the famous picture showing Charcot's psychiatric theatre (Martin, 1977). This is the only picture of the three that also shows the researcher himself. He stands in front of an audience of men with bright heads and dark suits (some of them have white aprons which make them look like butchers). They all sit or stand in listening positions, taking notes or gazing straight towards the stage. On stage Charcot stands, pointing to a woman who is in a convulsive seizure (probably hypnotically produced). The position of the demonstration object is twisted, her head is thrown backwards, and one of her hands is in a fist. Her eyes are closed. Her bodily position is in stark contrast to the carefree, listening and – first and foremost – *wide-awake* men who surround her. The sexual connotations are also obvious (see Williams, 1990, who has shown that the photographic sequences of hysterical females produced by Charcot have direct counterparts in early pornography). Contrary to the men, who are dressed in buttoned up dark suits, the woman is in a low-cut blouse and one of the sleeves has slipped down revealing her naked shoulder (Martin, 1977: 34).

This picture is different from the other two in several ways. It is from a different time and a different discipline (medicine) – a time and a discipline where the central position of the researcher/clinician was underlined and made heroic. The object is reduced to an immobile body. She might be cured, but can she hope to be part of the epistemophilic project? There is an insurmountable gap between her and the researching men in the auditorium – she cannot just wake up and become one of them (like Asch's student), nor hope to grow up and join their ranks (like Heckhausen's little boy). There is not just a difference in degree between researcher and object, there is a difference in kind – a difference between knower and known. It is reasonable to believe that this has something to do with her gender, as we are introduced to an object who, on the one hand, is completely 'the Other' to these men, and, on the other hand, arouses a fascination that in any other context would be defined as sexual.

MALE RESEARCH-PASSION

This last picture might be seen as a sort of résumé of the male version of the epistemophilic project: a researching subject, directing an intense gaze as well as a phallic index finger towards an object that is totally different from himself – an object who seems to close herself around her own great secret. Let us take a closer look at this male epistemophilic project which often seems to be associated with a romantic scientist hero. There are two prominent figures in literature who can be interpreted as representatives of this heroism, namely Goethe's *Faust* (published in 1808) and Mary Shelley's *Frankenstein – or the Modern Prometheus* (published anonymously in 1818; here the edition from 1992 is used). Both works are produced in a modernity where the Enlightenment's belief in endless growth and progress is mixed with the Romantic demand that subjective experience should be recognized. The conflict between the old stuffiness of scholastic knowledge on the one hand, and the new demands for empirical knowledge and action, on the other, is demonstrated already in the first scene of Goethe's play. Faust, who is prematurely old and grey, bemoans his dusty and wormy so-called knowledge – a sort of scholarly midlife crisis where magic and finally the devil himself seem to be the only solution. This tragedy gives ample opportunity to analyse the researching body (Faust, for instance, becomes strikingly young, energetic and sexy through his new search for knowledge). However, I concentrate on Shelley's *Frankenstein*, partly because it more directly concerns the modern scientist's aspiration to become a sort of technical god – one who creates the world and not just understands it – and partly because it so evidently shows the significance of the body as the centre of all secrets.

The Story of Victor Frankenstein

Victor Frankenstein was born in Geneva, and his childhood was a happy one. Not least the relationship with his foster sister, Elizabeth, is depicted as 'exquisite pleasure' – they are always together and she is 'more than a sister'. But it is in this happy childhood that he finds the source of his own ruin – his burning interest in natural philosophy. He had 'a fervent longing to penetrate the secrets of nature', but alas, he often felt that no one could tell him anything new. Fifteen-year-old Victor is already hit by that old Faustian spleen: 'It seemed to me as if nothing would or could ever be known' (Shelley, 1992: 40). At university he finds out that the professors have nothing to offer. The closed (dusty, wormy, cf. Faust) atmosphere is embodied by M. Krempe, who is a professor of natural philosophy: 'M. Krempe was a little squat man, with a gruff voice and a repulsive countenance' (1992: 45). However, soon Victor meets another professor, M. Waldman – who is in every way the opposite of M. Krempe – a combination of erect body, forceful activity and friendliness. And he makes Frankenstein realize that it is not the alchemists which young Victor had studied (just like Faust), but the down-to-earth empiricists who are the real heroes:

> these philosophers, whose hands seem only made to dabble in dirt, and their eyes to pore over the microscope or crucible, have indeed performed miracles. They penetrate into the recesses of nature, and show how she works in her hiding-places. (1992: 47)

The result is that Frankenstein is converted to natural science, an experience at least as ecstatic as other religious conversions: 'soon my mind was filled with one thought, one conception, one purpose' (1992: 47).

Nobody who has not experienced them themselves can understand 'the enticements of science', Frankenstein says. In the research itself one finds the nourishment of discovery and wonder – a sort of totally intrinsic motivation, characterized by an almost obsessive intensity. For Frankenstein this obsession is oriented to exploration of the human body and, of course, the question of life itself. He goes about his business systematically and energetically – and it is only because of his 'overnatural enthusiasm' that he does not give up. For this is undoubtedly also a rather repulsive affair. He studies not only anatomy, but also observes the decaying processes of the human corpse: 'I saw how the worm inherited the wonders of the eye and brain' (1992: 51). And suddenly he understands the secret involved in the principles of life and death, and he himself is now able to give life to dead matter. His plan is to make a human being (anything lower on the evolutionary ladder would have been beneath his dignity), and he collects his building material from cemeteries, morgues, slaughterhouses and dissection-rooms.

Just like Faust he emphasizes the grandness of being a godlike creator – and a variety of feelings sweep him along like a hurricane. But in contrast to Faust, who seems to become younger through his deal with the devil, to create a body for Frankenstein seems to imply that his own is dried out. Pale and weak he goes on, following an irresistible impulse: 'I seemed to have lost all soul or sensation but for this one pursuit' (1992: 53). After a while the first enthusiasm seems to be replaced by mere compulsion – he feels as if he is condemned to 'slave in the mines'. Every night he is suffering from high fever, and he begins to avoid the company of other people as if he was in fact guilty of a crime. The researching process has never been as evidently connected with passion as in the sad story of Victor Frankenstein.

Scientific Ethos and Domestic Happiness

Victor Frankenstein describes a process that resembles the torments of passionate love – all the way from the nourishing discovery of the other (or perhaps rather the discovery of one's own desire?) through obsession, where everything else becomes pale and insignificant, to the compulsive need for something that is detrimental to both health and sanity. Or perhaps this obsession has more in common with masturbation, which at the time was considered even more destructive. Anyway, it is the forbidden character of this project that is underlined – the passion for knowledge is a secret vice in Frankenstein's case, something he does in the dark hours of night, behind locked doors in an isolated attic. The connection between knowledge and sexuality is evident. The fact that the research-passion is equivalent to a secret vice also implies that there are some laws that Frankenstein transgresses. Evidently, he violates the laws of religion (but just like Faust, he does not pay much attention to that). More importantly, he also violates his own scientific code. The emotional neutrality that according to R.K. Merton (1949, referred to in Mitroff, 1974) is the essence of the scientific ethos, is also celebrated by Victor: 'A human being in perfection ought always to preserve a calm and peaceful mind, and never to allow passion or a transitory desire to disturb his tranquillity. I do not think that the pursuit of knowledge is an exception to this rule' (Shelley, 1992: 54).

Against the obsessive quest for knowledge, Frankenstein (or Mary Shelley) puts calm and warm domestic affections. All destruction in world history is depicted as the result of the untamed research-passion; the fall of great civilizations could have been avoided if only this passion had been counteracted by a greater appreciation of the simple, domestic life among the great explorers/generals:

> if no man allowed any pursuit whatsoever to interfere with the tranquillity of his domestic affections, Greece had not been enslaved; Caesar would have spared his country; America would have been discovered more gradually; and the empires of Mexico and Peru had not been destroyed. (Shelley, 1992: 54)

At this point it might be Shelley's female voice that is heard: harmony connected with the domestic sphere is ranked above the passionate explorations of the world out there. The scientific ethos usually expresses the Cartesian split between body and soul in a slightly different way, demanding public rationality cleansed of bodily contamination. Or as Habermas has put it: 'reason . . . has no body, cannot suffer, and also arouses no passion' (Habermas, 1982, cited in Marshall, 1994: 103). As we have seen, Victor Frankenstein himself aspires to such a coolness, but to his own dismay he constantly fails to abide by the rules of this reasonable and disembodied sphere of researchers. He is not only possessed by knowing the body in a manner that almost resembles necrophilic passion (all the graveyard visits and putting together of dead limbs). He also uses his *own* body in the project: he digs, dissects, 'dabbles in dirt' and stench – it is really a dirty handicraft that is described, far away from the refined scientific distance, where the object is explored by the inspecting gaze itself.

According to the scientific ethos everything will be solved with the right amount of self-control. The good researcher does not let his passions govern his research, even though the fact that there *is* an ethos tells us that it is not all that easy. However, the prerequisite for this universal, reasonable and disembodied research subject is the fact that he is particularly, emotionally and bodily taken care of elsewhere, namely in that small domestic sphere. That the male modern subject can go out into the world as an explorer/researcher/entrepreneur because others – generally women – are taking care of the bodies of men and children, has been pointed out by many feminist critics of modernity (see Bjerrum Nielsen and Rudberg, 1994). Passion (in varying degrees) is not eliminated, but (more or less) built into the domestic infrastructure serving the great male mind. This process is also evident in the fact that the ideal for the male scientist changes: the romantic loner is in a way substituted by the researching family father (see the happy families on the first row at the Nobel prize ceremony). To be married to one's research is a problematic merit in a culture where knowledge and passion shall be kept apart.[2] At the same time the passionate scientist seems to glow right beneath the cool surface of the scientific ethos. The American theorist of science Mitroff (1974) interviewed physicists in the Apollo project in the beginning of the 1970s. There was a substantial agreement when it came to pointing out the ones who were the most prominent researchers in the field. Those chosen were not the loyal experimentalists, but rather the ones who seemed married to their own hypothesis. This type of researcher stirred up ambivalent feelings among their colleagues – they were depicted as both extremely irritating and admirable. So, even though the scientist hero (like Frankenstein) seems to be given a status as oddball, he will also function as a sort of counter-norm in a research community which will become more and more stamped by the disenchantment of modern bureaucracy.

The Research Result – The Monstrous Body

The destructive consequences of the untamed research-passion have never been more clearly illustrated than in the case of Frankenstein. Frankenstein himself gets completely hysterical when he sees the being that he has created start moving. He had tried to make him beautiful, he says, but even though some parts were perfect (for instance 'the pearly white teeth'), the totality is monstrous. Filled with horror and disgust Frankenstein escapes to his room where he immediately falls asleep and dreams 'the wildest dreams'. In these dreams acts of love are consequently mixed with images of death: when he kisses his flourishing Elizabeth her lips turn into the hue of death, and all of a sudden she is transformed into his dead mother's corpse – 'a shroud enveloped her form, and I saw the grave-worms crawling in the folds of flannel' (Shelley, 1992: 57). It gets even worse when he wakes up, and suddenly sees the monster pull the curtain of the bed aside:

> and his eyes, if eyes they may be called, were fixed on me. His jaws opened, and he muttered some inarticulate sounds, while a grin wrinkled his cheeks. He might have spoken but I did not hear; one hand was stretched out, seemingly to detain me, but I escaped, and rushed downstairs. (1992: 57)

Frankenstein develops a whole series of bodily symptoms: his pulse is beating, he breaks out in cold sweat, he falls to the ground in convulsive fits. Sometimes his bodily reactions make him rather similar to the 'fainting lady' of the nineteenth-century novel (he spends a lot of time in bed with high fever). But he also pulls himself together in a manly manner by taking long, exhausting walks.

The monster as symbol of horror is of course well known to us – and in many versions it is only as a grunting, stiff-legged creature with his arms stretched out that he is presented to us (Hindle, 1992). In Shelley's book, however, the monster is much more complex, and in fact rather touching. One has to be made of stone in order not to sympathize with this awkward being, who tries to climb into the bed of his creator: for what is this hideous grin if not the first sociable smile of an infant? The hubris of Frankenstein is undoubtedly that he plays at being God (he should have been more humble), the *ruin* of Frankenstein is caused by his obsession (he should have controlled himself), but his *crime* lies in the fact that he does not take responsibility for this creature, but abandons his newborn and helpless child. The whole story from now on concerns how this innocent orphan, who does not know where he comes from and who he is, tries to be accepted within the human community. And to Shelley that means being loved and taken care of within the tender relations of a family. The monster tells about his painstaking efforts to make contact, mainly through learning the language of men (both by listening in on conversation and reading). This however proves not to be possible, he is too hideous for anybody to love. The monster therefore decides to revenge himself on mankind: 'If I cannot inspire love, I will cause fear' (Shelley, 1992: 140). The monster hunts down Frankenstein's family, kills Victor's little brother and causes a beloved servant girl to be accused of the crime. Eventually the monster gives Frankenstein an offer he cannot refuse: the monster will leave Frankenstein and his dear ones in peace, if Frankenstein creates a female monster with whom he can share his lonely life. Frankenstein hesitantly agrees to this deal, if the monster promises afterwards to leave Europe (!).

Now there is no escape left for Frankenstein (an important theme of the Gothic novel is the anxiety of not having any way out; see Hindle, 1992). The monster follows him like a horrid shadow: 'Yes, he had followed me in my travels; he had loitered in forests, hid himself in caves, or taken refuge in wide and desert heaths; and he now came to mark my progress, and claim the fulfilment of my promise' (Shelley, 1992: 161). In other words, the monster has been there all along, but he now comes forward at the horizon like 'the return of the repressed'. And the image of him reminds Frankenstein all too clearly of his former mistakes, and he tears the female monster which is nearly finished, apart. The monster gets furious and for the first time he calls Frankenstein his slave:

> Slave, I before reasoned with you, but you have proved yourself unworthy of my condescension. Remember that I have power; you believe yourself miserable, but I can make you so wretched that the light of day will be hateful to you. You are my creator, but I am your master – obey! (1992: 162)

This reversal of positions, where the creator suddenly finds himself in the power of the creation, has been interpreted politically as a symbol of a capitalism which brings forth its own destructors – the modern proletariat (Moretti, 1983), as well as a symbol of 'the compulsive character of masculine science' (Easlea, 1983). This reversal of power also informs us that subject and object, creator and creature are dialectically related to each other: the monster who follows Frankenstein like a shadow is after all part of Frankenstein himself – and that is why it is impossible for Frankenstein to get away. It is in fact a common mistake to confuse Frankenstein with the monster (the monster is often called Frankenstein), and maybe this is not only a question of the public being uninformed. By creating the monster, Frankenstein has made himself monstrous; the object reflects the subject, the product of knowledge tells us something about the knower, as well as setting conditions for what the knower might know about himself. When realizing that the monster has killed his little brother, Frankenstein characterizes the monster as 'my own vampire, my own spirit set loose from the grave and forced to destroy all that was dear to me' (Shelley, 1992: 74).

The monster is not just the horrid product of science. It is part of Frankenstein himself, and then perhaps that part of himself that is hardest to acknowledge – his own unreasonable body. The modern project implies that the body, just like the monster, is exiled to a prediscursive region (see Turner, 1980; Morgan and Scott, 1993), from where it talks back at us in a language that we cannot completely grasp. It is a body that Frankenstein has been forced to push back in order to become a knowing subject – in the sort of abjection that Julia Kristeva (1982) claims is a prerequisite for being inscribed in the symbolic order. But it is also a body which he longs to recreate (just as the abject is rejected as well as tempting). This recreation seems only to be possible through his 'dabbling in dirt' and his putting together leftovers (reminiscences) that are already dead and buried. And when he starts digging into the secrets of the body – however grim they turn out to be – this body will no longer keep calm. Every time Franken-stein pushes the monster away, it comes back even more horrid, even more satanic and deadly to reason. The tragedy is that there is neither an escape from the body, nor a way to integrate it into the knowing process itself – even though this project was aimed at revealing the inner secrets of this body.

The Unreachable Secret – The Psychoanalytic Story

We are now at the 'final point' of the male epistemophilic project, as we summarized it when looking at the Charcot picture: the male researching subject, looking at an object which is different in kind – an object that seems to lock itself around its own secret. So what is this secret? The object in this picture was a woman, and I suggested that her sex was not insignifi-cant. Is the secret that the epistemophilic project seeks to disclose in fact something that resides in the female body? When we look at the metaphors of science in both Shelley's time and afterwards there most cer-tainly often is a woman involved. Nature itself is depicted as a woman, even a 'resisting' woman whom the researcher tries to both 'conquer' and 'penetrate' (see Keller, 1986). To reveal her secrets is in fact to undress her. Humphrey Davy – a scientist who was partly used as model for Franken- stein – expresses the glorious possibilities of chemistry in the following way: 'The skirt only of the veil which conceals these mysterious and sublime processes has been lifted up and the grand view is as yet unknown' (cited in Easlea, 1983: 28). If one gets to know so much by just lifting up the hem of the skirt, what cannot be expected higher up?

Is then the monster in the story of Frankenstein a symbol of the female body? The monster might not just be the scientist's own body – but some- thing which refers to all sorts of impurity that has to be kept in check in order for culture to evolve (see Douglas, 1969). The monstrous part about this body is that it cannot be categorized. It stands outside linguistic cat- egories, it is completely ambiguous and horrid both with regard to its origin (dead limbs that *move*) and appearance (a *human-like* freak). The ingredients are 100 percent 'natural', but the making of this body is the result of human delusions of grandeur. The monster is both 'postnatural' and 'precultural' (Brooks, 1993). Such characterizations are in our culture closely associated with a feminine position: 'Woman' is said to be pos- itioned outside the symbolic order, she represents 'the Other', the ambigu- ous and abject (see Kristeva, 1982). Peter Brooks (1993) has therefore argued that it is possible that the monster in this text symbolizes 'woman', a woman who also protests against this definition as 'other'. A point in case is that the authoress seems to identify more with the monster (see the moving portrait) than with the hero Frankenstein. The monster is also one who frantically tries to escape from a position where he is only a visual object to others, by trying to learn the language that is a necessary con- dition for entering the symbolic order. The entrance into this order is at first attempted by imploring glances and outstretched hands, and when that strategy fails, the struggle moves into a more militant phase – not a completely unknown process in women's fight for recognition. However, it is problematic to press the equation woman = monster (however tempt- ing it is!) in relation to *this* text – as the monster is depicted as male, wanting a female companion. So, perhaps, the monster should not be interpreted as symbolizing the female body in itself, but rather the relationship between Frankenstein and his own body – a relationship which is *mediated* through a female body in particular ways.

In order to understand the effects of this alleged mediation, let us turn to the psychoanalytic story of the epistemophilic project (which almost literally parallels the metaphor of research used by Humphrey Davy). My intention here is not to reduce scientific endeavour to this story – it evi- dently does not tell it all. There are, of course, both internal scholarly tra- ditions as well as other social/historical factors at work in the construction of scientific knowledge. However, I suggest that a psychoanalytic frame- work might contribute to our understanding of the psychological motives involved in this process, and thus make at least some sense of the striking intensity, as well as the inertia, of science.

The starting point for the psychoanalytic story about the development of epistemophilia, is the fact that the relation between a man and his body is mediated through a female body in at least two different ways. First, the body of the mother is the psychological point of departure for every man, and second, there is a social arrangement where women have taken care of the bodies of children and men, at least in our culture. It is perhaps this fusion between the male and female body which seems to make the question of sexual difference so important in the developmental story of the little boy. According to psychoanalytic theory, the discovery of the anatomical sexual difference represents a trauma to him (in contrast to the little girl who just sulks and becomes envious). The little boy's curious inspection of his mother's sex is, according to Freud, the prototype of all later explorations of the world (Freud, 1923). The epistemophilic project is therefore from the very beginning 'scopophilic', i.e. connected to vision (see Irigaray's [1974] criticism of Freud's sexism on this point). What the boy discovers, i.e. the fact that mother lacks a penis, has of course consequences for his conceptions of gender, but it also influences the knowing process in general. From now on this process will be characterized by strong ambivalence: the boy discovers that the one he loves is not 'complete' (the phallic mother is an illusion). According to the theory this does not only imply anxiety about one's own body (the mother's lack can of course afflict this little boy as well) – but also anxiety about the process of *looking*. To 'look at' mother is tempting, but dangerous for the boy; it is not just a dazzling experience, it might in fact 'blind' him (compare the myth of Oedipus), just as the sight of the tabooed in general blinds or kills the transgressor. In this oedipal drama 'father' is of course the one who can punish the boy for looking.

The epistemophilic project of the little boy is therefore frustrated from two sides. First, the body does not exist as a *whole* object – and his search for totality will always be frustrated. Second, his vision (which is full of desire) is governed by the law of the father, who prohibits him from looking into the most secret hiding-places. Whatever the reason, the result is that the boy can never (and dare not) see everything – just as he feels that he is close to the core of the matter or begins to glimpse the outline of a totality, he must turn his gaze away and concentrate on more marginal phenomena and parts. The passion that is connected with vision also loads those fragments with intense emotions, so that some of the bits and pieces (foot, shoe, ankle, panties) often turn into clear-cut fetishes for the little boy. The fetish is a sort of libidinous compromise (in fact, a spare penis), the result of an effort to deny sexual difference. Through the fetish the boy can maintain the illusion that there is no difference and therefore no threat to his own phallic intactness (bodily or culturally). The problem is of course that this denial of sexual difference is an illusion, and that the epistemophilic project therefore will be characterized by a certain partial blindness and fetishistic fragmentation. Frankenstein's monster might actually be interpreted as such a fetish that implies a *denial* of sexual difference (this is also a point made by Brooks, 1993). As pointed out, the monster is a man in the text, but his maleness is not overly convincing, there are for instance no hints of sexual functioning, and the wish for a female companion seems to represent the need for a mother rather than the need for a sexual partner. The monster of the text is also a linguistic neuter – 'the being', 'the creature' – indicating a kind of unassortedness when it comes to gender. And this unassortedness is in fact an important part of its monstrosity. The megalomaniac project of Frankenstein has not just been to create a being in his own image, but a being who transcends the threat to bodily intactness/wholeness that a recognition of sexual difference seems to imply.

What are the consequences of this for the researching process, as well as the character of scientific knowledge? Although we must be careful not to make simplistic assumptions about causal relations in this context, there are at least some interesting parallels between the structure of scientific knowledge and the psychoanalytic story of fetishist vision: there is the traditional valorization of experimental observation (in contrast to sloppy interviewing); there is the disdainful rejection of any possibility to see it 'all' (the thing-in-itself); there is the fragmentation of knowledge (see the textbooks) which is not just a virtue of necessity, but often fetishized as *the* way of knowing; and last but not least there is the so-called 'gender-blindness' of traditional social science, a term that might in fact be more apt than we have imagined because it represents an active denial of sexual difference and not mere oversight of women. (This is an interpretation that has been overlooked in feminist epistemology, as far as I know.) But of course the psychoanalytic story also informs us of the frustration of it all – like Isaac Newton who, according to Frankenstein, admitted to feeling 'like a child picking up shells beside the great and unexplored ocean of truth' (Shelley, 1992: 39). Although our discoveries and findings are connected together in ever new ways – in new theoretical models or painstaking empirical cumulation of knowledge (or as in the case of Frankenstein – in a brand new being) – it is also an inherently frustrating project disturbed by the gnawing feeling of never really hitting the target. Just as the phenomenon that we want to grasp always seems to be a bit to the side of all our refined indicators and operationalizations. And finally there is the defence against all passion resulting in a genre of stories and texts that have at least one thing in common – they are usually monstrously boring.

In such a perspective the *goal* of the male epistemophilic project might be to disclose the inner secrets of the female body (in order to understand and keep one's own body intact), and the *monster* – in this case the perversion of scientific knowledge – might be seen as the result of the fact that this 'original' project is always frustrated. The unhappy end of Victor Frankenstein is a case in point. Frankenstein repeats over and over again that the researcher is to follow nature (which is always a 'she') into her most secret hiding-places, caves and recesses. But he has great problems when it comes to reaching this centre of all secrets: every time he is near a disclosure, he is, as Brooks (1993: 216) puts it, hit by something monstrous – just like the little boy who is blinded by the sight of his mother's body and obliged to turn away. The sexual attraction that Elizabeth represents is systematically mixed with death: when he kisses Elizabeth in his dreams she turns into his dead mother – full of crawling worms. The final sexual fusion with Elizabeth is something that he sees as his 'reward' after having finished his last wicked project – the female monster. But when Frankenstein refuses to fulfil his part of the deal with the monster, the deadline that the monster sets up for his total destruction is exactly his wedding-night: '*I shall be with you on your wedding-night*' (1992: 163) – this monstrous sentence is repeated as in a Greek tragedy. After the wedding ceremony Elizabeth is killed by the monster, and the union of love is again associated with violent death: 'I rushed towards her, and embraced her with ardour; but the deadly languor and coldness of the limbs told me, that what I now held in my arms had ceased to be the Elizabeth whom I had loved and cherished' (1992: 189). Victor Frankenstein never gets his reward. The epistemophilic project is frustrated in the cruellest possible way: he never gets to know the secret of the female body, and due to the mediation between this female body and his own, he is never to know the secret of his own body either.[3]

The Epistemophilic Project – Destabilized

The theory of the fetishist/phallic gaze has been very useful to feminist film theorists (see Mulvey, 1989) in order to analyse the character of 'to-be-looked-at-ness' of female film actors (see also the Charcot picture, analysed above). At the same time, however, this Freudian version has been criticized for unduly universalizing this story. It seems reasonable to ask to what extent this sexual secret is a secret any more – perhaps this epistemophilic project is connected with more puritan times? The American film theorist Linda Williams (1990) shows in her analysis of hard core pornography that today no one seems to turn his gaze away, but rather stares intently straight at the female sexual organs: the epistemophile has become gynaecologist. Possibly, the new trivialization of sexuality may result in the disenchantment of the epistemophilic project itself. Nudity becomes nakedness; the body is not portrayed, it is staged – both in hard core pornography and in the so-called superrealist art, where naturally sized wax dolls are exhibited. Peter Brooks (1993: 282) comments this trend in the following manner: '[It] reduces the epistemophilic project exercised on the body to a kind of tautology, or a mere gesture of pointing; *that* is the body.' But the mere fact that we can find that interesting implies that the epistemophilic project is not yet dead. In fact there might even be an opposite trend at work here, a sort of remystifying – as the postmodern conception of the body asserts that it is *not* a symbol of something else, *not* a story which makes sense.[4]

Today the body which is staged is often a male body, i.e. men have achieved a new character of 'to-be-looked-at-ness'. This is often under-stood as a result of the fact that women have conquered a new status as subjects in our culture. However, it is also possible that the passionate (and fetishist) gaze never was as rigidly gendered as the Freudian analysis implies – women have of course also been fascinated by female objects (for instance on the screen) and often identified with the male gaze. When it comes to the story about Frankenstein, I suggest that many female readers will waver between identifying with Frankenstein and the monster – but seldom with Elizabeth. On the other hand, it is important to note that the monster itself is not an immobile object, which is only to be looked at. It is in fact the gaze of the monster which Frankenstein finds so intolerable from the first moment – these yellow, watery eyes! Although the researcher might celebrate the scopophilic distance, this does not stop the research object from scrutinizing the researcher – an interaction that has often been depicted as almost as disturbing as the monster's gaze. In addition, even the starting point of the epistemophilic project – the curios-ity about mother's body – will probably at first be frustrated by the stern and reproving gaze of mother herself. A gaze that also contains a dash of condescension that efficiently informs the boy about his own bodily lack, his ridiculous smallness. There is of course power also in the female gaze – in the seductive version as well as the reprimanding/condescending one. This female gaze might also change historically in a manner that resembles the development of the monster's gaze: from the begging look which only wants to be acknowledged by the intact and powerful subjects, to the all-seeing inspection which seems to coolly dehumanize men. Who now is whose monster?

The most important criticism of Freud's theory about the fetishist gaze is in fact that it does not take into account that gender relations are dynamic. It is striking that Freud seems to think that the boy is right in existentially abhorring the female 'lack', even though he regards fetishism as a poor solution (see Williams, 1990). Such a viewpoint implies that the present gender order is static, and intactness (both bodily and culturally) *is* in fact identified with the male sex. If this were true, the epistemophilic project would only be possible as a male project, as the difference in kind between knower and known is made a natural given. Today the academic world has lost the homogeneity of gender that made the male bodily history an unquestioned condition for the researching process. The fact that the body today is such a hot topic is perhaps partly due to women having made this body salient in a new way. They contribute to this salience by their mere presence in high enough numbers and in high enough positions. In contrast to the 'male' horror of sexual difference, most women seem to cope rather well with this bodily fact. Today, there is even a passion for difference (see Moore, 1993) that women can make use of in the public, academic world: they can play out their own bodily otherness, and through their gaze put the bodies of male colleagues on the agenda without being overly inhibited either by the scientific ethos or accusations of being sexist. The Norwegian sociologist Karin Widerberg (1995) tells a story about an important meeting of professors where she is the only woman. The story about her own deliberations about what clothes to wear (a black blazer, jeans, metal belt and cowboy boots), as well as her reflections about the bodily performances of the assembled men, are summed up in the following celebration of difference.

> Why should I be afraid of them? The fact that they are 'ugly' and so very much men in their strivings to show off in front of each other, makes me calm. I want to be different, not one of them. And by my being just different, they can never place me, never 'get me'. (Widerberg, 1995: 95, my translation)

FEMALE RESEARCH-PASSION?

Evidently, the body can still be exiled to a prediscursive region, refused as the abject that every knowing subject must transcend – and women who play at their difference must always beware that they do not become *too much* body, too much gender. Nevertheless, this rejecting of the body does not seem to happen in the same way any more. It is for instance striking that the depiction of the female body given by Simone de Beauvoir some 50 years ago in *The Second Sex* seems to be almost impossible today:

> man dives upon his prey like the eagle and the hawk; woman lies in wait like the carnivorous plant, the bog, in which insects and children are swallowed up. She is absorption, suction, humus, pitch and glue, a passive influx, insinuating and viscous; thus, at least she vaguely feels herself to be. (de Beauvoir, 1972: 407)

But even though the epistemophilic project of de Beauvoir seems to parallel the male one – with the female body as 'the other' – the central position that the body has in her texts also reveals important differences.

In a female epistemophilic project the own body will be incessantly thematized.[5] Evidently, one reason for this is that femininity is culturally associated with body and sex, in a way that is not the case for masculinity (see Morgan and Scott, 1993). But perhaps it is also because the connection between knowledge and body has been more obvious to women (which does not imply that it is less problematic to them). Not because women *are* more 'embodied' than men, but because their relation to their own body has not been mediated by the opposite sex, but by their own. The desire of knowing the secrets connected with the *male* body has not been especially dominant in feminist discourse (and the efforts to reverse the roles, for instance in 'male stripping', seem rather to inspire giggling than frantic pleasure in women). Men are not depicted as great enigmas by women, but as rather uncomplicated creatures. This has often been associated with a somewhat condescending tone: oh, we *know* those bodies – they are not very interesting! But it could of course also imply idealization, which actually means that men are disembodied by women themselves – male bodies are seen as pure prolongations of male rationality. While de Beauvoir describes the female body as a smelly swamp, the male sexual organ is referred to as a fine, uncomplicated and neat finger (de Beauvoir, 1972: 406). In short, a woman is not obliged to go via the male body in order to understand her own, and maybe that is why the sexual difference will not be experienced as such a bodily threat to her.

The relation of a woman to her own body is of course also mediated, but then through another woman – mother (and as Toril Moi shows in her analysis of Simone de Beauvoir, the swamp metaphor tells us something of Simone's relationship with her mother). The female epistemophilic project does not begin with a father's categorical prohibition, and therefore it might never become as obsessive and monolithic as the male passion for knowledge – just like the girl's solution of the oedipal conflict does not seem to be as total as the boy's, but results in a sort of bisexual wavering between mother and father. The male metaphors of knowledge centring around penetrating gazes will perhaps never be really appropriated by her. Toril Moi calls attention to the fact that Simone de Beauvoir as a little girl never associated knowledge with formal training or fatherly discipline, but with eating:

> If only the universe in which we live was completely edible, I thought, what power would we not have over it! As a grown-up I still want to crush blooming almond trees between my teeth, and take a bite of the rainbow chocolates of the sunset. I saw the neon-signs like gigantic candies against the night sky of New York, and I felt frustrated. (cited in Moi, 1995: 39, my translation)

According to Moi, there is a clear influence from Sartre in this equation between knowing and eating (thus, the gender of the epistemophilic project is far from unambiguous). Still, Sartre's theory of knowledge is even more strongly associated with the possession as well as the destruction of the desired object – while the candy knowledge seems to imply a slow melting on the tongue – and perhaps the sweet taste is the most important thing? Karin Widerberg (1995: 22ff.) also associates her own lust for knowledge with vegetative processes, like lying in bed and 'devouring' books from the local library. To 'devour' something is often associated with a somewhat unrefined project of knowledge – where the knower indiscriminatingly and gullibly 'swallows' everything. And perhaps the female epistemophilic project does connote some of these things in our culture?

In this perspective the female epistemophilic project might be seen as less obsessive, more oral (is that why we love interviewing?) and also less tormenting than the male one. Positively defined, that would perhaps imply that it is also less defensive and therefore with the possibilities of becoming less boring and more pleasurable. However, the importance of the maternal relationship may result in problems of the same magnitude as the ones that made the boy turn to fetishist vision. Mother is also the invading mother – the one who not only supplies the child with candy, but also the one who forces the overcooked vegetables down her throat. Knowledge is not just something that you can devour, it is also something that threatens to choke and devour *you*. To be engulfed – the very sign of passion – might therefore arouse ambivalent feelings in a female epistemophile. And this is an ambivalence that is not only due to the fact that she lacks the opportunity to become absorbed in her research. The passionate monomania of Frankenstein would of course be even more unforgivable in a woman (she cannot leave her newborn and helpless children – and if she did, who would then take care of Frankenstein?). Still, a woman might have motives of her own to keep her passions at a manageable size, so that she will not vanish completely. If her epistemophilic project is both about recreating the maternal relation as well as breaking out of it – it will of course be a rather ambivalent affair. To be engulfed by mother is to renounce the possibility of being a knowing subject, to reject mother is to renounce the very nourishment on which the female epistemophilic project seems to thrive. Somewhere in this female project it is perhaps possible to recognize the melancholic position that according to Julia Kristeva (1989) characterizes many women, because the work of sorrow required in the separation from the mother's body is never completed. In Moi's analysis of Simone de Beauvoir, this is made into a significant point. De Beauvoir's project of knowledge seems to be constructed from a depressive psychological position, where the 'black hole' after mother is filled with almost compulsory writing. To Kristeva the solution for such women is often found in the erotic-theoretical relationship with a man (and she seems to recommend both vaginal jouissance and childbirth) – a relationship which through the use of language in a way makes her 'born again', disposing of her need for mother. To de Beauvoir the lifelong relationship with Sartre undoubtedly had such qualities (although we can be shocked at the grim aspects of it). Perhaps, this applies to other women as well, if their epistemophilic project has the bodily basis that I have suggested. Of course, we do not really know how the female version of the epistemophilic project will turn out – and what I have said here is nothing but more or less educated guesses. And even though I have stressed the differences between the male and the female versions, I am almost certain that the female epistemophile will learn a trick or two from Frankenstein. But even more certain that she will create some kind of monster of her own.

NOTES

1. In this paper I treat 'the body' in a naive, realist way – well aware of the fact that the main theme in today's discourse on the body is the conflict between essentialism and social constructionism (nominalism): do our bodies determine us, or is culture victorious vis-a-vis our flesh? Such questions have been highlighted not least in feminist theory, where the traditional dichotomy

between biological sex and socially constructed gender has been seen as increasingly problematic (see Butler, 1990). The body is no longer standing uninvited outside scholarly discourse, and yet in the anti-essentialist warfare the body seems to become a somewhat lofty affair (we could *learn* to desire almost *anything*). It is not always easy to *believe* in this construed body, because when it comes not to *the* body, but to *our* body we remain incurably naive realists. There is therefore a clear tendency of re-erecting the body as materiality or corpo(re)ality in gender studies (see Braidotti, 1991): bodies are not merely surfaces for inscription of cultural messages and signs – a sort of signifiant without signifié or a name looking for its thing. Bodies do in fact 'talk back' at us all the time, reminding us of our mortality and cooling us down in the midst of all our self-constructing projects.

2.   What might happen when they are *not* kept apart is shown in the sad story about J.B. Watson, the founding father of behaviourism. According to an introductory book on the history of psychology (Schultz, 1981) it was Watson's charismatic and charming personality which eventually brought on his ruin. He did evidently not leave his body at home. He used his body directly in the research process, putting electrodes on it in order to measure sexual response and went to bed with his assistant. The result was both divorce and dismissal from his university position. In the textbook this is seen as a regrettable lack of understanding for the leeway that genuine research talents must be given in order to create great things.

3.   This reminds us of Sartre's conception of knowledge as something that always destroys the known object. The inherent frustration of this project is also expressed in the famous last sentence of *Being and Nothingness*: 'Man is a useless passion' (Sartre, 1969: 615).

4.   And even in hard core pornography there is still an obsession with disclosing the innermost secret, a project that is no less problematic today, regardless how much one stares straight at the 'thing'. According to Williams (1990), the problem is associated with the unsure signs of female pleasure, and this pleasure can only be demonstrated indirectly by male penetration ('the meat-shot') and ejaculation ('the money-shot'). In other words, signs of male pleasure are fetishized in order to cover up the 'lack' of the female.

5.   Feminist theoretical discourse is in the avant-garde when it comes to problematizing the body (see Davis, 1995), and the relationship between sexuality and knowledge is a dominant theme when it comes to analysing 'the becoming of intellectual women' of our time; compare the texts used here: Moi (1995) about Simone de Beauvoir, Widerberg's (1995) memory work on her own growing up.

REFERENCES

Bjerrum Nielsen, Harriet and Monica Rudberg (1994) *Psychological Gender and Modernity*. Oslo: Scandinavian University Press.
Braidotti, Rosi (1991) 'The Subject in Feminism', *Hypatia* 6(2): 155–72.
Brooks, Peter (1993) *Body Work: Objects of Desire in Modern Narrative*. Cambridge, MA: Harvard University Press.
Butler, Judith (1990) *Gender Trouble*. London: Routledge.
Davis, Kathy (1995) *Reshaping the Female Body*. New York and London: Routledge.
de Beauvoir, Simone (1972) *The Second Sex*. London: Penguin.
Douglas, Mary (1969) *Purity and Danger*. Harmondsworth: Penguin.
Easlea, Brian (1983) *Fathering the Unthinkable: Masculinity, Scientists and the Nuclear Arms Race*. London: Pluto Press.

Freud, Sigmund (1923) 'The Infantile Genital Organization', in *Standard Edition*, Vol. 19. London: Hogarth Press.
Harding, Sandra (1986) *The Science Question in Feminism*. Milton Keynes: Open University Press.
Hindle, Maurice (1992) 'Introduction', in Mary Shelley *Frankenstein – or the Modern Prometheus*. London: Penguin.
Irigaray, Lucy (1974) *Speculum et l'autre femme*. Paris: Editions de Minuit.
Keller, Evelyn Fox (1986) *Science and Gender*. New York: Yale University Press.
Krech, David, Richard S. Crutchfield and Egerton L. Ballachey (1962) *Individual in Society*. New York: McGraw-Hill.
Kristeva, Julia (1982) *Powers of Horror – An Essay of Abjection*. New York: Columbia University Press.
Kristeva, Julia (1989) *Black Sun*. New York: Columbia University Press.
Marshall, Barbara (1994) *Engendering Modernity*. Cambridge: Polity Press.
Martin, Barclay (1977) *Abnormal Psychology*. New York: Holt, Rinehart and Winston.
Mitroff, Ian I. (1974) 'Norms and Counter-norms in a Select Group of the Apollo Moon Scientists: A Case Study of the Ambivalence of Scientists', *American Sociological Review* 39(8): 579–95.
Moi, Toril (1995) *Simone de Beauvoir. En intellektuell kvinne blir til*. Oslo: Gyldendal.
Moore, Henrietta L. (1993) *A Passion for Difference*. Cambridge: Polity Press.
Moretti, Franco (1983) *Signs Taken for Wonders*. London: Verso.
Morgan, David and Sue Scott (1993) *Body Matters: Essays on the Sociology of the Body*. London: Falmer Press.
Mulvey, Laura (ed.) (1989) 'Visual Pleasure and Narrative Cinema', *Visual and Other Pleasures*. London: Macmillan.
Sartre, Jean Paul (1969) *Being and Nothingness*. London: Methuen.
Schultz, Duane (1981) *A History of Modern Psychology*. New York: Academic Press.
Shelley, Mary (1992) *Frankenstein – or the Modern Prometheus*. London: Penguin.
Smedslund, Jan (1967) *Psykologi*. Oslo: Universitetsforlaget.
Turner, Brian S. (1980) *The Body and Society*. Oxford: Blackwell.
Widerberg, Karin (1995) *Kunnskapens kjønn* (The Sex of Knowledge). Oslo: Pax.
Williams, Linda (1990) *Hard Core*. London: Pandora Press.

Index